Henry Parry Liddon

Clerical Life And Work

A Collection of Sermons With An Essay

Henry Parry Liddon

Clerical Life And Work
A Collection of Sermons With An Essay

ISBN/EAN: 9783744743495

Printed in Europe, USA, Canada, Australia, Japan

Cover: Foto ©Thomas Meinert / pixelio.de

More available books at **www.hansebooks.com**

Clerical Life and Work

A COLLECTION OF SERMONS

WITH AN ESSAY

By H. P. LIDDON, D.D., D.C.L., LL.D.
LATE CANON AND CHANCELLOR OF ST. PAUL'S

SECOND EDITION

LONDON
LONGMANS, GREEN, AND CO.
AND NEW YORK: 15 EAST 16TH STREET
1895

All rights reserved

ADVERTISEMENT

ALL that is contained in this volume, with the exception of Sermons VIII. and IX., was published on different occasions during a period of forty years. Dr. Liddon himself collected and arranged most of the Sermons, and chose the title under which they are now reprinted. It will be seen that they express the ideal of the clerical life that was before his mind from the earliest days of his ministry. He appears to have wished for their republication, so that he might help a larger number of the clergy to share his own belief and aims.

EMBERTIDE,
September 1894.

CONTENTS

AN ESSAY.

THE PRIEST IN HIS INNER LIFE	PAGE 1

Originally published in "The Ecclesiastic and Theologian," October 1856, and January 1857.

SERMON I.

THE WORK AND PROSPECTS OF THEOLOGICAL COLLEGES.

ISAIAH l. 4.

The Lord God hath given Me the tongue of the learned, that I should know how to speak a word in season to him that is weary: He wakeneth morning by morning, He wakeneth Mine ear to hear as the learned 46

Preached at the Anniversary Festival of Cuddesdon College, June 10, 1868.

SERMON II.

THE MORAL GROUNDWORK OF CLERICAL TRAINING.

JOB xxviii. 12.

But where shall wisdom be found? and where is the place of understanding? 73

Preached at the Anniversary Festival of Cuddesdon College, June 10, 1873.

SERMON III.

OUR LORD'S EXAMPLE THE STRENGTH OF HIS MINISTERS.

St. Matt. iv. 19.

And He saith unto them, Follow Me, and I will make you fishers of men 93

PAGE

Preached at the Ordination of the Bishop of Oxford, in the Cathedral Church of Christ, on the Fourth Sunday in Advent, December 23, 1860.

SERMON IV.

THE WHOLE COUNSEL OF GOD.

Acts xx. 27.

I have not shunned to declare unto you the whole counsel of God . 119

Preached at the Ordination of the Bishop of Salisbury, in the Abbey Church of St. Mary, Sherborne, on the Second Sunday in Lent, February 21, 1864.

SERMON V.

THE SECRET OF CLERICAL POWER.

Acts i. 8.

Ye shall receive power, after that the Holy Ghost is come upon you 149

Preached at the Ordination of the Bishop of Salisbury, in Salisbury Cathedral, on the Fifteenth Sunday after Trinity, September 24, 1865.

SERMON VI.

FATALISM AND THE LIVING GOD.

Psalm viii. 4.

What is man, that Thou art mindful of him? 172

Preached at the Ordination of the Bishop of Salisbury, in Salisbury Cathedral, on the Seventeenth Sunday after Trinity, September 23, 1866.

SERMON VII.

THE MORAL VALUE OF A MISSION FROM CHRIST.

St. John xv. 16.

Ye have not chosen Me, but I have chosen you, and ordained you, that ye should go and bring forth fruit, and that your fruit should remain 207

Preached at the Ordination of the Bishop of Oxford, in the Cathedral Church of Christ, on the Fourth Sunday in Advent, December 22, 1867.

SERMON VIII.

CLERICAL MOTIVES.

1 Cor. xvi. 8, 9.

But I will tarry at Ephesus until Pentecost. For a great door and effectual is opened unto me, and there are many adversaries . 232

Preached at the Ordination of the Bishop of Winchester, in St. Philip's, Battersea, on Trinity Sunday, May 26, 1872.

SERMON IX.

FAITH WITHOUT MIRACLES.

St. John x. 41, 42.

And many resorted unto Him, and said, John did no miracle: but all things that John spake of this Man were true. And many believed on Him there 247

Preached at the Ordination of the Bishop of London, in St. Paul's, on Trinity Sunday, May 31, 1874.

SERMON X.

APOSTOLIC LABOURS AN EVIDENCE OF CHRISTIAN TRUTH.

ROMANS x. 18.

But I say, Have they not heard? Yes verily, their sound went into all the earth, and their words unto the ends of the world . 266

Preached in the Chapel of Lambeth Palace at the Consecration of the Bishop of Nassau, on the Feast of St. Andrew, November 30, 1863.

SERMON XI.

A FATHER IN CHRIST.

1 COR. iv. 15.

For though ye have ten thousand instructers in Christ, yet have ye not many fathers: for in Christ Jesus I have begotten you through the Gospel 288

Preached in St. Paul's at the Consecration of the Bishop of Lincoln and the Bishop of Exeter on the Feast of St. Mark, April 25, 1885.

SERMON XII.

BISHOP SAMUEL WILBERFORCE.

1 COR. ix. 22.

I am made all things to all men, that I might by all means save some 311

Preached at the Parish Church of Graffham, Sussex, November 2, 1875.

SERMON XIII.

JOHN KEBLE.

COL. iii. 10.

The new man, which is renewed unto knowledge, after the image of Him that created him 332

Preached at Keble College, Oxford, on occasion of the Opening of the Chapel and Laying the Foundation-stone of the Hall and Library, on the Feast of St. Mark, April 25, 1876.

SERMON XIV.

EDWARD BOUVERIE PUSEY.

St. Matt. v. 19.

Whosoever shall do and teach the same shall be called great in the kingdom of heaven 355

Preached in St. Margaret's Church, Prince's Road, Liverpool, on the Second Sunday after the Epiphany, January 20, 1884.

THE PRIEST IN HIS INNER LIFE.

IT is a matter for just complaint with candidates for holy orders, that many books which profess to treat of pastoral work address themselves almost exclusively to the external duties of the Christian Priest. They enter at length upon a consideration of such points as the composition of sermons, visiting the sick, schools, ritual; and they continually insist upon the necessity of bringing the inward life to bear upon the discharge of such outward and visible ministries. The existence of an inward life is indeed assumed, but no attempt is made to determine its specific character, or the laws of its formation. Thus a recent writer on the duties of a parish priest remarks by way of appendix to one of the most practical and valued of his lectures, that,—

"After all is said and done the parish priest never can be thoroughly effective in the sick-room, till his own heart shall be in a condition to furnish him readily with the language he should employ in it. He cannot work conviction in another of the heinousness of sin in itself, or of his participation in it, till he has arrived at that conviction himself, and in his own particular instance. He cannot impart to him an adequate sense of the unspeakable comfort contained in the doctrines of the Cross, till in his own very self he has tasted what that comfort is. And if, when sitting by the sick man's side, he finds his ideas stagnant, and his feelings unmoved,—no power to address him, and no knowledge what to say—he has reason to suspect that he has work to do nearer home, before he can be of much use there, that he must *first* be converted himself and *then* strengthen his brother. This however," continues Professor Blunt, "is not a province for a lecturer

---

[1] This Essay appeared originally in the *Ecclesiastic and Theologian*, October 1856 and January 1857.

to enter upon; this is not a lesson to be learned from a professor in the schools, but is to be gathered by self-discipline and self-restraint, in the silence of night and the chamber, amidst the disappointments, the disasters, the vanities, the distresses of life, consecrated all of them to edification by the Spirit of God, Whose good offices are to be sought for and won by purity and prayer."[1]

Is it indeed so? Are the profound experiences of the religious life only to be gained by rude contact with the vicissitudes of the world? Is it indeed true that the soul can only truly know and love God when everything less than He has been tried, and has failed to satisfy her? We venture to think otherwise. Perhaps, indeed, the most familiar type of conversion is that in which sinners first apply themselves to all systems and theories of life which promise happiness and peace, and which cannot confer them, till in despair they at length turn to Him Who created the soul for Himself, and Who makes it restless till it rests in Himself.[2] To whom should they go when all else has failed them, but to Him Who has the words of eternal life? Yet, surely, God can be known by His creatures without making Himself the result of a negative induction. He can, if He will, attract the soul more powerfully by a display of His own surpassing Beauty and Perfections than by discovering the worthlessness of all that disputes His empire. He can win the heart of the youth who has not entered upon life, no less than that of the aged to whom the world has played false. Samuel is a creation of His grace no less than St. Peter, and His hand is as discernible in the long training for their respective labours vouchsafed to St. John Baptist or St. Timothy, as in the conversion of the publican or the harlot.

Moreover, "self-discipline and self-restraint," "in the

[1] Blunt, *Lect. on Duties of a Parish Priest*, p. 239.
[2] St. Aug. *Confessions*, I. i.

silence of night and the chamber," are most necessary, and quite in keeping with that spirit of Primitive Christianity to the illustration of which the late Margaret Professor of Divinity at Cambridge so laudably devoted himself. But they will share the fate of all abstract excellencies, in being admired and eschewed, so long as they are not thrown into a concrete and practical form by those who recommend them. And as for "purity and prayer," it cannot, unfortunately, be assumed by any one who has an intimate knowledge of the moral statistics of our Universities, that a majority of those who yearly leave these seats of learning to devote themselves to the service of the altar will have retained the one grace, or formed habits moderately proportioned to the moral and intellectual development of the other.

Yet they do pass—a continuous stream of life and energy—from the lectures, the boats, the unions, the college chapels, the haunts and associations which are often too degrading to bear mention,—to the pulpits, the deathbeds, the altars of the Church of Jesus Christ. They may have escaped in its most repulsive forms "the corruption that is in the world through lust." They may in better moments have made a real effort to rise "on eagles' wings" and in renewed strength to Him Who made the soul for Himself, and Who alone can unfold and satisfy its complex faculties and its mysterious instincts. But the atmosphere in which they move chills and repels the efforts of Divine grace; the well-pointed sarcasm, the suppressed look of pity of some intellectual acquaintance of whose society they are proud, no less than the rude joke of the boon companion to whom they defer without respecting him, all this does its work in counteracting influences which might help men at our Universities on the road to heaven, and even prepare them in a measure to acquire the temper and experience of the guide of souls.

It is therefore too generally the case that men with closed hearts, and scanty insight into truth, and palsied wills, find themselves suddenly in a position which demands sustained resolution to act for God, and tender charity for the souls of sinners, and piercing intuition into the depths of Divine justice and Divine compassion. They are placed at the centre of the religious life of a parish. From their personal devotion to, and union with, the Source of Life, His healing virtue is to go forth and cleanse and strengthen; they have a part in that priestly commission which inevitably bestows the prominence of a city set on a hill on all who bear it. Sinners cry to them for help, penitents for guidance, aged Christians for consolation and support. "Out of the abundance of the heart the mouth speaketh"; and conversely, where the inner life is faint or languishing, there is, as a matter of course, little or nothing to say.

Of course deadly sin severs the soul from God, and destroys its supernatural life. "The soul that sinneth, it shall die." But many who have not thus fallen, or who, having fallen, have returned to God by formal reconciliation with Him, only do not lead a devotional life, because they do not comprehend the truth that such a life is a work in itself, and, being so, must be treated methodically. They imagine religion to be a sentiment to which they occasionally surrender themselves, rather than a service which lays all the energies of the soul under perpetual obligations to achieve it. They are so alive to the danger of inward or outward formalism, that they forget to do anything with their souls or bodies "decently and in order." The great Apostle took special care to run " not as uncertainly," and in combating his spiritual enemies to aim his blows with definiteness and precision; but some who claim at the present day a somewhat exaggerated right to represent his teaching, seem very lamentably to beat the air, and to suppose that their prospects of reaching heaven are dependent on the irregularity of the efforts they make while upon earth. Such persons will naturally feel little interest in the subjoined observations, if indeed they do not consider them mischievous, as tending to methodise those energies of the supernatural life of a Christian priest, which seem to them more excellent when left to develop themselves and when characterised by an erratic and wayward independence of rule and system. But it may be hoped that a contrary impression prevails more and more increasingly with earnest clergymen, and it is to such that we address ourselves.

I.

The Church of England has not left her clergy to choose for themselves absolutely and without restraint or direction, all the devotions with which they will daily approach the Throne of Mercy. On the contrary, " All Priests and Deacons are to say DAILY the Morning and Evening Prayer, either PRIVATELY or openly, not being let by sickness or some other urgent cause."[1]

Now the principle that to obey is better than sacrifice seems to invest this direction with the dignity of a primary obligation for the consciences of clergymen. They are not thus enjoined to attempt any other nameable devotional exercise. And, *cæteris paribus*, it would be the unhesitating instinct of a religious mind to accept, as the safest course, that which duty may suggest, rather than to seek for something on its own responsibility. It is of course very possible that the time devoted to the daily office

---

[1] Rubric: Concerning the Service of the Church. That the *private* recitation of the Daily Office was not regarded as an improbable case by the compilers of our Prayer Book is further proved by their explicit statement that, "when men say Morning and Evening Prayer *privately*, they may say the same in any language that they themselves do understand."

might be spent in prayers more adapted to elicit, in the case of this man or that, a passionate and tender emotion towards the Person of our Lord and Saviour. Yet this will hardly counterbalance the consideration that obedience is a surer test of love than emotion, even when men seem to check the ardour and impulsiveness of love that they may win her distinguishing and primal characteristic. Like her Divine Master, the Church says to her Priests, "If ye love Me, keep My commandments."

If this be so, it is of importance to observe the extent and definiteness of the obligation. The clergy are not bound to say the Daily Office only at times, when they can enjoy the privilege of joining with a congregation in saying it. They are always and everywhere bound to say it. It is, of course, better to join with others, if possible, but if they cannot do this, they are bound to say it alone. The newly-ordained deacon, who finds himself in a parish where there are two Sunday Services, and an incompetent Rector, is no less bound to say the Daily Service than the stalled member of a Cathedral Chapter. Nor is the obligation discharged, if he puts asunder what the Church has joined together, and reads one chapter and some prayers to his servants, and says the rest alone. For by a certain combination of confessions, psalms, canticles, lessons, and intercessions, the Church designs to produce at one and the same time a double result, one upon the faithful generally, and one upon the soul of the reciting Priest in particular, from the efficacy of such a combination. It might be scarcely possible for any man to appreciate the moral result upon his character, which, however delicate and imperceptible, undoubtedly follows upon his carefully complying with or violating an injunction such as that in question. But in the lapse of years, who will not see the large and very serious influence which such a habit formed under such a sense of responsibility must of necessity produce upon the life of the soul? This result is forfeited when, by an act of self-will, the priest selects from the Daily Service such portions of it as suit the domestic needs of his family, and says, or neglects to say, the rest apart from them. In any case he would use family prayer; and he has an instinct in favour of the daily Church Lessons. But if he thinks that he is complying with the direction of the Church, because he uses portions of its Daily Service in his domestic worship, he is simply deceiving himself, the truth being that he is consulting his own convenience. If he says *the whole*, as enjoined in the Prayer Book, and his family join him, the case is widely different; so long as he *obeys*, there can be no reason against his being joined by all lay Christians who are ready to associate themselves with him, in an act, which may not be with them a matter of duty, but can hardly be other than a source of edification.

It may, perhaps, be thought that the duty is stated in a harsh and technical way, and so is at variance with the spirit of freedom and sonship which ought to characterise all Christian devotions. But let it be considered, that in saying the Daily Service, whether in Church or out of it, whether alone or with others, the Priest acts as a Priest, and makes a solemn act of intercession. In his private prayers, he treats of the needs of his own soul, and its eternal prospects; in the Daily Office, self is almost, if not quite, dismissed, and he acts for others. In the Confession he associates himself with the penitents; in the Psalms and Canticles with the communicants of his flock; in the Creed and "Our Father," and concluding intercessions, he is praying and protesting with all and for all his spiritual family. He may be in his chamber, and they at their several occupations, but, in the Communion of Saints he is acting with them and for them. The Priesthood of the Great Intercessor has descended upon him; and the spirit of that marvellous chapter, S. John xvii., is the spirit of the Daily Office. Even the lessons are not for himself alone; from them he culls and lays up treasures of warning and encouragement and consolation which he cannot keep to himself, but he must go forth and dispense to the sinful, and the faltering, and the broken-hearted. Like the converted thousands of S. Paul, his parishioners are ever in his heart; he is always thankful, joyful, anxious, even agonising, all at once, on their behalf; and the full expression of this ministerial temper he finds in a careful use of the Church's appointed Matins and Evensong, and it may be added—not elsewhere.

Let it be further considered that each separate portion of the Daily Service is meant to bear a distinct relation towards what follows or precedes it. The confession and absolution cleanse the soul from venial sins, before it sings God's praises; the psalms express its gratitude for past mercies, before more are received in the instructions of the appointed lessons, or asked for in the prayers which follow; the lessons, like "letters from the heavenly country" (as St. Augustine used to called Holy Scripture), make the repetition of the creed intelligent and vivid· the creed precedes the concluding intercessions, because he that cometh to God must believe that He is, and that He is what He has revealed Himself to be.[1] By the time the collect for the day is said, the soul has been prepared for this act of formal intercession by confession, by praise, by instruction, by protestation of Catholic belief. It is presumably in a condition widely different from that in which it would have been had it not passed through this varied preparation; and not the least valuable of its qualifications for effectual intercession is the spirit of obedience to the Church's injunctions in which it thus draws nigh

[1] Heb. xi. 6.

to Him Who giveth grace unto the humble. This last advantage is utterly forfeited; the rest, more or less, when —instead of saying the *whole* Daily Service, as a solemn offering to God on behalf of His Body and Spouse, the Church,—a Priest contents himself with "a selection from the Prayer Book adapted for Use in Families," or, with the Psalms and Lessons for the day, or in fact with any possible stratification of prayer, praise, and instruction, which, not being that of the Church, although taken from her formularies, is in fact, a compilation of his own.

But, the Rubric contains a clause, which is not unfrequently understood to amount to a dispensation from observing it altogether. We allude to the words, "not being let by sickness or any other urgent cause." Who is to say what is an "urgent cause"? or who is to say that any reason which Mr. A. thinks sufficiently "urgent" is not so?

Of course, in the present state of discipline, the clergyman who disregards the duty without giving it a moment's consideration is as little likely to be interfered with as he who mistakenly thinks that he *has* good reasons for neglecting it. But the history of the Rubric will assist any honest conscience to discover the sense in which it was imposed upon the Church of England by those Savoy Divines, from whom the English Formularies received their final and still surviving impress. Every tiro in liturgical studies will recognise in this Rubric a continuation of the rule by which the clergy of the Church of England four hundred years ago were bound to the repetition of the Sarum Breviary.

"In 1549," says Mr. Procter, "the direction was limited to those who ministered in any church; but in 1552 the Common Prayer was directly substituted for the Breviary by the order that 'all Priests and Deacons should be bound to say daily the Morning and Evening Prayer, either privately or openly, except they were letted by preaching, studying of divinity, or by some other urgent cause,' and provision continued to be made for the public service by the further order, that curates being at home and not otherwise being reasonably letted, should say the same in their parish church or chapel."[1]

To the same effect Wheatley :—

"The occasion of our rubric was probably a rule in the Roman [*i.e.* English ante-Reformation] Church, by which even before the Reformation and the Council of Trent, the clergy were obliged to recite what they call the Canonical Hours," etc.[2]

It will have been remarked, in 1549 the injunction was not in force—the Sarum Hours were probably still in general use. In 1552 the present rubric was attached to the reformed offices, with one very important variation from its present form. "Preaching," and "studying of divinity" were cited as "causes" of an urgency which might be held sufficient to dispense with the obligation. This was practically to allow men, at their pleasure, to substitute one duty for another; and, as prayer, particularly prescribed prayer, has none of the excitement of "preaching" and "studying of divinity" to recommend it, and its results can only be appreciated by faith of a higher order than that of average clergymen, it was natural that the rubric should become a dead letter. Besides which the whole genius of the Elizabethan age was against prayer and in favour of preaching; it was an age impatient of devotional contemplation, and eager in its treatment of religion under an almost exclusively speculative and intellectual aspect; and men, therefore, who would stand well with their age (and when has such a motive not had power with the majority ?) would be easily persuaded that there were other calls upon their time more "urgent" than the obligation to say daily service.

When, therefore, the Savoy Divines undertook the

[1] Procter on Common Prayer, p. 178.
[2] Wheatley's *Rational Illustration*, chap. ii. § 1.

revision of the Prayer Book, they cancelled the clause by which preaching, or studying of divinity, were held to be sufficiently "urgent causes" for a neglect of this first of clerical duties, and they substituted another by which sickness was declared to be such a cause. It would seem that they proceeded upon a principle which may be recognised pretty clearly. The rubric of 1552 made the suspension of the duty to depend on the will of man, that of 1662 referred it to the will of God. The clergy were not henceforth to decide that other duties might be more important to them than the solemn tribute of their daily service; He alone, to Whom that service was due, was by the course of His providence to suspend its payment. While their predecessors had legislated as if the personal edification of the clergy was the one end and purpose of the Daily Office; the great Caroline Divines regarded that office as a tribute exacted from His ministers by the Lord of Life Whose glory was promoted by it, and Who must be left to signify for Himself, when He would waive His rights—and further as an act of charity towards souls perpetually obligatory on the Christian priest,—the omission of which was fraught with injury to the vitality of the Church, and with danger to the souls of her pastors. And this is indeed the actual meaning of the existing rubric which embodies the mind of the English Church of the seventeenth century on this subject, as distinct from that of the latter part of the sixteenth. If the history of the rubric be allowed to throw light upon its intention, we cannot doubt that the Church of England, when she last considered the question, deliberately phrased it in a manner which should make the Daily Office a sacred obligation upon all her conscientious ministers when they were not *physically incapacitated* from saying it.

1. But, it will be asked, how is such a representation of this obligation consistent with the fact that of those

whom it mainly concerns, a vast proportion have never observed it? Here is a sacred duty—incumbent upon an order which is the teacher and guardian of morals—not merely notoriously neglected, but in many quarters absolutely ignored. This fact, it will be argued, must be accepted as an interpretation and comment upon the meaning of the rubric, illustrating its actual force by the general and practical sense of the Church, and reducing its proportions from those of a sharply defined precept, wielding an empire in the well-regulated conscience and over the disciplined will, to the limits of a more or less valuable suggestion addressed to the individual judgment, taste, or sense of religious expediency.

In reply, it may be remarked that the non-observance of this rule of the Church has been unduly exaggerated both by its opponents and advocates. Such exaggeration is a natural mistake. Religious men do not parade the habits which bind them to God; they are more or less "hidden secretly in His tabernacle from the strife of tongues" and public scrutiny. The kingdom of God did not originally come "with observation," and it is set up in individual hearts as unostentatiously as may be consistent with the terms of submitting to it. This feature of unobtrusiveness and retirement as characterising the practices of the Christian life, although estimated at its true moral value in the Sermon on the Mount, is held by the world, and sometimes by religious men who are looking on, to argue weakness, or failure, or inefficiency, or even more, in men and institutions among whom it prevails. We too often believe only in what we see; and we take it for granted that excellence which does not display itself does not exist, or it would be forward to proclaim the fact of its existence. How false this principle is, they will best know who are at all intimate with the lives of the saints of Christendom. And it is not to be supposed that we can at all judge of the extent to which the present precept was observed in the seventeenth century (for example), from the records of its observance which happen to have been transmitted to us. To do so would be to ignore the general instinct of religious men, and therefore of a conscientious clergyman, bound as he would be by the example and precept of our Divine Lord to say little and do much. It would be to forget how this tendency to keep religious practices out of sight had received a new impulse from the Reformation, in consequence of its real or alleged apprehensions of formalism, and that therefore an English clergyman's religious life would, under almost any circumstances, be less public than that of a French ecclesiastic. Moreover it would be a fatal miscalculation, from its omission to take into the account that peculiar εἰρωνεία of the Englishman's character, which mantles in privacy and reserve his religious no less than his domestic and social habits, and which has always been an important element in the past, as it will be in any future practical developments of English Christianity.

Some few years ago a catena of authorities on this subject was published in Oxford;[1] and, although we believe that it might be added to on further research, it is in its present form a very sufficient attestation of the fact that the rubric under consideration cannot be described as having been a dead letter, since it has exerted a very powerful influence on the past mind of the English Church. And, although it should be admitted that a large proportion of the clergy have ignored this direction, it must not be forgotten that when the Church last addressed herself to the subject in her corporate capacity, she increased the definiteness and obligatory character of the duty—a fact which more than counterbalances, in a moral point of view, the licence and neglect of Puritan or Latitudinarian

[1] *Tracts for the Times*, No. 84.

sections of the clergy, however respectable, numerous, or influential.

2. But, secondly, it will be objected that the Service itself witnesses against its being used in private. The plural pronoun in the prayers and collects, the invitation, "Let us pray"; the Versicles which imply a Response, still more the Absolution, and Exhortation, forbid the supposition that the compilers of this Service actually contemplated its being said in private and by way of intercession. This is what may be said; and it would be sufficient to urge in answer the fact that the Sarum Breviary was similarly used, yet that it was equally congregational in its structure. The Reformers passed on a principle which they found in existence without discussing it. That principle maintained that the fittest private devotions for the interceding priest in his closet were precisely those which he would use if he were in choir. Why was this, but because the Communion of Saints was most vividly brought before the mind by an office which will not allow its reciter to believe himself alone? He is alternately priest and people: he confesses and he absolves; he addresses and he listens; he prays, and he ratifies his own intercessions by the solemn "Amen"; he sustains throughout a double capacity, and it is the Church's intention that he should do so. She will not allow him to forget that he is a member of a body, and has duties towards it. In the life of faith, as in the eternal world, time and space are reduced to being mere conditions of human thought; they cease to separate as in the world of sense. The priest is never without a congregation; though it be far away, and have chosen an earlier or later hour than his own, or none at all; like St. Paul, he is separated from it, in person only, not in spirit and reality; for men of all times and countries meet in Catholic communion before the throne of God, drawn by

the principle of life, ever energetic and one in its operations,—the sacred Manhood of our Divine Lord, as diffused in His Church through the agency of the Co-equal and Eternal Spirit. And therefore so far from its being matter for surprise that the Daily Office of the solitary clergyman is the language not of an individual, but of a Church; it is almost inconceivable that the Church could ever have sanctioned a different arrangement, without weakening her sense of the truth that her clergy pray not for themselves, but for and with her to whom they minister. "We are to remember," observes Bishop Cosin, " that we which are priests are called 'Angeli Domini'; and it is the Angel's office, not only to descend to the people and teach them God's Will, but to ascend to the presence of God to make intercession for the people, and to *carry up the daily prayers of the Church* in their behalf, as here they are bound to do."[1]

3. But, where, after all, it will be asked, does this injunction occur? It is not in an Article, not even in a Canon,—it is embodied in a Rubric. And is it not, it may be urged, sufficiently notorious that in the judgment of the living Church of England—the overwhelming majority of her Bishops and Clergy—the Rubrics can be kept only so far as custom, or the local impulse of the Church prescribes? Rubrics, then, it will be said, belong to questions of taste and propriety, to archæological and ecclesiological dilettantism: but to give them weight in a question of moral obligation is to offer a deliberate insult to strong minds, and to lay a mischievous snare for weak consciences.

Waiving the large question as to the obligatory character of the Rubrics as a whole, as irrelevant to the present discussion, it is nevertheless obvious to remark, that any injunction which proceeds from authority

[1] *Works*, vol. v. p. 2.

cannot be set aside without moral injury to the person doing so, unless it be set aside upon a principle—the principle of an intercepting law or higher obligation. The servant who is sent on a message is not morally at liberty to remain at home because he wishes to do so; he is unquestionably right in remaining if the house were suddenly on fire, or the order countermanded. Any authority, however weak, provided only that it exists at all, imposes precepts which have power in the forum of conscience, and which a religious man will not therefore disregard because the subject-matter is thought trivial or the imposing authority weak and incompetent to enforce obedience. This needs insisting on, considering the cavalier manner in which Rubrical questions are discussed at present, just as though they were purely matters of taste, and in no sense matters of morality and upright adherence to obligations of a formal character. If a Rubric be set aside at all, it must be set aside upon a principle. It is a further question, which need not now be entered upon, whether any sufficient principle for neglect of rubrical observance can in truth be pleaded. Possibly not. But clearly, if the Church has power to decree rites and ceremonies, as our Article affirms that she has, her decrees can only cease to bind, when some sufficient reason has been adduced, which will hold good in the court of conscience. Men confess this, when they say that they neglect the Rubrics, because to observe them would offend others, and so, that they defer to the law of charity, or again when they plead want of explicitness on the part of the Rubrics themselves, and say, that they contradict or seem to contradict each other. *Such* pleas prove at least the conviction that some plea is needed; and a plea can only be needed where what is a *primâ facie* duty is to be overruled. Let us apply the above-named pleas to the matter in hand. Grant that to preach in the surplice would lead to a breach of Christian love, and that a clergyman who substituted Saints'-Day for Sunday Lessons would be liable to the charge of having acted without very definite instructions. Can it be said, that any, the most sensitive anti-Tractarian, could be offended by the curate's compliance with the law of the Daily Service in the privacy of his home? or can it be maintained, that the direction to say the Daily Office *privately*, if public opportunities do not present themselves, is not as explicit as words can make it? The ordinary pleas for non-observance of the Rubrics in general do not apply to the direction before us; it therefore retains its character of an obligatory command addressed to all priests and deacons of the Church of England, and it can only be set aside, by doing violence to the conscience, if it is in the least alive to the moral bearings of the question.

And it is difficult to suppose that if, on the one hand, men believe with the Great Apostle, that every priest taken from among men is ordained for men in things pertaining to God, that he may offer gifts and sacrifices for sins,[1] and on the other, that great perils are necessarily incidental to the endeavour to discharge this work of intercession,—that to live perpetually on the vestibule of heaven has dangers no less than blessings—that to approach the everlasting God with words of our own, or selections of our own from His Word, involves an element of risk,—if this were felt, the Daily Office would appear not in the light of a bondage and a law, to free itself from which the clerical conscience must engage the services of a questionable casuistry, but rather would it be hailed as a merciful and welcome provision, enabling the priesthood, with diminished responsibilities to discharge daily that work of intercession, which God awaits at their hands, on which depends the destiny of souls, and

[1] Heb. v. 1.

for which they must most solemnly give account hereafter.

"We" (observes Bishop Cosin, in a passage written before 1638, and speaking in the name of the English clergy), "we are also bound, as all priests are in the Church of Rome, daily to repeat and say the public service of the Church. And it is a precept the most useful and necessary of any others that belong to the ministers of God, and such as have the cure of other men's souls."[1] The grounds of the first of these assertions have been already in a measure discussed. The truth of the second can only be fully tested by individual experience. Many a living priest of the English Church will fervently echo the assertion of the great Caroline Bishop of Durham, that the precept which enjoins the use, whether private or public, of the Daily Office is "the most useful and necessary of any others that belong to the minister of God."

It is most useful to those to whom he ministers, not merely because it makes interest for them with the All-merciful God, but because it further does or may promote to an almost indefinite extent the ministerial capabilities of their pastor. It deepens his familiarity with the words of Scripture, and the formularies of the Church. He is constrained, almost in self-defence, to make continual efforts to penetrate more and more thoroughly the deeper meaning of what he repeats so frequently. Divine truths are stamped upon his soul, not merely as on that of a mature intellect by enforced concession to conviction and argument, but as on the soul of a little child, by way of frequent repetition, and almost of physical indentation. This will make itself felt in his sermons and in his private ministrations, illustrating thereby the original mind and purpose of the Church as declared in the Preface to the Prayer Book of 1549. "The Fathers," we are told, "so

[1] *Works*, vol. v. p. 9.

ordered the matter, that all the whole Bible, or the greatest part thereof, should be read over once every year; intending thereby that the clergy, and especially such as were ministers in the congregation, should (by often reading and meditation in God's Word) be stirred up to godliness themselves, and be more able to exhort others by wholesome doctrine, and to confute them that were adversaries to the truth."[1] And in fact, the Daily Service "reverently, attentively, and devoutly" said, contributes most effectively to store the soul with matter from which meditations, sermons, private counsels, may draw an ever fresh and plenteous supply. Earnest men are pretty generally agreed as to the value, almost as to the necessity, of extempore preaching, uniting as it does the advantage of popularity to that of accordance with Catholic instinct and ancient prescription. But to attempt this, if the soul be not daily fed with the nourishment of psalm, and creed, and prayer, would be rash, if not disastrous. It would be difficult for a man who does not habitually breathe the Church's atmosphere and utter her words, to speak in public without departing from her mind and temper.

Again, the priest who is much among his people knows how effective is a reference to the lesson or psalm *of the day*, as proving to his flock that he has been with God, even though they have not followed him; and men often remark how the daily services seem to coincide, as if by a providential guidance, with the needs of their daily parochial work, and how the very psalm or the lesson for the day, suggest themselves irresistibly as most opportune when a sinner has to be warned, or a penitent to be cheered, or a deathbed to be visited—prescribing to them at the needful hour "what they shall say and what they shall speak." Or again, when travelling, and exposed to the many temptations which occur in the domestic circle

[1] Concerning the Service of the Church.

or in general society to lay aside the keen and collected spirit of an ambassador from heaven, the clergyman is recalled to his true and never-ceasing relation to God and the Church by the recurring office which must be said, and which, by the difficulty he has in saying it, enables him to test the degree in which he has admitted to his heart a worldly and un-Christlike temper.

This is the value of the precept. It obliges the minister of God utterly to realise His presence at least twice in the day. Either he must do this or be guilty of a miserable hypocrisy. It will be said, perhaps, that the Church has no right to force her clergy to the risk of such a sin ; but no religious duty can be prescribed without such risk. Every religious gift and grace may be profaned and become a "savour of death unto death." To some our Lord's own most gracious words were addressed only with the result of depriving them of any cloak for their sin. Of course the Daily Office *may* make some clergymen formalists and hypocrites; but the Church runs this risk, deliberately, with some that she may make many "remembrancers who keep not silence, and give the Lord no rest until He establish, and till He make Jerusalem a praise in the earth."[1] Like the unvarying ritual in heaven which is uttered by spirits who move incessantly before the very throne of God, the Daily Service of the Church befits and expresses the temper of those who ask one thing of the Lord, that they may renounce all for His most gracious and winning Presence, that they may dwell in His courts, and be satisfied with the pleasures of His house, even of His holy temple. To others it may seem unreal and formal; to the living soul of him who bears Christ's commission, it helps to generate that reverent love and piercing knowledge of the Being of Beings which makes men angels, and fits them for eternity.

Isa. lxii. 6, 7.

II.

It may be safely asserted that, generally speaking, no one practice of the Religious Life can exist alone. In dogmatic theology, we know, that each separate article of the Faith implies with more or less distinctness, that whole cycle of teaching of which it is a part. In morals, a single defect is held sufficient to vitiate an action or a life; and excellence must be complete " if it is to exist, in any true sense, at all." " Bonum ex causâ integrâ, malum ex quolibet defectu."[1] So the religious life is a whole, and to its continued existence the integrity of its essential elements is absolutely necessary. A solitary religious practice, isolated from the other acts and temper of which it is at once the expression and complement, will dwindle first of all into a formalism, and at length be abandoned in disgust.

The Church of England then, in prescribing for her clergy the daily use of Matins and Evensong, has, in effect, prescribed to them the Religious Life. For the efficient discharge of this one duty a devotional and collected temper is required, which must be developed by other expedients. The case of a man who should ignore or neglect the formation of such a temper, and yet attempt to obey the Church's rule, would be lamentable, but certain. He would first of all be distressed by the contrast between his own inward life, its aims, tone, and atmosphere, and that of the formularies, from periodical contact with which his sense of duty would not allow him to escape. Gradually, this sense of contrast would weaken and die, and the service would be said more and more mechanically. At length a crisis would arrive, however

---

[1] Compare St. Thom. Aq. *Prima Sec.* qu. 18, art. 4, 3; or Sanderson, Serm. i. *ad Pop.* § 14. *De Oblig. Consc. Prælect.* ii. § 9.

originating: nature would revolt at a degrading and hypocritical mechanism claiming to represent the soul's aspirations towards its Maker; and the practice would be abandoned, without a suspicion that it might have become the stimulus and centre of vital religion, and not without a sneer at the Church which did not erase such a stumbling-block to earnest and honest men from its authorised formularies.

But in truth the sense of contrast between the language of the Prayer Book, and the inward life of the clergyman —created as this is by the grace of God—is meant by Him to issue in a widely different result. He makes us thus uneasy, at the existence of an admitted evil, that He may guide us to the remedy. It is His gracious purpose, that the soul should be continually approximating to the devotional type which is set before it in the Psalter, and that as it expands with ever-increasing tenderness and awe towards Him Who is its Centre and Sun, it should more and more perfectly appropriate and feel at home with that inspired language in which the saints have, for three thousand years, learned to know and to love Him. But how is this to be effected? We reply, by Meditation.

Now Meditation is a duty, with which every person who is attempting to lead a religious life, is supposed to be familiar. The Bible says so much about it, that in a Bible-reading country like ours, everybody takes it for granted. But the popular idea of meditation is, we apprehend, as indefinite as it is general. It supposes at least this, that the mind is exercised on a religious subject. But beyond this it cannot advance. You see a worthy clergyman in his study,—he is resting his elbow on the table, and reflecting on some portions of his Bible —making remarks at intervals to his wife. This is indeed better than nothing, although it be a feeble and dreamy effort, failing in reverence, in intellectual address, in analysis, in stimulating the imagination, in challenging and coercing the will, in opening the soul in very truth to the eye of its God, and making it court His gaze,—in short, failing in all the great purposes of meditation. It fails in these because it fails in *system*; meditation to be real MUST BE systematic; and the soul should be taught to move just as systematically and reverently when in the Divine Presence as the body. Such a meditation as this bears the same sort of relation to that of the well-instructed Christian, as does the rant of a meeting-house to the ritual of a well-appointed church. It is indeed an effort in the right direction, but an effort at once undisciplined, aimless, fruitless,—because "not according to knowledge," because without "decency and order."

Meditation is popularly conceived to be an act of the soul when in a state of partial passivity and listlessness. It can think, contemplate, speculate, when through circumstances it is debarred from action. To meditate when a man can act is to lose time, and to be unpractical. Such is the popular idea on the subject: but we maintain, on the contrary, that meditation implies an active exertion of all the powers of the soul,—that it is impossible when the intellect is wearied, and the will languid, and the memory overcast—that it demands, in short, intellectual and moral activity, and that in return, it illuminates the intellect, and nerves and braces the will. Meditation is an act of the whole soul, rising in the fulness of its energy towards its God. It is not merely systematic thought about Divine things, because such thought can exist when one power only of the soul is exercised, whereas meditation exercises all. Still less is it mere resolution to live justly and holily, resolution being sudden, and not always implying the exercise of thought. Nor is it mere action of the memory, however well-stored and docile,—for memory does not necessarily lead to intellectual or moral analysis, which is of the essence of meditation. Least of all is it mere indulgence of the imagination or religious fancy: for this is compatible with utter paralysis of the will, and with feeble and desultory apprehension of Divine Truth on the part of the intellect. None of these powers can meditate alone: but in their conjunction the understanding, the memory, the imagination, and the will, do effect that interpenetration of the soul by the atmosphere of Revealed Truth, that living simultaneous apprehension of its severities and its beauty, that sensitiveness which cannot but act upon what is known, and does not shrink from knowledge lest it should involve action; results—which lie at the basis of the true priestly character. The mental powers were given us that we might return them to God, and this is best done by meditation. The reason has a higher subject-matter than mathematics; the memory than Horace and Virgil; the imagination than poetry and works of fiction; the will than the effort to live and rise in life. The true object of the reason is the Incomprehensible; His Revelation of Himself is that of the memory: the imagination was meant to gaze in perpetual fascination on His surpassing Beauty; and His Holy Law is the one correlative of the human will. Man, in short, was made for God; and so far as the human soul is concerned, this truth is expressed by meditation.

Of course it is only gradually that the Christian soul learns how to apply her natural faculties to supernatural ends. At first the soul moves awkwardly and indecorously in the presence of God. Fluttered and confused, like a negro entering a Christian church for the first time in his life, she cannot reconcile her own activity with the Presence of Him Who is eternal Rest. She is too excited to lie quiet and adore; too awestruck to move with collectedness and self-possession. She is alternately attracted and repelled,—first won by the beauty of the supernatural world, then scared by its exceeding fearfulness. As she gazes, mysteries are transacted which confuse her apprehension; groups of beings throng around, with movements which she cannot interpret; voices sound, which, though the familiar words of Holy Writ, seem to her purposely unintelligible; she is in a blaze of light, but she is simply oppressed by it, unable to appreciate its piercing beauty, or to note its discoveries, or to mark its varying scintillations, or to pursue it with adoring love to its Source and Fountain. She shuts her eyes, and, while moving where all else is order and devotion, she alone is distracted, almost to being irreverent, and she begins to feel that the Presence of God, as revealed in meditation, demands from the soul the manners and bearing of those who move habitually around His Throne, and that it is beyond her present education and attainments.

Every parish priest knows how different is the hasty walk, the excited gaze, the uncontrolled prostration, the rapid and unmeasured words of the new communicant, from the calm, collected, restrained, yet profound devotion of the man who has for years been constant in his attendance at the foot of the altar; and such is the difference between the beginner in meditation and the Christian who has made some progress.

We will endeavour to describe a meditation, in its leading features, premising that any such description is necessarily very general, and may need much adaptation to the wants and eccentricities of particular cases.

You first of all place yourself on your knees. This is *essential*; it reminds us that the attitude of the soul towards Divine Truth is one not of criticism, but of utter, prostrate, adoring self-surrender to God's assertions and commands. "Let God be true, and every man a liar," is the motto of the temper of mind which befits meditation. Meditation supposes the natural reason to have yielded to what St. Paul delighted to call "the obedience of faith": and proceeding on this assumption, it advances to "subdue every thought to the obedience of Christ." The world of time and sense, its transient and deceptive appearances, are left behind, and the soul and body lie motionless before Him Who is the Truth itself,—incapable alike of deceiving and being deceived,—and before that Revelation which is at once an attestation of His having spoken, and a record of what He has vouchsafed to say. "Taceant omnes doctores: sileant omnes creaturæ in conspectu Tuo; Tu mihi loquere solus,"[1]—is the language of the soul as she places herself in the Presence of the Ever-Blessed Trinity, with a view to meditation.

Before and above her is the Almighty, Everlasting, Infinite God, Three and yet One, "dwelling in light which no man can approach unto," surrounded by the whole company of Heaven, the four awful creatures, the twenty-four elders, the thousand times ten thousand. The Word made Flesh is there: His Sacred and Immaculate Manhood is adored by Archangels, Apostles, Prophets, Martyrs, Confessors, Virgins, Innocents. On this side lies the narrow path to Paradise, steep, thorny, unfrequented; on that the "facilis descensus Averni," the descent to the Eternal Pit broad and inviting, thronged with its countless multitudes. This presence when realised forces the soul involuntarily to preparatory prayer. In a few heartfelt petitions, she (1) protests to God her utter distrust of self, her firm trust in His boundless compassion, her resolution to attempt in His strength that to which nature is so unequal, and next (2) she resigns herself to His Will, as to the results of meditation,—assuring Him of her readiness to accept cheerfully from Him mental

[1] *De Imitat. Christi*, i. 2.

darkness, or dryness of spirit, or a sense of being deserted by Him, or distractions, no less than His illuminating and consoling grace. The earnestness with which this last petition can be urged will enable a man to test how far he is seeking God because He is God, or only because meditation is a distinct source of intellectual pleasure to His intelligent creatures.

So much for the first step in meditation : the second consists in a careful consideration of the particular subject which is to furnish material on the present occasion. As the meditation will be attempted, if possible, early in the morning, when the powers of the soul are fresh, vigorous, and undistracted, the materials will have been perused over-night. The fact, whether mystery or doctrine, parable or miracle, which is to be approached, now comes before the soul, and while the memory carefully gathers up the fragments of the sacred narrative, the imagination, although under rein, mantles the object of meditation in appropriate scenery, gives life and vividness to scenes, persons, and actions concerned, and seizes with eager penetration on everything which can render the object of contemplation more real, lifelike, and fascinating to the mental powers. For, as Hooker remarks, "the mind, while in this present life, whether it contemplate, meditate, deliberate, or howsoever exercise itself, worketh nothing without continual recourse unto imagination, the only storehouse of wit, and peculiar chair of memory."[1] And if it should appear dangerous to admit a faculty which has for its object-matter beauty as distinct from truth to a conference with the truth itself —a faculty so erratic and creative as the human imagination ; let it be considered by those who feel the objection to have weight, that if God as the Eternal Truth is the Object-matter of the intellect, and as Archetypal Purity is that of the moral sense, so there is a faculty which He has

Eccles. Pol. v. 67. 7.

created that it might seek and find Him, as the Uncreated Beauty. Men are led to Christ from the world, sometimes because He alone has the words of eternal life, sometimes too, because He alone defies the criticism of the moral sense, but sometimes also because in His Body Mystical, no less than in the days of His Flesh, He is "fairer than the children of men." And it may further be remarked, that if the imagination were to be denied *any* share in helping the human soul to find and enjoy its God, it is, at least, singular that He should have spoken to it in language of a structure and phraseology calculated to stimulate it to peculiar activity. It is singular, we repeat, that Revelation, which might have been thrown into the form of hard prose or formal propositions, should be imbedded in poetry such as that of the Psalter, or Isaiah, or the Canticles, if God were unwilling to be sought by His servants through the action of their imaginations as well as through that of their intellects.

It is the intellect which is next summoned to the Divine Presence. Memory has recalled the subject of meditation; imagination has surrounded it with circumstance and detail; but to stop here would be to reduce meditation to the proportions of an imaginative reverie. The understanding accordingly proceeds to grapple with the subject, and to do this effectively, it must analyse it. It breaks up the sacred narrative or message, which has just been contemplated as a whole, and apprehends it piecemeal. There is, of course, some danger here, lest mere intellectual speculation should take the place of intelligent apprehension of Divine Truth; and, to guard against this, it will be found necessary to have a constant eye to practical points, and to lay emphasis upon them. There is danger, even in practical people, of an over-anxiety to grasp many truths at once, so as to contemplate them in their symmetry and relative independence: and this will best be obviated by a resolution to be content with one point at a time, and sternly to exclude conterminous subjects which press, however invitingly, for consideration. It should also be observed that the temptation to give exaggerated attention to a favourite dogma, and so to violate the analogy and due proportions of the Faith, is one against which a man must be on his guard while engaged in meditation, more than at any other time; because the soul is not then under the control of external restraints, as in the Church Service, where we are obliged to move forward, and is particularly likely to surrender herself to the guidance of a temporary preference connected with the controversial or other circumstances of the day. And to do this would be very fatally to forfeit that religious discipline which is one of the most valuable results of systematic meditation. On the other hand, if this be borne in mind, it may very fairly be assumed that to follow the guidance of God the Holy Ghost, should He vouchsafe any special illumination, would be the part of Christian prudence, no less than of Christian reverence.

But the end to which the intellect will direct its energies is this,—the selection of some one point *for action or imitation*. This is indispensable. It must be *one* point, not many: and, when chosen, no time must be lost in acting on it. Most men will, or ought to know enough about themselves, to be anxious for something bearing on the improvement of their own character, or on their besetting sin. It is the privilege of saints to meditate with a view to acting upon others,—although it certainly ought to be the practice of clergymen. But most men "hide God's image within their heart, that *they* themselves should not sin against Him."

This done, the intellect retires, and the point upon which it has fixed as cardinal is transferred to the will. This is the soul—the crisis, of the meditation. That the will may embrace the duty or practice selected by the intellect from the materials which have been considered, it becomes necessary that the affections should be forced to act upon what as yet has been only contemplated intellectually. Will, as we all know, results from the union of desire and reason; but while it is their joint result, it can control them separately. Hence it is, that as men are responsible for what they believe, so they will have to answer for what they love. In the well-disciplined soul of the Christian, the affections are all perfectly under control; he is as little the creature of impulses proceeding from within as of circumstances pressing from without; and, moreover, when conscience bids, he can concentrate his affections upon a given object, not artificially, and as though under constraint, but with the full play, the gushing freshness of a natural impulse. Some modern writers who seem to think that human nature is only respectable when it is lawless and undisciplined, are incapable of understanding the belief of the Church that the powers of the soul only enjoy perfect freedom when self has been annihilated, and impulse is enslaved to the law and will of Jesus Christ. Such, however, is the fact: the perfect Christian offers and presents unto God himself, his *soul* and body, "to be a reasonable, holy, and lively sacrifice unto Him." Our Lord Jesus Christ was never subject to impulse: His every affection was under perfect restraint: He only loved when He willed to love: He only felt sorrow when He willed to feel it; He was never surprised into an exercise of His affections which His will did not sanction; He "looked on the young man," and "loved him"; He appointed a time and place for His Mental Agony, and then with full consciousness of what He was going to breast, He "began to be sorrowful"; He walked to the grave of Lazarus, and when there, "He wept." His inner life, no less than His Sacred Body, was perfectly His own, and beyond the reach of external or internal circumstance; but He did not love, grieve, compassionate with less intensity, because He felt pity, grief, and love, only when He perfectly willed to exercise these affections. And in such proportion as the Christian becomes conformed to the image of Jesus Christ, his inner life is characterised by this same feature of perfect self-control; he suspends and he exercises affection when he wills to do so, and he wills when conscience bids him: but his affections are not the less genuine, vigorous, and hearty, because they are held in obedience to the governing principle of the soul, and are projected at its bidding upon rightful objects. Train any natural power, and you *may* either cripple or develop it: but men would long ago have been savages again if the former had been the normal and the latter the accidental result of training: and experience has shown that mind and body gain strength, when nature is kept somewhat under check and discipline, —instead of losing it.

We need therefore be under no apprehension of artificiality in proceeding to direct the affections upon the object of meditation. Our power of doing so will depend upon the discipline of the soul, not upon the natural peculiarities of our individual psychology. We CAN do so, if we will. We *can*, as Christians who have God's grace, love Him; we *can* hate His enemy the Evil Spirit; we *can* abhor sin; we *can* grieve over that which grieves our Lord; if we only *will* to grieve, to hate, to love.

This exercise of the affections will often atone for the deficiencies of the understanding. Emotion in uneducated men has often supplied the place of culture. "A strong and pure affection concentrates the attention on its objects, fastens on them the whole soul, and thus gives vividness of conception. It associates intimately all the ideas which are congenial with itself; ... it seems to stir up the soul from its foundations, and to attract to itself and to impregnate with its own fire whatever elements, conceptions, illustrations can be pressed into its own service. ... Every minister can probably recollect periods, when devotional feeling has seemed to open a new foundation of thought in the soul." [1] We quote this remark of a Socinian writer, who is not generally prone to undervalue the office of the intellect in religion, or to exaggerate that of the affections, by way of showing that when spiritual writers on meditation recommend us to give great attention to the exercise of the affections, they do it on this ground, that while the intellect can never do the work of the affections, the affections, under the guidance of the will, may achieve that of the intellect. Love implies knowledge: but knowledge does not imply love.

Here then the soul must linger in the presence of our Lord, laying her inmost being before Him, and entering into reverent, yet confiding and affectionate conferences with Him. Here, like Moses, Christians may talk to Him face to face, as a man speaketh with his friend: here, like children, the brethren of the Only Son, Christians may seek and embrace their Father, in the full liberty of the Spirit. Here, if a penitent, the soul will renew acts of faith, hope, love, and contrition; she will renounce and accuse herself; she will distrust, blame, humble, hate herself; she will implore the Divine mercy, and in fear and trembling will admire the love of Christ which passeth knowledge, and which has spared one so guilty and defiled. Here, if advancing in the religious life, she will give expression to the graces of love, joy, peace—for, in, and with God; long-suffering, gentleness, goodness, towards others; faith, meekness, temperance; admitting very heartily her sad shortcomings in not

[1] Channing, *Works*, Part II. page 454; London and Glasgow, 1855.

corresponding with the gracious agency of the Holy Spirit. She will sigh to God for more perfect unworldliness, more purity of intention, more zeal for the salvation of others, more sensitiveness of conscience. Here, if living near to God, she will boldly claim His Friendship, and His Blessing; will insist on the Power of the Blood of Jesus Christ, with which she has been sprinkled at Baptism and in Penitence; will assure God that she desires to live for Him, to die for Him, to rest perfectly in Him, to be utterly conformed to Him, to glory in Him alone, to offer self to Him without reserve, to do all to His greater glory, to be perfectly united to Him. And in any case it would be desirable here,—(1) by casting oneself upon God, to nerve the soul for future sufferings; (2) to resolve to sacrifice any cherished inclination or pursuit which is at variance with clerical or Christian perfection; (3) to make a perfect oblation of self to the Blessed Trinity, as the End and Lord of the Soul by Creation, by Baptism, by Confirmation, by Ordination.

In closing the meditation it will be of importance to pause for any further suggestions of God the Holy Spirit, —to pay particular attention to the *practical resolution* to which the exercise of the intellect leads, and which the will confirms, and to pray that God will give strength manfully to abide by it.

It is not easy to recommend a good book for beginners in meditation. Indeed, such a book has long been a desideratum in our devotional literature. Dr. Hook's *Meditations for Every Day in the Year* would be better described as pious reflections; they lack the method, the nerve, the point of meditations. The *Daily Steps towards Heaven* is a valuable work for those who have made progress, and can supply from the stores of their inward life what is wanted to give substance and development to its suggestions. Beginners complain of it as not sufficiently suggestive;[1] and in its English dress it is only intended for lay use. We want a book of clerical meditations, more formal and systematic than Mr. Pinder's work on the Ordinal—more distinctly clerical than the adaptations of Nouet and Avrillon, edited by Dr. Pusey. The model seems to be furnished by the great work of L. De Ponte; but it should be of English growth, and should teem with references to the English formularies, otherwise it will always pass for an exotic, and will fail to touch the heart and influence the mind of the English Church.

Meanwhile it may be suggested that the parables and miracles of our Blessed Lord, the Messianic Psalms, and, above all, the history of the Passion, as they stand in our English Bibles, may, by the application of an adequate method, become materials for meditation.[2] It is a very good plan to keep a Psalter and New Testament for the purposes of private devotion, as the margin may easily be used for analysis in pen and ink; and in this way the Church of England precept " by daily reading and WEIGHING of the Scriptures to wax riper and stronger in the " priestly " ministry," would be obeyed in a much more satisfactory manner than, it is to be feared, is at present generally the case.

We have said thus much on meditation because it lies at the root of the priestly life, and is of primary importance. We have seen that it is practically implied by the injunction to say the Daily Service, which else is likely to lead to habits of formalism. But it also implies self-examination. For unless the soul knows her own

---

[1] The *Meditationes* of Avancini, from which the *Daily Steps* is an adaptation, was written specially for priests; and if we allow for Roman peculiarities—is a very valuable work.

[2] As an assistance to the analysis of Scripture on Patristic principles, we would recommend Kilber's *Analysis Biblica*, recently reprinted at Paris. The Psalter is analysed so as peculiarly to fit it for meditation.

deformity and weakness, she never will project herself with sufficient constancy and resolution upon the thought of God, and the phenomena of the supernatural world. "I thought upon my ways; and turned my feet unto Thy testimonies." A priest's self-examination will, of course, have to cover a larger ground than a layman's in proportion to his larger and more serious obligations; it will have to consider the same duties under more complex relations; it will have to keep an eye on the tendency to certain deep and very subtle sins (such as the love of power and influence for their own sake, and apart from the work of Christ, or certain disguised forms of spiritual pride) incidental to the ministerial position and its temptations.

But meditation, when systematically pursued, contributes very materially to promote other features of the devotional life. It must have occurred to most thoughtful persons, that the practice of ejaculatory prayer is one peculiarly adapted to meet the requirements of the present day. We live in an age and country where the energies of those who seriously labour for the cause and kingdom of Jesus Christ are over-taxed to an unprecedented extent. Those who give most time to prayer give but little when it is meted in the measure of antiquity. But perishing souls cry for succour, and the forces of Satan never consent to an armistice during which the Christian priest may draw more plenteous draughts of water from the wells of salvation, to supply the needs of his own soul. Certainly pastoral labour may be prayer if it is offered to God, but it must be sanctified by this intention of doing it for Him, and in His strength, however hurried and informal may be the movement of the soul by which such an intention receives expression. Again, there are many intervals during the day which the clergyman who knows the truth of

Leighton's remark, that "the grace of God in the heart of man is like a tender plant in an unkindly soil," will be careful not to lose, when they may be devoted to short but earnest intercourse with our Blessed Lord. In passing from cottage to cottage, or while waiting at a railway station, or in the sacristy of the parish church, the soul of the pastor ought to rise spontaneously to the throne of God; and the morning meditation will have supplied materials for doing this, culling from Holy Scripture or from the Prayer Book some choice and piercing words, praying for mercy, or for the gift of Divine Love, or for Christ's continued presence, or for spiritual discernment; petitions such as, darted up to Heaven, to win in the very labour and heat of the day supplies of grace and consolation from the Divine heart of our compassionate and ever-present Lord.

Again, although as a general rule it is wise in praying with the sick and poor to use only the Church's words, there are occasions when extempore prayer becomes a matter of necessity. It is impossible, or almost so, that the research of the parish priest should have been able to anticipate every variety of mental and moral weakness by his selections from the copious stores of antiquity; and the risk of using general language when there is need of pointed applicability to a particular case is very great. A soul must be led to God, not under cover of a general formula, but, as she is, in His Presence. It is to be feared that many, who do not hesitate to approximate to the doctrinal errors of dissenters on such vital questions as that of Baptismal Regeneration or the Eucharistic Presence, feel nevertheless a sort of superstitious scruple against such a use as this of extempore prayer as being dissenting; verily they strain at a gnat and swallow a camel. Extempore prayer is dangerous, if not almost impossible, in the mouths of those who are strangers to systematic meditation upon dogmatic truth; it is a very efficient aid in the hands of the clergyman whose inner life is fed by meditation, who may be himself drinking of God's pleasures as out of a river, but who "can have compassion on the ignorant and on them that are out of the way," and who knows what it is to lie with a broken heart at the feet of Jesus Crucified.

It is obvious, moreover, that meditation will furnish capacity for prayer during periods which may elapse before the commencement of service, or between the several parts, or, again, after all is over. The importance of collectedness in those who pray for the Body of Christ rather than for themselves cannot be exaggerated; and distraction will be best guarded against by the occupation of mental prayer during the intervals of service. Especially is meditation of importance to him who would at all adequately discharge the highest service which a creature can offer to the Supreme Being—the celebration of the Blessed Eucharist. This is indeed the central and supreme act of the Christian ministry, by which it is directly associated in the mediatorial work of Jesus Christ. As the Christian priest "by Christ's authority committed to him absolves" a penitent "from all his sins";[1] as he teaches in the Name of Christ, and "as though God did beseech men by him"; so he shares the interceding work of Christ,—partly in the daily office,—partly in his private devotions,—but particularly and emphatically in the Holy Eucharist. St. Paul charged St. Timothy that "supplications, prayers, intercessions, and giving of thanks be made for all men," adding as a reason, "that this is good and acceptable in the sight of God our Saviour." St. Augustine (*Ep.* 59, *ad Paulin.*) shows that the apostolical precept receives its fulfilment in the Eucharistic service, and the Church of England evidently follows the leading of this

[1] Form of Absolution in the Office for the Visitation of the Sick.

great Father, by quoting St. Paul in the opening words of the Church militant prayer, a quotation to which there is nothing that corresponds in the Latin Canon. The priest then prays for the universal Church, for its truth, unity, and concord, for all Christian kings, for all bishops and curates, for all Christ's people, for all in trouble, sorrow, need, and sickness,—he commemorates "all God's servants departed this life in His faith and fear," and prays that "we with them" may partake His heavenly kingdom. And in the Post-communion prayer, while the unconsumed Body and Blood of our Lord lie before him on the altar, he entreats the Eternal Father, that "by the merits and death of His Son Jesus Christ, and through faith in His Blood, we and *all His whole* Church may obtain remission of our sins and all other benefits of His Passion." S. Augustine held meditation to be a necessary preparation for all prayer; but it must be peculiarly so for a due discharge of that august worship compared with which the intensest and lowliest prayer is but an earthly familiarity. At least ten minutes or a quarter of an hour (independently of any more formal preparatory office, or needful examination of conscience) should be spent by the celebrant alone with God, in such earnest and confiding colloquy as the practice of meditation will have rendered easy and delightful,—a time in which to pass in review the many who hang on his intercession, in which to offer himself and his offering to the Divine glory, in which to concentrate all the powers of his soul for an act at which, as St. Chrysostom says, attendant angels tremble, and which thrills irresistibly through the courts and ranks of heaven up to the very throne of God.

Much might be said about the private devotions of the celebrant, at the intervals of the service, and particularly as to the expediency of connecting the successive pauses which occur with the several stages of our Lord's Passion.

Here however there is so much room for the legitimate play of diverging religious idiosyncrasies that we forbear making more particular observations—remarking only that the method of devotion best calculated to assist each man will be most quickly and effectively discovered by himself in meditation.

III.

A complemental yet most useful practice of the clergyman's life (if time allows) is the observance of the lesser canonical hours, and particularly the use of the service for Sext, by way of noonday prayer. Of course such a practice as this rests on very different grounds from that of the daily office, and even from meditation, of which the former is positively, and the latter implicitly, enjoined in the English formularies. It is simply an act of the individual judgment, undertaken with a view to edification. While therefore it may undoubtedly be declined by any who have conscientious reasons for doing so, the advantages of such a practice appear to us very considerable. Matins, indeed, and Lauds are very fairly, and Vespers very fully represented in the English Prayer Book; so much so, that the repetition of these offices in their original shape might appear to some minds to involve an act of disloyalty towards the actual services of the English Church. The elements of Prime and Compline which are embodied in our Prayer Book are less considerable; and the three lesser hours are wholly unrepresented there. On this ground, it may be held that they together form a natural complement to the Matins and Evensong of the English Church, as illustrating the spirit and extending the principle of these services without superseding them. And here it is impossible not to express a decided preference for the Sarum use of the 119th Psalm in Prime, and the three following Hours, over the other Psalms which Bishop Cosin in his devotions and the various Gallican breviaries of the reformed type, have in deference to Eastern precedent substituted for it. If the *Venite exultemus* will bear daily repetition, as in the judgment of the Church of England and indeed of the whole Western Church it will, as much may at least be said for that marvellous Psalm, the 119th—of which St. Augustine observes that its wonderful depth seemed to him proportioned to its seeming simplicity, and that he only undertook to expound it at the urgent request of those who had listened to his other lectures on the Psalter.[1]—The 119th Psalm does indeed represent in the very highest degree the paradox which is more or less true of all Scripture—the paradox of seeming simplicity overlying fathomless depth. It conveys at first an impression of tautology, when compared with the rest of the Psalter; it seems to reiterate with little attempt at variety the same aspirations, assurances, prayers, resolutions; but a man must use it *daily* for months and years together before he can understand its true value as expressing with consummate beauty the language of a soul which is "alive unto God through Jesus Christ our Lord," which basks in His presence, and rejoices in His law. Draw a number of lines from the centre of a circle to its circumference, and the nearer you get to the circumference, the more clearly will you perceive the divergent directions of the radiating lines. On the other hand, as they approach the centre, these lines perpetually approximate, till we forget that if produced they will diverge into infinity. If we may use the illustration, the rest of the Psalms approach God, each from its own direction, and rest at a sufficient distance from Him,—the one Centre to which all converge—to leave their separate characteristics clear and well defined; while the 119th Psalm winds itself

[1] Cf. Aug. *proœm. in Ps.* 118, ed. Ben. tom. IV. p. 1277.

around Him, appropriating and embodying something from all the streams that lead to Him, yet clinging to Him so closely that the infinite variety which it contains seems merged in a single strain of obedience and adoration. The Church on earth has a varied ritual; the angels sing only Holy, Holy, Holy; variety is a condescension to the instinct of change, which, as Aristotle knew, is characteristic of a state of imperfection:[1] but the 119th Psalm is at once infinitely varied in its expressions, yet incessantly one in its direction: its variations are so delicate as to be almost imperceptible, its unity so emphatic as to be inexorably stamped upon its every line; it is the language of the Catholic Church, gathered out of every people, and nation, and tongue, and therefore so various, it is so apparently tautologous, because spoken beneath the very Throne of God.

Nothing, we believe, so expresses the true spirit of ecclesiastics as the 119th Psalm—the pure intention to live for God, the zeal for His glory, the charity for sinners, the enthusiastic love of the Divine law and the Divine perfections, the cheerfulness without levity, the gentleness without softness, the collectedness and gravity which is never stern or repulsive; in short, the inward and outward bearing of the Priest of Jesus Christ.

IV.

But we must bring these remarks to a close, and by way of summary will endeavour to sketch the *dies sacerdotalis*—the clergyman's diary.

Of course he has a fixed hour for rising: he knows the importance of rule in such a matter to his own soul, and to all around him. We will suppose that, at latest, it is six in the summer, and seven in the winter months. On

[1] *Arist. Nic. Ethic.* vii. 14: εἴ του ἡ φύσις ἁπλῆ εἴη, ἀεὶ ἡ αὐτὴ πρᾶξις ἡδίστη ἔσται· διὸ ὁ θεὸς ἀεὶ μίαν καὶ ἁπλῆν χαίρει ἡδονήν.

waking he will give his first thoughts to God, thanking Him for preservation during another night, and his thankfulness will be quickened by the reflection that, taking an average, 12,000 souls have during this very night passed to their account. While engaged in dressing he will, with a view to giving his thoughts to God, recite the 51st Psalm, or the *Te Deum*, or some Christian hymn. And this ended, he will engage in mental prayer or meditation for half an hour; and if his heart is really in the work, he will find half an hour a short allowance of time to be spent with the Source of Light and Love. "A te tua consideratio inchoet, ne frustra extendaris in alia, te neglecto," said St. Bernard to Eugenius; he will begin with himself, but he will remember before God all to whom and for whom he ministers, and for whom Christ has died. "The oftener," says Bishop Wilson, "we renew intercourse with God, the greater will be our devotion."[1] The habit of meditation will grow on a man; if he is really in earnest, it will train him sooner than any other for the eternal presence of God. If it is Sunday, or there is a daily celebration, he will endeavour to extend his meditation, making it a preparation for the great service of the Church. If he is a curate in a parish where there is no daily service, he will say the morning service before he leaves the room, and when meditation has quickened the powers of his soul; because as Bishop Wilson remarks, "they whose hearts desire nothing, pray for nothing";[2] and as the same authority reminds us, it is well to make it a law to ourselves to meditate before we pray, as also to make certain pauses to see whether our hearts go along with our lips.[3] But the great lesson which ought to be stamped indelibly on the clerical mind is the preciousness of time,—its brevity and irrevocableness,—the strict

---

[1] *Sacra Privata*, p. 3, Denton's edition.
[2] *Ibid.*   [3] *Ibid.*

account which must be given of it,—the overwhelming interests which hang upon its due employment. Labour is the portion of the servants of God, leisure is a misery, —for it is an invitation to Satan and an easy avenue to deadly sin. These considerations will regulate the distribution of the day. It will be well to give an hour in the morning to theological study, as distinct from meditation and from preparation of sermons. The intellect is a gift of God, which is as glorious when it promotes His cause and kingdom, as it is hateful and satanic when it opposes Him; it is therefore to be developed to the utmost of our powers, and exercised on the highest subject-matter. The distribution of the remaining hours of the day must depend in a great degree on parochial necessities: but the conscientious clergyman will feel that it is absolutely necessary to seek God in prayer in the middle of the day, and that two hours is an amply sufficient allowance of time for a walk or recreation, if indeed his parish does not give him sufficient exercise. He will dine at an early hour, with a view to declining the habits of society, as a rule, and to better devoting his evenings to visiting, especially in the winter months, when the men will be found at home,—a rare contingency at other times. He will make meals a matter of as little ceremony as possible, and will study simplicity in his table and household. He will offer each visit, each meal, each conversation, each walk, to God. The evening office will be said at a fixed period, and he will be careful to devote some time to spiritual reading or study of Holy Scripture, of which it is wise to commit to heart a portion every day, with a view to the exigencies of preaching and the possibilities of sickness. He will say Compline with his servants,[1] and will spend a quarter

---

[1] It is desirable that in every house there should be an oratory or room specially set apart for prayer.

of an hour in general and particular self-examination; for he will learn others best in the abyss of his own heart. He will offer the day to God, and pray for mercy on his many falls; and for more perfect devotion to the cause of Jesus Christ. He will lay him down in peace, anxious yet light-hearted, commending his spirit into his Father's Hands, and resigning himself to the Will and protection of his gracious Saviour.

There can be no doubt among sensible Churchmen of the duty and expediency of restoring to religion that outward and visible majesty, which asserts its existence and position in the world, which was freely conceded to it by the wisdom of Antiquity, and which it has only lost in an age of indifference and laxity. And we live accordingly in an age of Church-restoration, and may rejoice that in some places the temples and ritual of the Body of Christ bid fair to rival the beauty which characterised them of old. But it is of the last importance that we should recognise a danger, of which dissenting opponents so often (with whatever animus) remind us, that, namely, of substituting a devotion to the externals of religion, for a supreme anxiety about the state and prospects of the soul,—its freedom from the empire of sin, its actual reconciliation to God, its supernatural life, as exhibited in the exercise of the infused graces of faith, hope, and charity, its cheerfulness and peace, its readiness for death. Those who are looking on, and whose criticisms are sharpened by unfriendly dispositions, often detect in a body of men, or in an individual, defects of which they themselves are unconscious. "Fas est et ab hoste doceri." It is a warning for all, Priests and people, who have the true interests of the Church of England at heart, and who know that of the many theories which, in this busy age, claim attention, the full Sacramental system of her Prayer

Book alone is true, and alone worthy the energies of an immortal soul. It is a warning which comes from God, through whatever intermediate agencies, and while it cannot be neglected without the greatest peril, it may, if vigorously acted upon, convince the world, before many years have elapsed, that they that are with us are more than they which be against us, and that it is now, as in the days of the Apostles, a miserable portion for any " to be found fighting against God."

SERMON I.

THE WORK AND PROSPECTS OF THEOLOGICAL COLLEGES.[1]

ISAIAH l. 4.

The Lord God hath given Me the tongue of the learned, that I should know how to speak a word in season to him that is weary: He wakeneth morning by morning, He wakeneth Mine ear to hear as the learned.

IT would not be difficult to predict the differences which are to be found among commentators, as to the original application of passages like this. A dry criticism, such as that of Grotius, can never hear in these words aught save the Prophet's voice, describing his mission and daily inspirations from heaven. But great Teachers of the Ancient Church, followed herein by thoughtful moderns and by our own translators, refuse to recognise in so sublime an inspiration anything else or less than the very words of Christ. And that construction of this, and of other passages in the later portion of Isaiah, is, even on principles of criticism which are very far from Patristic, the most natural one. Here, as elsewhere, the personality of the Prophet himself, if it has ever mingled in his thought with that of the Speaker in the text, has certainly melted away before that higher Personality, and has thus been practically superseded. Here is an illustrious Teacher of the future Israel, to Whose school the Isles and the people from afar are summoned as listeners.

[1] Preached at the Anniversary Festival of Cuddesdon College, June 10, 1868.

His mouth is like a sharp sword;[1] the Spirit of the Lord rests upon Him, that He may preach good tidings to the meek and bind up the broken-hearted, and give to them that mourn in Zion beauty for ashes, the oil of joy for mourning, the garment of praise for the spirit of heaviness.[2] This Elect Teacher, in Whom the soul of the Lord delighteth, will not fail or be discouraged till He have set judgment in the earth.[3] All this, and much else to the like purpose, points to an Ideal higher than any which could be realised by the greatest prophets of the old Theocracy. The relation of each of these prophets, of Isaiah himself, to the Ideal Teacher, was only that of typical and partial anticipation. They had a limited, He an unlimited inspiration:[4] they had a restricted sphere of action, He was to act throughout all races and all time:[5] they were the instructors of the ancient people of God, He was to be the Doctor of doctors, the Teacher of Humanity.[6] If it was true, in a sense, of Isaiah, that the Lord God had given him the tongue of the learned, that is, the power of instruction, that he should speak, across the intervening centuries, a word of seasonable comfort to the captives in Babylon; if, morning by morning, the Prophet's ear was wakened from on high to receive some new disclosure of the Mind and Heart of God, yearning with a Love and Mercy which Justice had not eclipsed over the actual and the predestined sufferings of His Israel; this is but a foreshadowing in earlier time of the Ministry of the Prophet of Prophets; in Whom dwelt all the treasures of wisdom and knowledge; Whom to have seen was to have seen, in His perfect Counterpart, the Everlasting Father; Who could open wide His Arms to the whole human Family, and bid men come unto Him, weary and heavy laden as they were, since He would give them rest.

[1] Isa. xlix. 2. [2] *Ibid.* lxi. 1-3. [3] *Ibid.* xlii. 4. [4] St. John iii. 34.
[5] St. Mark xvi. 15; St. Matt. xxviii. 20. [6] St. John i. 9.

It is indeed pre-eminently true of the ministry of our Lord, that while His Human Ear was ever wakened to hear as the learned, His instructions were generally directed, not to stimulate the intellect, but to solace the woes of man. His teaching indeed contained within its compass the final and authoritative solution of the chief problems that can engage and embarrass human thought. But the form of His Teaching was popular as distinct from scientific, concrete rather than abstract, religious and not philosophical. It was addressed to the wounded heart rather than to the anxious intelligence of man. Sin, actual and inherited, had made man weary of a burden which he could not bear, and in view of which life and death were alike unwelcome. And Christ, our Lord, throughout His ministerial Life, was the speaker of a word in season, whereby He not only gave light to them that sat in darkness and in the shadow of death, but actually guided the feet of humanity into the true way of peace.[1]

Like His Regal and Priestly Offices, our Lord's Prophetical Office is in a measure delegated to His Ministers.[2] Since the day of Pentecost, it has been permanently put into commission. As the celebration of the Eucharist is only and really an act of Christ's Priesthood, and the administration of discipline in the Church, only and really an act of Christ's Royal Authority, so is the perpetual communication of Christian doctrine a continued exercise of His Prophetical power. But herein He is Himself His own Doctrine and His own Message; and the word in season which the weary need is what He is, and what He has done and suffered, no less than what He has said. We, His Ministers, do not merely echo and expand the Sermon on the Mount; we preach the Person and the work of the Preacher. For Christ our Lord is the Object as well as the Author of Christian Doctrine; and His best

[1] St. Luke i. 79.   [2] St. John xx. 21.

word of consolation to human hearts is the announcement of Himself.[1]

The prophetical office then lives on, although its message is stereotyped for all time since the appearance of the Redeemer. This is the real gift of the tongue of the learned. It is given from on high. It is given, less with a view to intellectual gain, than with a view to spiritual relief. This is ever the double character of Christian, as distinguished from secular or Pagan learning; it is acknowledged to have been given from above, and it is cultivated, not chiefly for the sake of doing so, not even chiefly for the personal advancement of the student, but for the relief of the ignorant, the erring, the suffering, the poor. The heavenly origin of the message and the disinterested philanthropy of its promulgation mark off the prophetic office of the Church from all human teacherships. And as the tongue of the learned is given still from heaven, and the word in season is still spoken to the weary; so still, as of old, morning by morning, in the Church of God, the ears of Christ's ambassadors are wakened to listen, if perchance they may hear it, to new applications of His one, once-for-all given message of mercy, or of new and, by them, unsuspected treasures contained within the vast storehouse of His healing Truth.[2]

And if on such a matter an opinion may be ventured, it might seem that Holy Scripture contains few passages which furnish so appropriate a motto to be graven over the gateway of a Theological College as is the text before us. For in preparing for Orders, it is the prophetical, rather than the other aspects of the ministry, to which, of necessity, most attention is directed. A theological college endeavours, so far as human agency can do this, to give the tongue of the learned, the power of spiritual instruc-

[1] St. John ix. 5; 2 Cor. iv. 5.
[2] 2 St. Peter i. 3, iii. 18; 2 Cor. v. 17; 1 Cor. xiii. 9.

tion, to the future ambassadors of Christ. It proffers this gift, not for the self-satisfaction of the students, but in the interests of souls. It aims not merely at the intellectual bettering of the clergy, but at the spiritual solace and strength of their future flocks. It would fain teach them to listen, morning by morning, for the Divine Voice, explaining, deepening, fertilising within them the truth which is thus committed to their guardianship.

I.

The first function of a Theological College is obviously to teach Theology. Of late years the paradox has been advanced that, properly speaking, there is no such thing as Christian theology to teach. Christ, our Lord, it is broadly asserted, was a teacher, not in any sense of theology, but only of religion. Theology is described as an aftergrowth; it is said to be the product of an age of reflection, or an age of controversy, when philosophy had really taken possession of the rudder of the Church's life, and was shaping the fresh utterances of living Christian feeling into truant compliances with its own rigid intellectual forms.

This theory is so entirely at issue with fact, that it would be undeserving of notice if it were not very acceptable, or indeed little less than intellectually necessary to a powerful school of thought, partly within and partly without the Church at the present day. For what can be less true than this assertion in its relation to our Lord's teaching? I say nothing for the moment as to that of His Apostles, St. Paul or St. John. Where, in the whole of Holy Scripture, is the doctrine of the Divine Providence affirmed with greater explicitness and detail than in the Sermon on the Mount?[1] What other portion of the New Testament enables us to say, with such certainty as does

[1] St. Matt. vi. 25-34.

our Lord's last discourse, that the Holy Spirit is not only Divine, but a distinct Subsistence or Person in the Godhead?[1] Who does not see that our Lord's whole teaching is saturated with theology? that His Parables (it may suffice to mention the Prodigal Son) are peculiarly theological, as revealing new features of the Divine Character, new truths about the range of the Divine attributes? that if we follow His popular conversations, such as that with the woman of Samaria, we find ourselves listening to theological statements touching, for example, His own Omniscience,[2] or the immateriality of the Divine Essence;[3] that appeals to the heart and conscience of man so simple as, "Come unto Me, all ye that labour and are heavy laden, and I will give you rest,"[4] can only become practical forces acting upon and changing deep currents of human life, when grave questions like, "Who dares to invite us thus?" and "How will He give us rest in our lifelong weariness?" have been asked and answered; and that the only satisfactory answer to these questions must be purely and profoundly theological?

The truth is that Religion and Theology are inseparable. We are bound to God in the secret recesses of our spiritual being, by the truths about God, of which we are certain. If no such truths exist, then there is no possible basis for any such thing as religion at all. If such truths do exist, then it is of vital importance to the strength and earnestness of religion, that they should be exactly ascertained and stated. Therefore, proportioned to the strength of the religious tie must be the intellectual anxiety respecting the facts which warrant it. What are these facts? upon what do they rest? where is their real frontier? what do they exclude and contradict? what

---

[1] St. John xiv. 26, xvi. 15.
[2] Ibid. iv. 18, l. 48.
[3] St. John iv. 24.
[4] St. Matt. xi. 28.

do they imply, and sanction, and necessitate ? These questions are not the cumbrous weapons of a stupid scholasticism, which would fain imprison a heavenly poetry within the bars and bands of its graceless syllogisms: they are the irrepressible voice of the human spirit, face to face with the awful, the absorbing problem of its destiny, and refusing to be satisfied with sentiments when it craves for truths. The conception of an untheological religion is one of those desperate shifts to which men are driven when they have lost all vital, intellectual hold upon the bone and substance of the Faith, while yet they shrink, for a variety of reasons which I forbear to analyse, from breaking with the many associations which have still more or less power over their imaginations and their hearts. It is contrary to experience to suppose that human beings will knowingly either live in the contemplation of, or die out of devotion to any shadows, however beautiful; and if the truths which are the life of religious feeling and action are to stand the wear and tear, the perpetual cross-questioning, the play of hostility, of curiosity, of apprehension, of hope, necessarily and incessantly directed upon them, some science of theology is, from the nature of the case, not other than inevitable.

Enough, however, respecting a paradox, which will only be referred to in another generation as a quaint curiosity of our own. It may indeed be truly said that the most accurate theology without vital religion is of little worth; and this position is one of which, as will presently be shown, a theological college cannot afford to be unmindful. But at least the proper business of an institution such as this is not based upon a gigantic misconception. A theology is the correlative of a real revelation. There is such a science as Christian theology. And it is the task of a theological college to teach it.

And, doubtless, such a college should teach theology in

that narrower but profound sense which the word bore in the ancient world, and which it is always healthful and stimulating to recall. The Pagan Greeks reserved the august title of "Theologian" for those devout bards of a remote antiquity who, as Orpheus, Hesiod, Homer, had not conceived of the genesis of the universe without reference to that of the gods, and who thus were distinguished from the physiologists, such as Thales and Anaximander and others, since these were occupied with theories respecting the organisation and combination of matter, without any reference to the Divinity. With Aristotle, theological philosophy means what we should now-a-days call the science of the absolute, or that department of metaphysics which deals with the primal and most abstract principles; and here we see the word already wellnigh prepared for its future Christian use. Some of the early Christian writers indeed, such as St. Justin and Tatian, termed the science of Christian Faith simply philosophy. They meant that the Christian Faith was the truest wisdom for man; they hinted, moreover, indirectly that the Christian teachers could take rank side by side with the greatest sages of the ancient world. But the word philosophy was not really fitted to do this work. It was too inextricably intertwined in that age with Pagan associations; and it further suggested a process of perpetual inquiry, as distinct from the study and exhibition of a fixed, ascertained, absolute truth. Accordingly, in other writers of the second and early part of the third century, we find the "God-taught wisdom" (σοφία θεοδίδακτος) frequently contrasted with the philosophy of Paganism; and this expression almost leads us up to the briefer word theology. As the employment of the word by Aristotle had suggested, theology meant in the first days of its Christian use only that part of the Christian doctrine which treats of the Being and Attributes of

God. In such writers as St. Athanasius or St. Gregory of Nazianzum, " theology " stands for an explanation of the doctrine of the Holy Trinity ; their common expressions, theologising the Son, theologising the Holy Spirit, are condensed terms for stating that each of these Divine Persons is truly God. Thus St. John the Evangelist was commonly termed the Theologian, because he so emphatically asserts the Divinity of our Lord : and the " theology" was in this sense opposed to the " economy," that is to say, to the gracious Dispensation whereby God took His place as never before among the things of time and sense through the Incarnation of the Eternal Son, and to the various results of that stupendous mystery, as seen in the powers and organisation of the Church or in Christian history. In St. Augustine we find the word "theology" used in the wider modern signification,[1] as practically inclusive of all Christian doctrine ; although he, too, sometimes restricts it to that portion of Revelation which directly concerns the Essence of God.[2] In the middle ages, the sense which it bears among ourselves had already become general.[3]

This is not a mere point in the history of language, or a matter only of antiquarian learning. It may serve to remind us that an institution like Cuddesdon College is by the very name which it bears especially devoted to teaching theology in the sense of the science of the Supreme Being. To amass, to examine, to analyse, to exhibit in its collective force and in detail, that body of truth respecting the Being of beings, of which, through the Christian Revelation, superadded to the activities of conscience and natural observation, mankind is in possession ;—this unrivalled, this sublime occupation, is the proper central intellectual work of a theological college. To that work

[1] *De Trin.* xiv. 1.   [2] *De Civ. Dei,* viii. 1.
[3] Cf. Wetzer u. Welte, *Dict. Encycl.* art. " Theologie," by Mattès.

all else is subordinate, all else is accessory, all else ministers. Dogma, history, evidences, morals, language, criticism, fathers, councils, commentators, liturgiology—all are but varied means of approaching, contemplating, (dare I say it ?) investigating God : all lead up to Him, or lead down from Him, or circle round Him, or at any rate base their sole claim to interest on the reality of His Life. In all departments of theology, God is the real Object of study. His truth, His guidance of His people, the proof that He has really spoken, the moral law of His Being, His written word, whether expounded by the masters of Christian doctrine, whose words are heard with respect and deference in all the Catholic Churches now as in days when all were visibly one, or as explained by an accurate analysis of language, the traditional laws and language of the service which expresses Christian devotion to Him— all this centres in or radiates from Him ; from His Life and Presence, from His awfulness and His love, all draws the secret of its undying interest. But what He Himself is in the inner law of His everlasting Being, what He is in His general relation to His creatures, so far as He has made these things known, is properly the subject-matter of theology.

Inextricably bound up with the study of this Theology proper, is the study of what the ancients call the Economy. There are familiar words in our Communion Service, to which in past days the author of *The Christian Year* used to point as summarising our Christian faith on this head with an exhaustive clearness. " Above all things ye must give most humble and hearty thanks to God, the Father, the Son, and the Holy Ghost, for the Redemption of the world by the death and passion of our Saviour Christ, both God and Man, Who did humble Himself even to the death upon the cross for us miserable sinners, who lay in darkness and in the shadow of death, that He might make us the children of God and exalt us to everlasting life."[1] The Holy Trinity, the terms of the Incarnation, the Redemptive object of the Passion, man's condition after the fall, the filial dignity of his regenerate life, the exaltation of his life in glory hereafter;—it is a summary of God's love in the gift of His Blessed Son. It suggests that the Christian teacher of the Science of God must add to it the science of Man, as Man actually is. If the word in season is to be spoken with effect to him that is weary, it is necessary to discover and to state the deep secret of this permanent weariness. The loss of the supernatural robe of grace in Eden, the resulting dimness of man's intelligence and the weakness of his will; the inheritance of guilt attaching, in the eyes of Divine Justice, to humanity considered as an organic whole; the pervading taint and the wrongful acts which disfigure man's personal and social life; in short, modern human nature must be studied, ere we can appreciate and duly set forth the Divine Medicine which is to heal its wounds. "With the Bible and Shakespeare," it has been said, "a man may consider that he has all that is necessary for an effective ministry." This is a rude and inaccurate statement of a substantial truth, of the truth that God and man are the two terms of any practical theology. Human character in its broad, common features, and in its individual peculiarities, is well worth the closest, the severest observation; and to stimulate this observation, to train the eye in taking note of all that reveals the soul within, is an indispensable part of an adequate clerical training. Much, doubtless, can only be learnt by actual intercourse with other men. Much, too, may certainly be learnt from books and from the experience of those who have lived longer than we, and who hand on to us something of the accumulated wisdom of the centuries behind them. But

[1] Communion Service.

however we may study him, man, on his ethical as well as on his mental side; man, in his strength as well as in his weakness; man, in his phases of bitterest hostility to God, as well as in his saintliest moods of conformity to God's word and will; man, at the dull stupid level of his average action, as well as in his most exceptional and heroic efforts, is a study only less important for our purpose than is God Himself. For it is when human nature is seen in its many-sidedness, in its greatness, in its littleness, that the word in season, God's Revelation of Himself in the Life and Death of His Blessed Son, can be spoken to some serious purpose. Our ministry is not the random proclamation of a scientific discovery, involving nothing but an intellectual interest; but the careful adaptation of a Divine Remedy to the wants of a patient, whose case and symptoms we have accurately considered. To show that in Jesus Christ, Incarnate, Crucified, Interceding, given to us in Sacraments, presented by us again and again to the Father, there is grace which can more than cure all human woes;[1]—this is the proper business of men who have, in the Evangelical sense, to speak a word in season to wearied humanity.

II.

But if a man is to set about this work with any prospect of success, he must be something more than a teacher of theology, and a lecturer on human nature. The most accurate knowledge will be powerless unless the speaker be himself of a certain spiritual type which, in the instinctive judgment of those whom he addresses, gives him a moral, as well as an official, right to speak. Hence, the work of a theological college is to mould character as well as to teach truth; nor is this formative duty by any means the least important sphere of its activity.

[1] Rom. v. 20; Col. iii. 11; 1 Cor. i. 30.

(*a*) First of all, such a college as this has to set many of those who come to it seriously thinking on the great primary questions of life and death. Many a man enters here, with good dispositions, with a purpose to serve God in the Sacred Ministry, entertained, it may be, since childhood, yet with all that light-heartedness of temper and that hazy perception of the stern lines of truth which are natural at twenty-two.[1] He is in the position of the sons of Zebedee; he wishes to sit on the right hand or on the left; he knows not what he asks.[2] It is then the duty of a college like this to unveil to him the cup of which Christ once drank, and the baptism with which Christ was baptized, gently, considerately, yet sincerely. This, I say, is the part of a young man's true and best friend, who looks far ahead, even beyond the horizon of time. When a candidate for Orders enters these walls, Christ our Lord seems, if I dare so speak, to overtake him as He once joined the disciples on the Emmaus road, and to get him to think steadily on truths which as yet he only holds in solution. What does he mean by taking Orders? Why does he choose this rather than any other walk in life? Has he any real purpose deeper and stronger than his ordinary resolves? Is he intending to follow a respectable profession, or has he, in his secret soul, given himself to God? Unless and until such an act of sincere self-dedication is made, the whole teaching and life of this place ought to seem to him an unintelligible riddle. For it presupposes nothing less than this hearty devotion in those who come here. When this self-dedication has once been made, all falls into its place. God is seen to be the one Being for Whom life is really worth living, and a life which consistently points to God is simply the common-sense of the situation.

(β) And when this first indispensable and radical revolu-

[1] St. John xxi. 18.   [2] St. Mark x. 37.

tion has triumphed within the soul, it will be naturally followed up by an endeavour to cultivate all those great features of moral character which legitimately result from it. It is a noteworthy feature of our day that minds which are fanatically hostile to the claims of dogmatic truth, and to the orderly beauty and majesty of sacramental worship, are often keenly alive to the strong attractions of a lofty morality. What, for instance, has been the secret of the great popularity of such a book as *Ecce Homo*? Not the critical acumen of the writer: he would seem to think cheaply of criticism; he certainly pays little deference to it. Nor yet any great biographical power: he does not even attempt to present the events of our Lord's Life in an orderly sequence. Still less depth or accuracy of doctrinal statement; he discards doctrine upon principle, and he sins most grievously against some of its elementary requirements. Nor does his work appeal particularly to the devotional or spiritual instincts of the soul; his concern is with social and political truth, rather than with such truth as belongs to the personal life of individual men. Wherein, then, is the source of his power? It lies, I believe, in the writer's evident and enthusiastic devotion to a certain section of moral truth. Not of all moral truth: little or nothing is said by him about our duties towards God. But of that portion of morality which applies to the relations between man and man, as it is presented to us in the Gospels, the writer has, if a somewhat imperfect and distorted conception, yet, beyond doubt, a most enthusiastic admiration. And this admiration, based though it be upon a very limited apprehension of what Our Lord's moral teaching really was, has yet enabled him to produce a work which certainly has riveted the admiration of some minds of the very highest order, and of large masses among our most thoughtful countrymen.

Have we not in this fact material at once for warning and for guidance? It may be, it is true, that the clergy of the Church of England, during the last century, at times taught little else but a dry morality. But the reaction against that disastrous state of things, inaugurated by the Evangelical, and completed by the later Catholic movement, has not altogether escaped the danger of forgetting the sacred claims of an accurate morality. In its eagerness to re-assert the great truths of the Atonement and Justification through Christ, the Evangelical movement did not, at least in its better phases, depreciate morality; but it made no real provision for its practical culture. In its vindication of the real efficacy which belongs to Our Lord's Spiritual presence in the Church and to His action through the Sacraments, the Catholic movement was most powerfully aiding morality, by pointing to the real creative sources of high moral effort in the soul of man. But we have been perhaps in some cases too intent upon proving the reality of the assistance which is given us in these great means of grace, to do full justice to the purposes for which they have been given. At any rate, it is ever well to be reminded, however awkwardly or one-sidedly, of a forgotten or depreciated element of truth; and it is plain that the English people, just now, believe that enough attention has not been bestowed by their teachers on what are called, in the Collect, "the fruits of good living." But this attention must begin with practical self-discipline on the part of the clergy, if it is to be effectual. It is something to learn the full glory and the exigency even of the natural virtues, of justice, of courage, of temperance, of truthfulness, as occasions arise for putting them in practice. Yet more needful is it to take lessons (if I may so speak) in the virtues which do not belong to nature because they transcend it, in self-forgetting love, and in uniform brightness and joy of heart and soul, and in true inward peace amid troubles and distractions, and in long-suffering when there is much to provoke.[1] And surely this is a very proper part of the business of a theological college. Unless all are bent upon self-improvement in the highest sense, nothing of course can be done on a considerable scale; but this generous love of moral truth in action is not more than might reasonably be expected in each of those who are looking forward to the highest service of the Perfect Moral Being, while it should pervade the very atmosphere of the home in which they are preparing for their future work.

There are, indeed, two forms of moral excellence which seem to be especially necessary to a clerical order. It has been said by one of the opponents of Christianity, that a clergy, left to itself, is sure to ruin itself in time, partly through its general lust of promotion, and partly through its self-indulgence. This prediction may warn us especially to cultivate self-denying activity[2] and disinterestedness.[3] Such things do not come at once, as a matter of course, or in virtue of a general disposition to do right. But self-denying activity can be cultivated up to a point, at which to be occupied in something that shall help the cause of truth and goodness becomes a second nature; and disinterestedness may be trained into an instinct, which shrinks with unfeigned distress from the shame and degradation of conscious self-seeking in holy things. And who does not see that these virtues, even if, *per impossibile*, they could be isolated in the character, are the elements and instruments of nothing less than a great moral power, on account of the contrast which they present to the ordinary tenor of men's lives? Who does not see that these are the virtues of the Christian clergy of which, with pathetic sincerity, Gibbon

[1] Gal. v. 22. [2] 2 Tim. ii. 3. [3] Phil. ii. 20, 21.

complains, in a well-known passage, as having secured the success of the Gospel? Who does not perceive that men, who are thus engaged in the serious personal culture of moral truth, are alone able to understand it sufficiently to teach it in its fulness to their fellow-men, and moreover that in the long run they will alone be allowed to do so?

(γ) But there is a deeper work even than this which a theological college must attempt. I mean the systematic cultivation of piety, the strenuous devotion of the soul's purest and strongest affections to God. This work, if less obviously on the surface of such an institution than theological and pastoral instruction, is really much more vital. It presupposes of course in every student, a simple and strong desire to live for God. This unfortunately, cannot always be taken for granted, but it must always be laboured and prayed for with incessant energy. Where nothing of the kind exists, all prayer will appear to be more or less unreal and distasteful. But a theological college cannot afford to regulate its standard by the needs of those who are wanting in its fundamental requirements. And that devotion should be taught and recommended upon system in such a college, is a point which needs insisting on. Partly from our habitual national reserve, and partly from our dread of all unreality and cant in religious matters, it is usual even for religious Englishmen to avoid any reference whatever to their private spiritual life. The feeling is, that you would just as soon refer to a man's income, or to the character of his near relations, as to his daily prayers; it is, as we say, a strictly personal matter between each man and God; and any attempt to mould or guide it—I had almost said, any allusion to its existence—is held to be of the nature of a social impertinence.

It is impossible not to sympathise with the sincerity

which seeks to protect itself against exaggeration and imposture; and yet the general result, in the case before us, must be admitted to be nothing less than disastrous. What can be less like the spirit of the early Churches which met in the upper chambers of Jerusalem [1] or in the catacombs of Rome, than this frigid isolation of modern souls, who yet have been redeemed by Christ's Blood, and illuminated and warmed by His Spirit? What can be more in contradiction with the rule of pious Israelites in the days of the prophets, when they who "feared the Lord spake often one to another"? [2] What can be more obviously at issue with the natural and direct instincts of Christians really possessed with the love of God? [3] Too often, indeed, this reserve is but a screen which is thrown up to hide from a brother's eye what is really a spiritual ruin; but in any case, at a theological college, it ought if possible, to be breached. If men who are preparing to lead their brother-men to an eternity of communion with God cannot venture to discuss and to study the practical aspects of rudimentary devotion here, it is difficult to see how they are, twelve months hence, to recommend devotion to their flocks, with any such accent of authority as that which is based on a true personal experience.[4]

Is it too much to say, that, upon entering a theological college, a man would naturally set about the gradual reconstruction of his whole life of prayer? Probably his spiritual life at school and college has by no means kept pace with his intellectual life. The circle of secular interests, the horizon of secular thought, has gone on steadily widening, while the spiritual range of action is as contracted as it was eight or ten years ago. Now a theological college affords opportunities for recovering this lost ground. The old morning and evening prayers, used

[1] Acts i. 14.
[2] Mal. iii. 16.
[3] Heb. x. 25; St. Matt. xii. 34.
[4] 1 St. John i. 3; Acts iv. 20.

in private since childhood, will be best retained. But they will be enlarged, supplemented, paraphrased, overlaid. Like the old Norman columns in the nave of Winchester Cathedral, encrusted by the genius of a Wickham, the prayers of boyhood will be preserved, but over-built with much which the soul has found appropriate and needful since those few simple words were first breathed heavenward. Moreover, new habits and times of prayer will be carefully, thoughtfully, deliberately adopted. Especially at a theological college will a man make preparation for two indispensable features of every real ministerial life, first, some kind of systematic meditation upon Christian truth,[1] and, secondly, that daily use of the Morning and Evening Service, whether in private or in public, to which the conscience of the clergy is bound by the plain law of the Church of England.[2] To this must be added that solemn department of Christian devotion which centres in the celebration and reception of the Holy Communion. Some attempt, too, will be made to discharge, however imperfectly, the complex duty of intercession[3] for others, according to their several wants and claims, which forms so large a feature in the life of those who have the cure of souls. In fine, it will be seen that devotion is a vast subject, with experiences, difficulties, hopes, enthusiasms, failures, triumphs, all its own; and that nothing can be more in keeping with the objects of a college such as this, than an attempt to deal with it systematically. For, of a truth, both the moral rectification of the soul, and its devotional culture, are essential to that wakening of the ear of which the prophet speaks, morning by morning, with an ever-increasing sensitiveness to the

---

[1] 1 Tim. iv. 15.

[2] "And all Priests and Deacons are to say daily the Morning and Evening Prayer *either privately or openly*, not being let by sickness, or some other urgent cause."—Concerning the Service of the Church.

[3] Phil. i. 9; Col. i. 9; 1 Thess. v. 23; Rom. xv. 30-32; 3 St. John 2.

majesty and to the claims of truth. And for such work as this, diocesan colleges present advantages which cannot be rivalled elsewhere.

III.

To suppose that the true work of such a college as Cuddesdon can be effectively discharged by the Universities, is either to idealise the University-system as we of this generation have known it when taken at its best, or it is to underrate the essential conditions of any serious preparation for Holy Orders. Certainly, in respect of the mere apparatus of intellectual work, the Universities must be held to distance the efforts of any diocesan or provincial institutions. Libraries which have been accumulated during centuries, and professors, who are, presumably in all cases, and actually in most, representatives of the highest theological knowledge in the country, must of necessity produce lectures with which no private enterprise can presume to enter into direct competition. But, however this may be, it is certain that the University training for Orders addresses itself simply, and in the most business-like way, to the intellect. It does not touch the soul. It does not attempt to make provision for the development either of great moral features in the character, or of devotional tenderness and force in the affections and the will. The consequence is, that, even as to theology, it can only secure a speculative interest, that is to say, an interest, feebler and distinct in kind from that which is felt by men who have really devoted their whole mental and moral substance to the service of God. Moreover, the temper of our Universities is, as a rule, somewhat jealous of private personal influence; and no machinery of chapel services and of social discipline can of itself do the work of living hearts and wills, fired and braced by the love of God. When then, by its various devotional resources, by the familiar and open intercourse which subsists between its teachers and its pupils, and by the sincere effort, more or less general, of all who belong to it, to compass moral and spiritual improvement, a theological college endeavours to brace the will and to spiritualise the affections as well as to inform the understanding, it is occupying ground all its own, and ground from which, except by its own remissness or faintheartedness, it cannot be dislodged.

Nor can it be other than obvious to those who have the interests of the Church at heart, that in all probability theological colleges are destined, at no distant period, to act upon her mind much more powerfully than has hitherto been the case. Ten or fifteen years ago it might have been supposed that a recent University Commission, whatever else it might or might not have done, had, at least for the next two or three generations, secured the administration and government of our ancient seats of learning to members, although not to the clergy, of the English Church. But within the last two years it has become painfully evident that the most powerful party in the State is, as a whole, bent on utterly destroying the Church's position at Oxford and Cambridge. Unless matters take a turn, upon which it would be over-sanguine to reckon with anything like confidence, we may shortly expect to see the greater part both of Professorships and of the lay fellowships in our two Universities placed at the disposal of persons who professedly reject the claims of Christianity to be a revelation from God. It is indeed probable that for some time to come, men in communion with the Church will actually occupy the larger number of important academical posts. But they will have no right in virtue of their position to assume or teach the Church's creed, as a thing of course, when dealing with their pupils: while it will be perfectly open to any public instructors, who think fit to do so, to discuss either history or moral philosophy on an avowedly atheistic basis. In such a state of things, the only escape from bitter controversy among senior residents will lie in the direction of an organised indifference to religious truth. It is not difficult to predict that the present agitation, if successful, must logically be followed by another, having for its object the general suppression of clerical fellowships and of chapel services, as the last relics of what is strangely termed Church ascendancy. This done, that entire severance between the University and religion which, as has lately been proclaimed, is the aim of the most advanced section of anti-religious opinion, will have been completed; and Oxford will have ceased, both as a corporation, and as represented by the several societies which find shelter within it, to yield any public homage or honour to the name of our Lord Jesus Christ.

But before this point has been reached, will the University be any longer fitted even for that general preparatory training which should precede the serious study of theology in candidates for Holy Orders? Surely this may well be questioned. For in the coming time we may expect to see more frequently that saddest of sights to a Christian heart, now, alas! not altogether uncommon, when a lad who at his mother's knee has learnt to worship Christ our Lord, and who, after having been sent to a Christian school, has at length come up to the University, purposing to devote himself to the ministry of the Church, finds that the very studies which are necessary to secure his intellectual success, have, in proportion to his sympathy with them, as they are at present too often taught, sapped altogether his faith in a living and governing God, and have left him crowned indeed with his honours, but, instead of a postulant on the threshold of the sanctuary, a wanderer in the desert, a disheartened, despairing infidel. Nothing is more mournful than this waste of vocations, than this loss of noble hearts and well-stored minds, to the cause and work of Christ our Lord; yet nothing is more certain than that the University of the future, if the secularising influences have their way, and the denominational system is not adopted with a view to saving the Christian character of the Colleges, will be still more likely to enfeeble and kill down all religious aspirations than could possibly be the case in the University of the present.

And, if this be so, it is, I would submit to our Fathers in Christ who are present among us to-day, a matter for serious consideration, whether the Church in this land should not endeavour to provide, on a totally different scale from anything which has hitherto been attempted, an education at once efficient and religious, for her future pastors. Theological colleges will have, it may be, in future years to teach a great deal besides theology. A college, requiring a five years' period of residence, of which the three first are devoted to the humanities and to philosophy, treated from a Christian point of view, and the two last to theology, may produce a clergy which will not be inferior in point of culture and refinement to their predecessors or to their contemporaries at the University, while they will probably be greatly superior in sacred learning. Doubtless it is piteous even to think of turning our backs upon institutions which have been our home for some ten centuries, and to which a thousand ties bind us individually in reverence and love. Doubtless there is social and moral value in that mixture of clergy and laity, during the earlier stage of final education, which would be forfeited in the case I am contemplating. But sentiments cannot be seriously balanced against loyalty to Truth; nor can great social and educational advantages be preferred, at least by Christians, to the duty of maintaining in its integrity the faith of Christ. Most earnestly is it to be hoped, that, when the choice is once nakedly presented to the Rulers of our Church by our legislators, between a secularised University and Christian education elsewhere, no associations with the past, no sense of present injustice, no theories of national comprehension, will lead to hesitation between frank acceptance of what must be the path of serious sacrifice, and its plain alternative, the gradual but utter spiritual ruin of that class from which her ministerial strength is mainly drawn by the Church of England.

The future, however, with all its lowering anxieties is in the hands of God. But at least it is plain that theological colleges must be more and more important to the wellbeing of the Church of England, as the Universities are gradually felt to yield less and less support to the cause of religious Truth. May these colleges, may those who guide their destinies, be increasingly alive to the greatness of their work! They cannot indeed hope to escape from criticism. They must ever be attempting what is in many ways a thankless task. To the Church's enemies they will of course be the honoured objects of a particular dislike, and it is scarcely to be expected that her sons will always be sufficiently wise and generous to do them justice. Even a clerical order will not uniformly welcome influences which avowedly desire to promote its efficiency by raising its standard both of knowledge and of moral life; and on the other hand the best intentions cannot invariably protect the directors of these, or of any institutions, against errors of judgment which may reasonably be deprecated. Still on the whole, the criticisms to which theological colleges are exposed, do not always assail the mistakes which may or may not be rightly laid to their charge. Something will always be objected to them, do what they will. If they turn out a learned clergy, they will be told that after all the important thing is not learning but vital godliness. If they send into your parishes pious and earnest lovers of souls, it will be observed drily that in these days, when everything is questioned, men are wanted who can meet infidelity with its own weapons. If an impression is produced within their walls upon the mind and character of the students, it will be urged that these students only reproduce the phrases and mannerisms of this or that teacher, and that such influence is fatal to the healthy natural play of feeling and character. If no such impression is produced, then the question will be asked, somewhat triumphantly, whether it would not have been just as well if the persons who throng them had remained at the Universities for the purpose of reading theology. If such colleges elaborate and enforce something like system, they are certain to be warned against the danger of hypocrisy which will underlie any enforced or desired conformity to the rules which they prescribe; if they do nothing of the sort, they will be asked to produce a *raison d'être*,—to make some reasonable apology for presuming to exist at all. In short, the world dislikes them for the reason which makes it dislike all that really aids the cause of religion. They cannot be welcome to the general public until the general public is sincerely Christian. If you pipe in the market-place, the world will not forthwith dance; if you mourn to it, it will not lament. If a clergy is self-denying, after the manner of the Baptist, men hint now, as of old, that it is a dark power of mischief—in fact, that it has a devil. If it comes eating and drinking, like the Son of Man, the objectors to asceticism themselves declaim with virtuous warmth against such unprofessional self-indulgence, "Behold a man gluttonous and a wine-bibber, the friend of publicans and sinners!"[1]

[1] St. Matt. xi. 17-19.

In point of fact, religion, whether it be the vital principle of an institution or of a single soul, cannot afford to lend an ear to criticisms which, after all, left to themselves, are mutually self-destructive. If wisdom is justified of her children, it is all that can fairly be expected. A single eye to God's glory and to the claims of truth will indeed, in its majestic strength, act and speak with consideration for the prejudices and weaknesses around it; and it may be trusted to discern, with a tolerably unerring instinct, the point at which charity shades off into disloyalty to that which cannot be surrendered. And am I not right in saying that this college, under the guidance of the able and holy men who have ruled it, during the last nine years, has already outlived the stormy experiences, the failures, the disappointments, of its earlier history, and has fairly established its claim to the gratitude and confidence of all that is at once intelligent and believing in the Church of England? God has indeed given it the tongue of the learned, not that it may add one more to the centres of theological disputation, not that it may be a Christian Porch or a Christian Academy, but that, aiming higher, as a true Home at once of Knowledge and of Mercy, it may speak a word in season, through its ever-increasing band of students, to thousands of wearied souls. And this day's assembly shows that the warm brotherly feeling [1] which of old united its members in the strong bonds of a free devotion to a common work and a common Master, and which was referred to in those its younger days, as a token of God's grace and light resting upon its walls, has not, to say the least, been lessened in more recent years and under other auspices. How can those who knew and loved it well in its earlier and humbler phase fail to bless God for the wide prospects of work and of triumph which apparently He is now

[1] St. John xiii. 35.

opening before it? As they take note gladly and admiringly of its progressive victories, for what can they offer a more heartfelt prayer than that it may, in the years to come, be ever guided to combine the largest consideration for the difficulties of minds and classes in our difficult times, with a sincere loyalty to the uncorrupted, unmutilated Creed of the ancient undivided Catholic Church of Christ? And how can all of us, who are here gathered this day, better express our gratitude for God's mercies to this institution in the past, or our hopes for its greater usefulness hereafter, than by giving generously of our substance to its extension and support, in the confidence that its work is very dear to our Divine Redeemer, and of a value to souls for which He died, which the last day only will make known?

SERMON II.

THE MORAL GROUNDWORK OF CLERICAL TRAINING.[1]

JOB xxviii. 12.

But where shall wisdom be found? and where is the place of understanding?

THE idea of the Wisdom or Kochmah, as all careful readers of the Bible will be aware, fills a great place in the mind of the Old Testament. It is, indeed, the subject of a distinct literature, within the compass of the sacred Canon. In their different ways, the Proverbs, the Song of Solomon, Ecclesiastes, and the Book of Job are devoted to treating of it. Wisdom is no mere synonym for useful or general information; still less does it stand for practical knowingness, far-sightedness, shrewdness in the affairs of life. It is much more akin to what the Greeks, or some of them, meant by philosophy, and yet it differs from philosophy in some important respects. Like the Greeks, the Hebrews had an ardent longing to get to the bottom of things; but then the problems which exercised the Greek thinkers so largely were settled, and settled on the highest authority, for the Hebrews. The revealed doctrine of a creation—that is to say, of a creation out of nothing—made a good half of early Greek speculation superfluous. The Hebrew moved about the

[1] Preached at the Anniversary Festival of Cuddesdon College, June 10, 1873.

world knowing how it, and how he came to be; the Greek spent his life in feeling his way towards the truth which every Hebrew child had learnt in his infancy. But the Hebrew mind, satisfied as to the origin of things by the Revelation intrusted to the Patriarchs and the Great Lawgiver, turned its eye, with constant and earnest anxiety, in the direction of their final causes. A vivid and unquestioning faith in God's active Providence naturally gave this turn to Hebrew thought. God had made, God sustained all that was; but what was the purpose in detail of His creation? What was the intended relation of Israel to surrounding nations? What were the guiding principles and ends of all which in politics and society met the eye? what was the universal truth which might be traced beneath the varieties of the individual or the national? The answer to questions of this kind constituted the Wisdom or Kochmah; but then this answer was furnished, not by the enterprise and collision of human minds, but from above. Hebrew speculation, at least for some centuries, and in its highest and permanent forms, was itself inspired: and thus we are taught the general aspects of human life as exhibited in the Proverbs, or the nothingness of all earthly things, as in Ecclesiastes, or the mystical side and import of human love as in the Canticles, or some relations of suffering to demerit, as in the Book of Job. In a later age, at Alexandria, Wisdom and philosophy, the inspired and the human, the assured and the tentative, meet within the precincts of a great school of intelligence and culture. In the Books of Wisdom and Ecclesiasticus we see Israel thinking of the same problems as in Job and Ecclesiastes, and the Proverbs, but with a great store of revealed truth to fall back upon, and under the eye of Greek Philosophy. How to acquire wisdom; how wisdom will be rewarded; how the history of Israel and

Israel's saints and heroes, is a long illustration of the power of wisdom:—these are the topics of the book which bears the name. Wisdom becomes in its pages—as had been already hinted in the language of the Proverbs—less and less a quality, more and more a being clothed with the attributes of personality. And thus at last Wisdom is identified with its true Source, the Eternal and Personal Thought or Word of God; and we find ourselves in the prologue of St. John's Gospel, and face to face with the central Truth of Christianity.

Now, in one respect the Books of the Kochmah or Wisdom within the Hebrew Canon witness remarkably to the world-wide importance of their subject. Although generally of Israelitish origin, they are one and all remarkably free from the peculiarities and allusions which would connect them with the history, the worship, the home of Israel. Already they seem to belong less to Israel than to the whole human family. In the Book of Proverbs, which treats of the relations of human life in its most universal aspects, the name of Israel, the covenant people, is not once mentioned. In Ecclesiastes, which exhibits the proved nothingness of all earthly things, Jehovah, the covenant-name of God, does not once occur. If the background of the Song of Solomon belongs to Israel, the subject is of universal interest, at least, in its import, and mystic reference; and the Book of Job, dealing with a fundamental question of human life and experience, places us altogether outside the history, and in the main outside the thought and associations of Israel. There are no allusions to the Law of Sinai, to the promises, to the history, to the worship of Israel, in the whole compass of the book.[1] In this somewhat negative but very important manner, the writings of

---

[1] Cf. Delitzsch, *Das Buch Job*, Einleitung, § 2; *Der Chokmacharacter des Buches*, pp. 5, 6.

the Kochmah in the Old Testament are a direct anticipation of the Gospel. Jesus Christ our Lord, if we may dare so to speak, is peculiarly at home in them—not simply as One Whom they prefigure, or to Whom they lead on, but as their true complement and point of unity. They are universal and human in their range of interest; so is He. They grapple with the most fundamental aspects of life and destiny; He explains those aspects. They create immense moral wants, which He satisfies. They name and centre in a word to which He alone has done justice; it is His Name from Everlasting,—the Wisdom of the Father.

I.

Where shall wisdom be found? Job asks this question in his last address to his friends.[1] This address forms the transition from the complete entanglement of the thought produced by the three stages[2] through which the discussion of the relations of suffering to demerit has successively passed to the solution, begun in Job's soliloquy,[3] continued through the four speeches of Elihu,[4] and completed by the voice of the Lord acknowledged in the conscience of His suffering servant.[5] Job himself has been insisting, as his friends had insisted, upon the punishment which awaits the ungodly,[6] almost, as it would seem at first sight, making an admission which is fatal to his own logical consistency. But then he maintains unflinchingly that he is not an evil-doer in the sense of his friends. He admits the truth of their pictures of the destiny of the wicked, but he will not incur the guilt of falsehood, by allowing himself to acquiesce in their verdict

[1] Chaps. xxvii. xxviii.
[2] (I.) Chaps. iv.-xiv.   (II.) Chaps. xv.-xxi.   (III.) Chaps. xxii.-xxvi.
[3] Chaps. xxix.-xxxi.   [4] Chaps. xxxii-xxxvii.
[5] Chaps. xxxviii.-xlii. 6.   [6] xxvii. 11-23.

as to himself. And this leads him to appeal to and fall back upon the great gift of Wisdom, with which God had endowed certain of His servants, and which enabled those who possessed it to get far beyond the superficial idea that all the suffering around us is of a penal character. Suffering would be seen sometimes to have another and a higher purpose in a true philosophy of the universe; and what this purpose was, was taught, as much else was taught, by the Wisdom or Kochmah. Where was this Wisdom to be found? This larger and comprehensive insight into the nature of things could not come to man, Job maintains, from without, in the way of ordinary practical experience. It was not, for instance, to be acquired by the workers in those ancient mines, of which the traces are probably to be found in the Bashan country.[1]

> "For there is a mine for the silver,
> And a place for the gold which they refine.
> Iron is taken from the dust,
> And they pour out stone as copper.[2]
>
> . . . .
>
> They break away a shaft from him who remains above,
> There, forgotten by every foot (that walks),
> They hang far from men, and swing."[3]

And thus, as he pursues, human enterprise, even in these distant days, could open

> "The way that no bird of prey knoweth,
> Whereat the eye of the hawk hath not gazed;
> Which the proud beast of prey hath not trodden,
> Over which the lion hath not passed."[4]

And in language so vivid that it might seem to anti-

---

[1] Compare the interesting quotation from Wetzst in Delitzsch, *Das Buch Job*, p. 328. Besides these mines in North Gilead, the poet of the Book of Job may have witnessed mining operations (1) in Nubia, for gold; (2) between Petra and Zoar, for copper; (3) in the Lebanon.
[2] Chap. xxviii. 1-2.   [3] *Ibid.* 4.   [4] *Ibid.* 7, 8.

cipate the achievements of modern engineering, he tells how the miner

> "Layeth his hand upon the pebbles,
> And turneth up the mountains from the root;
> He cutteth canals through the rocks,
> And his eye seeth every precious thing.
> That they may not leak, he dammeth up streams,
> And that which is hidden he bringeth to light." [1]

And then Job pauses. His friends might have supposed that all this enterprise, in which they probably had shared, and which corresponded in that early age to the very foremost achievements of thinkers and practical men in our own day, was the high-road to wisdom; or that, at any rate, Job has in reserve some crowning word of praise for that which has wrung from him such sympathy and admiration. But Job only asks—

> "Where shall wisdom be found,
> And where is the place of understanding?" [2]

Job maintains that if man should search in every direction through the inhabited world;[3] if he even could penetrate to the subterranean waters;[4] if he could offer the things most precious in the judgment of that primitive age—the onyx and the sapphire, gold and glass, pearls, crystal, and corals, the "Ethiopian topaz," the pure fine gold [5]—yet wisdom, the profoundest perception of the nature of things, would still be beyond his reach. How, then, could it be attained? Job shall answer in words which we may not venture to condense—

> "Wisdom is veiled from the eyes of all living,
> And hidden from the fowls of the heaven:
> Destruction and death say,—
> With our ears we heard a report of it.
> God understandeth the way to it,
> And He,—He knoweth its place.
> For He looketh to the ends of the earth,
> And He seeth under the whole heaven;

Chap. xxviii. 9-11. [2] *Ibid.* 12. [3] *Ibid.* 13. [4] *Ibid.* 14. [5] *Ibid.* 16-19.

> When He appointed to the wind its weight,
> And weighed the water according to measure;
> When He appointed to the rain its law,
> And a course to the lightning of the thunder;
> Then saw He it and declared it,
> Took it as a pattern, and tested it also;
> And unto man He said, Behold!
> The fear of the Lord, that is wisdom;
> And to depart from evil is understanding." [1]

Wisdom is here the Ideal according to which God created the world. The idea of natural law as an integral portion of creation, regulating the wind, regulating the distribution of water upon the surface of the globe, regulating the rainfall, regulating the course of the electric fluid, could not be more clearly expressed; but Job maintains that this creation of the world, thus marshalled under the reign of law, was, at least in a certain sense, the unveiling of Wisdom. It was then that Wisdom—hidden eternally in God,—was "perceived"; it took substantial realisation and development; it was searched out and tested; its demiurgic powers were set in motion that it might clothe itself in an outward and visible form. It is the same idea of Wisdom as that in the Book of Proverbs;[2] the complex unity of divine ideas,—in which all the departments of creation, all its laws and processes, are seen from Eternity by the Infinite Mind, not as already actual but in a mirror. Here it is plain that we are not far from the full revelation of the Word or Logos: only the Logos is personal, while as yet the Wisdom of the Proverbs and of Job is probably an impersonal model of all creaturely existence.[3]

[1] Chap. xxviii. 21-28.
[2] Prov. viii. 22-31. On the general relation of the Proverbs to the Book of Job, compare Delitzsch, *Das B. Job*, Einleitung, p. 17 *sqq.*
[3] Delitzsch, *u.s.* p. 341. Die Weisheit ist nicht geradezu eins mit dem Logos, aber der Logos ist der Demiurg, durch welchen Gott nach jenein innergöttlichen Urbilde die Welt ins Dasein gesetzt hat. Die Weisheit ist das unpersönliche Modell, der Logos der persönliche Werkmeister nach jenom Modell.

When God thus gave outward form to Wisdom in creating the world, He also gave man the law by obeying which man corresponds to what he was meant to be in the archetypal world—and participates, after his measure, in wisdom. A comprehensive intellectual apprehension of the real nature of things is beyond man's mental grasp. What do we mean by matter, what by spirit, what by the universe, what by our own personal existence? The moment we begin to define these things, we see how little we know after all; how absolute knowledge everywhere eludes us. But eternal moral truth is not beyond man's moral grasp; and it is even more truly part of the Kochmah, than is intellectual Truth. Fearing the Lord, and renouncing evil—this is man's largest share in Wisdom; this is the best approach that man can make to what we should nowadays call a philosophy of the Absolute. He cannot without a revelation really contemplate things as they are,—as they are seen by God: but he can correspond to the realities as God sees them by obedience to elementary moral truth— by fear of the perfect moral Being—by practical renunciation of evil. It is the very motto of the Hebrew doctrine of the Kochmah which we have in the text— this substitution of obedience for ambitious speculation. "Be not wise in thine own eyes," says Solomon, "fear the Lord, and depart from evil."[1] "By the fear of the Lord men depart from evil," he says elsewhere.[2] "The fear of the Lord is the beginning of knowledge,"[3] says Solomon, "of wisdom," says the Psalmist:[4] "a good understanding have all they that do thereafter—the praise of it endureth for ever."

It is in accordance with this that when the Eternal Wisdom took human form, in Jesus of Nazareth, His

[1] Prov. iii. 7.
[2] *Ibid.* xvi. 6.
[3] Prov. i. 7.
[4] Ps. cxi. 10. Cf. Delitzsch *in loc.*

teaching followed this order. It began with moral and gradually ascended to intellectual or dogmatic truth. If we except our Lord's insistence upon the great dogma of the Divine Providence, the direct teaching of the Sermon on the Mount is moral teaching : it is a sketch, negative and positive, of the New Life which would befit the subjects of the New Kingdom. In the parables we trace the two elements; the doctrinal more and more asserting itself, yet being constantly based upon the moral, until in the last Discourse, in the Supper-room, we meet our Lord as a teacher of doctrines—doctrines about the Father, doctrines about Himself, doctrines about the Blessed Comforter,—accompanied by the significant intimation, "I have yet many things to say unto you, but ye cannot bear them now."[1] That sentence leads us on through the Apostolic Epistles, to the Creeds, to the Councils of the undivided Church, to the whole fabric and material of Christian Theology. But the basis of this glorious edifice was moral. "Jesus began to preach and to say, Repent: for the kingdom of heaven is at hand."[2] And to this hour "the foundation of God standeth sure, having this seal, The Lord knoweth them that are His. And, Let every one that nameth the Name of Christ depart from iniquity."[3]

Here we touch upon one of the most important principles which a man can grasp and lay to heart. The only safe basis in the human mind for the highest truths of faith—for the truths which satisfy and sustain the life of religion in the soul—must be a moral basis. On this point the Bible is utterly at issue with a large school of modern thinkers. All that is wanted, say they, for Wisdom, in its religious as well as in any other sense, for theological as well as physical or historical Wisdom, is intellectual activity—intellectual enterprise—intellectual

---

[1] St. John xvi. 12. [2] St. Matt. iv. 17. [3] 2 Tim. ii. 19.

downrightness. Moral prepossessions, moral sentiments, moral enthusiasm can do no good. Nay! moral earnestness may, by creating disturbing prepossessions, do much harm. The same qualities that make a man a good student or teacher of physical science will make him a good student or teacher of theological science. If not—they ask triumphantly—why not? The answer is, that religious truth addresses itself, not merely or chiefly to intellect, but to the moral sense; and it is justified, by the children of wisdom, at the bar of the moral sense. To understand God's Revelation to any real purpose, we must begin by fearing Him, by taking heed to His law. In the order of our religious education, although not necessarily in the order of time, the Decalogue precedes the Creed. Doubtless an intellectual interest in religious truth is possible without a moral interest. Bad men, like Henry VIII., have been good theologians; journalists, notoriously hostile to revealed religion, take the keenest and most discriminating interest in religious questions of the day. Ignorance would be bliss compared with such knowledge as this: what can be more piteous than the clear, hard, accurate knowledge of a soul, which has cultivated its intelligence without any corresponding cultivation of its heart and conscience? The absence of this fear of the Lord, which is Wisdom in the leading Bible sense of the term, is fatal to any living appreciation, if not to any appreciation whatever, of the doctrines of Redemption and Grace. What is the good of them in the judgment of a soul which has never felt the sting of sin, or which has never realised its own utter impotence to return to God? When such a soul comes into contact with the Creed of Christendom—when it finds itself face to face with the great truths of the Incarnation and the Passion of Christ, the Influence and Personality of the Holy Spirit, the sacramental channels of communication between God and our human life, the doctrine of the ever-blessed Trinity in which these several truths find their justification and their point of unity, it can only regard truths of this magnitude, truths which we know to be so unspeakably precious, as a hard block of dead dogma, weighing like an incubus upon all honest and earnest thought. It is conscious of no demand which they satisfy; it entertains no anticipations which they meet; it feels no deep-seated disease for which they provide the remedy. And therefore it is lashed into indignation at the statement that these truths are seriously necessary to salvation, although it is willing to take a patronising interest in them as monuments and landmarks of man's past intellectual history. The fact is, the soil in which such truths must strike root is a moral soil. It is only a sensitive and educated conscience that can recognise their urgency and value, and so sustain the intellect in dealing with the speculative difficulties which they present. Dogmatic wisdom has its root and beginning in the culture of those moral and spiritual sensibilities which Scripture calls the "fear of the Lord."

II.

Now, it was in view of this great principle that Cuddesdon College was founded. There are, of course, other forms which such a foundation might have taken. It might have been simply what the designation, "a Theological College," strictly taken, would seem to imply. It might have been only an institution in which Theological Lectures have to be given, and theological examinations periodically held. Theology being regarded only as a department of knowledge, addressing itself as attractively as it could to the intellect; when theological students had attended a regular course of lectures and had been examined, the work of such an institution would have been complete. Teachers of language, teachers of the natural sciences, teachers of history, teachers of pure mathematics, say what they have to say, ascertain whether what they have said is understood and remembered by their pupils; and then everything is over. Why should it not be so in an Institution for teaching Theology? The answer—let me repeat it—is because it is impossible in the case of theology to ignore morals, conduct, life, without the gravest risk. That risk may have to be run, to a very great extent at least, in the case of a secularised University; because a University, to be true to its idea, must deal with all departments of knowledge, as knowledge, and therefore with theology, whether above or among the rest. But in the case of an institution designed to teach theology to the future religious teachers of the people, with all that solemnity and urgency which should immediately precede a man's receiving the public Commission of Christ, to incur any such risk would be wholly indefensible. If a man would teach the power of religious truth, he must personally have felt the need of it. And this need can only be felt in the secret depths of the moral being, when conscience has been aroused to a sensitiveness which is often and most wholesomely not less than agony; when the strength of habit, old and bad, and the weakness of resolution, good and recent, has been fully appreciated; when men have recognised the simple justice of that solemn sentence of Scripture that the heart—that is the centre-point of moral activity in man—is, when man is left to himself, "deceitful above all things, and desperately wicked."[1] Until language such as this is real to a man, expressing not merely what he takes it for granted is conventionally correct, but what he knows and sees to be

[1] Jer. xvii. 9.

experimentally true, the Atoning work and eternal Person of Christ our Lord, and all the varied and blessed consequences of these facts in the Church and in the Soul, must belong to the region of phrase and shadow. These truths become real to men when the need of them is felt. Their reality is felt increasingly, as the moral life of the soul becomes more sensitive and strong. At last the passion for goodness and loyalty to the Faith may blend into a whole which absorbs and governs the whole inward being; each pulsation of moral enthusiasm throwing the soul upon revealed doctrine, each perception of dogmatic truth increasing the volume of the soul's moral force. "I am crucified with Christ, nevertheless I live; yet not I, but Christ liveth in me: and the life which I now live in the flesh, I live by faith of the Son of God, Who loved me, and gave Himself for me."[1] What better motto—to describe at any rate the ideal of its corporate life—could a theological college desire?

Now if a theological college is to recognise this principle, that spiritual and theological wisdom must have a basis in conduct, in life, in conscience, it will be necessary for such an institution to develop at least two things;—first, a system; secondly, a spirit or atmosphere.

It must first of all develop a system. Of course a system of instruction and study will be taken for granted; no one would endeavour to master less serious subjects than theology, by a few efforts at random. But what we require here, and chiefly, is a system of devotion, discipline, conduct, life. Not merely study, but prayer, meditation, if need be, confession, exercise, sleep, recreation, should, as far as possible, be ordered by rule. Men should learn to run, not as uncertainly, to fight their spiritual foes, not as one that beateth the air.[2] For the Christian life, however imperfectly and poorly, is yet in all who try

[1] Gal. ii. 20.   [2] 1 Cor. ix. 26.

to live it at all, a matter of rule; of rule which is the willing expression of love; of rule which, instead of confiscating, guarantees the blessed liberty with which Christ has made us free; of rule which reflects in the human soul something of that Eternal Order which is the law of the Divine Mind and Life. And therefore a House which has a religious purpose should be a House of rule; it should be governed by system. Afterwards and elsewhere, the exacting demands of public work may make very little of the kind possible. Happy they who make the most of such a blessing while they may!

What will system do? It will do this: it will, for the first time in the lives of most men who encounter it, set before them this great truth;—that life is given us to be disposed of and laid out from first to last under the eye of Christ our Lord. It will furnish them with an ideal of such an arrangement of life, together with opportunities of attempting to realise that ideal. A man cannot throw himself sincerely into a devotional system without being thereby braced and elevated; without feeling the power and beauty of moral law traversing and taking possession of all the wildernesses in his spiritual nature; without coming face to face with Him, Whose Presence and Will is everywhere implied in the rules which should govern Christian lives; with Him to Whom all leads upwards, from Whom all radiates.

Not that system alone will suffice. System, pure and simple, has no living power; it is only a shell which some living thing must have inhabited to give it existence, or which must have been made in artificial imitation of a natural growth. System, it has been truly said, if nothing more than system, is a "workhouse, whence escape is always welcome; wherein obedience and compliance are almost always forced and hypocritical." Besides system, then, a Theological College must develop a spirit—a moral and religious atmosphere—which will justify and interpret its system to those who live in it. Now it is much less easy to develop a traditional temper of thought and feeling in an institution than to lay down rules for its management; but in the case of a theological college, the spirit is more necessary than are the rules. A spirit which is earnest and practical tends insensibly to clothe itself with system; if earnest spirit without system involves aimlessness and waste of spiritual material, system without spirit is as dead as a soulless corpse. But who is to create the spirit? Certainly, *non cuivis contigit*. Certainly the difficulty of breathing into and sustaining in the members of any institution, the rare temper, the lofty enthusiasms which in deed become them, is the most rare and precious of the gifts of government; it belongs to what we term, in ordinary human language, moral genius. It is far too delicate and ethereal a power to submit to analysis, or to be bound down by conditions of time and place: it does not depend on formal relations, or emphatic occasions, or official understandings, for the secret of its empire; it makes the most of the by-play of incidental circumstance; it deals with life on its tender and unguarded side, in its moments of relaxation, at its intervals of despondency or frankness. It pours itself around others, when and how they know not; it saturates them; it impregnates them with its own fervour and impetuosity; it insensibly furnishes them with new points of view, new moods of feeling, new estimates of life; they learn, like the converted Franks, to adore what they had burned, and to burn what they had adored, before they know it.

Need I say, brethren, that such a gift is not really of human origin? Men may be its channels and administrators: it may attach to this man and not to that, to this character rather than to that; but He only Who governs and sanctifies the Church, the Divine and Eternal Spirit, is its real author. He seems to invest all Christ's greatest servants with the halo of some such power: St. John and St. Paul were each the centre-points of an atmosphere, strongly marked by their separate individualities, within which many souls grew and were sanctified. So in later ages was it with St. Basil and St. Chrysostom, and in an eminent sense with the great Augustine: these men were centres of moral and spiritual light and force, which constantly escaped from them, even without their meaning it, and which made companionship with them, of itself, a discipline. In a college such as this, as you know from its history during the last ten years, all depends, humanly speaking, on the presence of such a gift as this in its chief officer. It is this which explains the indescribable attraction and power of the place,—it is this which irradiates all else; which redeems everything here from the suspicion of triviality or wearisomeness; which gilds all the habits, all the associations, all the localities—the very roads, and hedges, and trees around, I had almost said—with a spiritual and moral beauty, at least in the eyes of those who amid these scenes have first learnt what life, and work, and death, really mean.

It is said, I know, that personal influences of this kind, in a theological college, tend to foster cliquism among the clergy. This is so far true, that nothing binds men together so closely as the felt power of a common enthusiasm. They who, sitting or kneeling side by side, have felt the illuminating, enkindling force of the same truths, dimly discerned, it may be, before, but thenceforth seen to be the very life of the soul, and, indeed, the one thing worth living for, feel towards each other as apostles must have felt, each of whom, in the upper chamber, saw the tongues of fire visibly resting on the head of every brother around him. There is no friendship so sincere, no bond of brotherhood so pure, so intense, I will add, so legitimate, as that which is rooted in consciously common convictions,—convictions traceable to a common origin. Such friendship may be termed cliquism; but the name is only deserved, if the objects of those to whom it is applied are selfish and narrow, or if their bearing towards others is exclusive or conceited. Surely what we want of all things in the Church of England is greater harmony among the clergy; more of that very sense of brotherhood which such a college as this conspicuously encourages; a more practical appreciation, to use the Psalmist's words, of the joy and goodness of dwelling together in spiritual unity.

Then there is that other criticism, that a theological college of this kind is really a hothouse. A hothouse, it is conceded, may do good work in the winter; but it is artificial work, at best. The plants which it rears will not stand the winds and frosts of the open air; they need a kindly soil and a high temperature. If a plant can be made to grow out of doors and alone, it had better do so; to shut it up is to weaken it; it is to give it a forced vitality at the risk of its future hardihood and vigour.

It is an old remark, my brethren, that if you wish to beg the question in an argument, your best way of doing so is to employ a metaphor. Under the cover and patronage of a metaphor, the logical fallacy glides past unnoticed, and too often takes its place unchallenged upon the throne of reason. I deny that a college of this description occupies any such position in the moral and spiritual sphere as to make the metaphor of a hothouse tolerably accurate. For what does such a metaphor assume? It assumes that human life as a whole—so sternly and inexorably condemned by our Lord and Saviour under the designation of " the world,"—interposes no dark shadows, presents no grave obstacles, offers no strong resistance to the highest development of the spiritual life; it assumes that the life of the world is the chosen home and natural mother of the Evangelical graces. Such an assumption needs only to be stated. To refute it, with the text of the Gospels in our hands, would be a waste of time. No doubt there are souls, at once pure, sincere, and hardy, which without preparatory discipline, so far as we know, of any kind, do sometimes pass unscathed through temptations which are the ruin of multitudes; souls which draw only strength and resolution from the ungenial atmosphere and active hostilities amid which they spend their day of life. But such souls are the exception; they are not the rule. The rule is, that all that is in the world, the lust of the flesh, and the lust of the eyes, and the pride of life—whatever else may be said of it—is not of the Father,[1] and does not help us to draw closer to Him. The rule is that to live in the world without being of it, still more to influence and improve it, you must have retired from it awhile, as did St. Paul into Arabia,[2] and in a Higher Presence have taken both the measure of its strength and the measure of its weakness. This is the moral object at which a theological college should especially aim. It is not a monastery, because in a monastery men are bound by obligations which last for a lifetime, and which differ altogether from the restraints involved in spiritual preparation for clerical work in the world. It is not, on the other hand, merely a literary society of men of blameless and retiring habits. It is emphatically a home of discipline and training for the most difficult work that a human being can undertake— that of teaching and feeding the souls of others. The world no more affords us such a home than do the wilds of Dartmoor yield us full opportunities for becoming botanists or geologists: Dartmoor yields many illustra-

[1] 1 St. John ii. 16. [2] Gal. i. 17.

tions of these sciences, but to appreciate them, to arrange them in the mental museum which we are gradually forming, we must most assuredly have placed ourselves under instruction, and have studied elsewhere. We cannot wisely attempt to begin *ab ovo*, and reject all the treasures accumulated by earlier observers and workers; we cannot ignore wisely either the ripe wisdom of science, or the ripe wisdom of our elders in the Church, because we may hope one day to add a little something from our own hardly-won observation and experience.

A hothouse indeed! In such a sense as—allowing of course for the immeasurable interval—in such a sense, I say, as our Lord's Companionship with His first disciples deserves the metaphor, but in no other sense, does it apply to institutions such as this we are considering; where the object is—to rest religious faith and life, not upon a forced and unreal, but upon the deepest and most solid basis—the plain and steady recognition of moral truth. We might, indeed, here appeal to experience. Is it not the case that the students who have left Cuddesdon, at least during the last ten years, have given proof of a knowledge of the world and of the hearts of men, at least as discriminating and true as that of others who have trusted to their own efforts or to the lecture-rooms of the University? Or rather, is not this statement felt by all who are acquainted with the subject to be very greatly below the real truth; and must we not dismiss, on the strength of such experience, an eminently foolish and misleading metaphor, which no one who had adequate ideas of the work in hand would have thought of employing?

To-day is an anniversary, in some respects, of more than ordinary interest. It is a day of many congratulations—natural and legitimate. Never before the present year has this College, in the person of any of its working officers, received such emphatic recognition from high quarters of the services which it has been permitted to render to the Church.[1] That recognition, many of you will feel, however grateful in itself, is purchased at a very heavy cost; and therefore to-day is a day, perhaps, of some great regrets and even of some inevitable misgivings. Brethren, at all such turning-points of life, whether public or private, it is well to reflect that, if men pass, principles, truths, means of grace, remain. Above all, He remains, Who is the author and the end of these things; Who putteth down one and setteth up another; Who, as being infinite in His resources, is not dependent upon this or that agent for the doing of His predestined work; Who disappoints alike, in His consummate Wisdom, our eager hopes and our feverish anxieties. The one thing to be really anxious about just now, is that the principle upon which this College was originally founded, by the piety and genius of your Lordship's predecessor, should be permanently and heartily recognised within its walls; that its religious philosophy should be moral before it dares to be speculative,—its students men who know something of their own hearts ere they preach to others.

[1] The allusion is to the appointment of the Rev. E. King, Principal of Cuddesdon College, to the Chair of Pastoral Theology at Oxford. The Bishop of Bloemfontein had left Cuddesdon College some time before his elevation.

SERMON III.

OUR LORD'S EXAMPLE THE STRENGTH OF HIS MINISTERS.[1]

S. MATT. iv. 19.

And He saith unto them, Follow Me, and I will make you fishers of men.

SUCH is the first notice of the Christian Ministry which meets us in the pages of the New Testament. Our Lord was standing on the shore of the lake of Galilee, and, if we may assume that St. Luke's narrative[2] refers to the same event as St. Matthew's, He had just wrought a miracle whereat all were filled with amazement, and in beholding which St. Peter had fallen on his knees while giving expression to his mingled fear and adoration. I need hardly remind you that this great Apostle, together with and by the influence of his brother St. Andrew, had for some months at least enjoyed the high privilege of Christ's companionship.[3] This, however, did not at first involve a final abandonment of their trade as fishers: unlike St. Matthew, they were allowed a period of preparation before their solemn call to the higher service of their Master. Our Lord had now opened His Ministry in Eastern Galilee, among those thickly scattered towns of Gennesareth, of whose comparatively large populations it has been happily said that "they were to the Roman Palestine almost what the manufacturing

[1] Preached in the Cathedral Church of Christ in Oxford, on the Fourth Sunday in Advent, December 23, 1860.
[2] St. Luke v. 1-11.   [3] St. John i. 37, 40, 41.

districts are to England."[1] The people pressed on Him to hear the word of God; the future Apostles had enjoyed a sufficient probation to meet this new demand on their faith and their obedience. Accordingly, "He saith unto them, Follow Me, and I will make you fishers of men."

I.

When Elijah called his future disciple from the oxen and the plough, there was the same kind of abrupt transition from simple physical labour to preparation for high spiritual office.[2] We may perhaps measure the greater exigency and imperativeness of the call of Jesus, by the fact that while Elisha's request that he might take leave of his father and of his mother was granted,[3] our Merciful Lord bade one who wished first to bury his father to enter on his discipleship without further tarrying,[4] and dismissed another, who desired to say farewell to his friends, as unfit for the kingdom of God.[5] Unlike these feeble, half-hearted proselytes, the Apostles seem to have asked for no delay: St. Peter and St. Andrew immediately forsook their occupation; St. James and St. John their father; as later, without their previous training, St. Matthew his receipt of custom.[6] The Voice Which they heard bade them leave nets and boat, and relatives and home; they were to break with the memories of youth, and with the hopes of manhood, and with the encrustation of habit that was already gathering around maturer life. Without reserve, without delay, without condition, without reluctance, they were to make a venture; they were to cast in their lot with One Who had no home, and Who as yet had promised only *this*, as the reward of obedience, "I will make you fishers of men." That promise surely meant that in a certain sense their past life would re-appear in the future before them. The

[1] *Sinai and Palestine*, p. 371. [2] 1 Kings xix. 19. [3] *Ibid.* 20.
[4] St. Matt. viii. 21, 22. [5] St. Luke ix. 62. [6] St. Matt. ix. 9.

love of enterprise, the careless indifference to danger, the keen interest which is awakened where success is beyond control and matter of speculation, the manifold exercise of skill and inventiveness, above all, the steady, patient, unrelieved, enduring toil,—in short, all the qualities which hitherto had spent themselves on that inland lake were now to receive a place and a consecration in the Heavenly Kingdom. All that they were leaving was to have a counterpart in that life to which they were called. The earlier gifts which they had received from God, His calling, by His Providence, to an earthly livelihood, might seem, like the privileges of the Race of Israel, to be "without repentance."[1] A new home, new fathers and mothers, and brethren and sisters, were to win their hearts:[2] there was the Gospel-net ready to their hands, and the sea of the nations was before them. David, the shepherd-boy, following the ewes, had been taken, in obedience to the same law of continuity between nature and grace, to feed Jacob the people of the Lord Jehovah, and Israel His inheritance.[3] If strangers to eloquence and human learning, if ignorant of the thoughts and ways of men, the disciples might rest in humble trust on that promise of Him Who spake, "*I* will make you." The seeming loss, then, was really gain; the past was not to be so much resigned as consecrated; they were ceasing to ply their earthly occupations to preside (as yet they knew not how) at the regeneration of the world. One strong act of love and resolution tore them from what as yet had occupied their understandings and enchained their hearts; That Voice had reached their inmost spirit, and they followed Its leading.

It may be difficult to determine how much of the fuller meaning of Our Lord's Words may have flashed across the soul of those fishermen, who already believed Him to be the promised Messiah.[4] *We* read those words by the

[1] Rom. xi. 29. [2] St. Mark x. 29, 30. [3] Ps. lxxviii. 70-72. [4] St. John i. 41.

light of His own subsequent declarations concerning Himself,[1] and of the witness of His inspired Apostles,[2] and of the Creeds of the Universal Church. We can dare to see in the Speaker none less than the Infinite and Eternal God. Yet, born and nurtured in the bosom of Christendom, we can never realise the full measure of that shock and wrench by which the Apostles passed from their lowly fishing-boat to the helm of the Vessel of Christ. As addressed to us, the words belong, it might seem, less to the day of Ordination than to that inner call to the sacred ministry, which must, at some time or other, have gone before. We can remember, perchance, how this message from God broke upon us. There was already a certain sense of the mystery and responsibility of life, and of the value of the soul; there was a deeper personal conviction of the hatefulness, misery, and end of sin, and of the greatness of our Lord's plenteous Redemption. The life of the plant or of the animal exists not in its perfection unless it be self-propagating; and every soul that is "alive unto God through Jesus Christ Our Lord," must endeavour, according to its opportunities, to give effect to this test and law of a true vitality, and to make other men share its blessings and its joys. Of this general tendency, the vocation to Holy Orders is a specific, perhaps not always, although generally, an intense manifestation. We beheld those to whom Christ our Lord and His love, and His promises, and His consolations were unknown; and though we ourselves knew little of Him, relatively perchance as little as did the fishermen of Galilee after that first companionship, the thought nevertheless came upon us, and took shape, and grew, and at length it whispered, "Follow Me, and I will make you fishers of men." No natural gift, we too may feel,

---

[1] St. John viii. 58; x. 30.
[2] Col. i. 15-17; Phil. ii. 6; Heb. i. 3; 1 St. John iv. 15; Rev. i. 11.

need be wasted: the work before us needs our every energy, it can hallow and employ the most common and trivial, as well as the most exceptional and brilliant gifts. Since that call until this day, when the promise is to be fulfilled by those hands to which Our Lord has delegated the bestowal of His high Commission, we have been following Him. Ay, brethren, you must be our Lord's true disciples in heart and will, before you may be His ministers. You must be fairly enclosed in the Gospel-net before you can help to bring in others. You must have learnt the habit, and tone, and culture which befit the court of the King of kings, ere, armed with His full credentials, you go forth as His ambassadors[1] to the world. It is well if, besides your letters of credit, you hold from Him an inner patent of spiritual nobility. You will find it hard to speak for Him with the tenderness, and firmness, and composure, and dignity, and earnest perseverance which befits His representatives, if you have (which God forbid) in any way forced yourselves upon Him. His words must surely falter and die away on your stammering lips, if He has not freed you from all bondage by His Divine enfranchisement,[2] if you lack inward loyalty and love, and are at heart the satellites of His enemy. None who is enslaved to sin, to any one ruling passion, whether it be lust, or covetousness, or pride, or envy, or subtle ambition, or fear of man, can proclaim in its majesty and its power the everlasting Gospel. Such an one, if placed in the ranks of the sacred ministry, will almost infallibly, and from a mere instinct of honesty, tone down the note of his prophecy to the grovelling level of his own experience.[3] Or it may be, from an opposite instinct of duty, he will draw exaggerated fancy pictures, because religion has never been real to

---

[1] 2 Cor. v. 20.   [2] St. John viii. 36.
[3] 1 Tim. i. 19, vi. 9, 10, 21 ; Tit. i. 11.

him. And therefore by prayer, and self-discipline, and practical piety, we must have followed Our Lord, if on the day of ordination we are to become in personal spiritual power, as well as by note of apostolic character and commission, fishers of men.

II.

But the words of the text admit of an application more adapted to our present circumstances. We cannot suppose that these words had lost their meaning when the Apostles had received their full Commission from the Lips and Hands of Christ. Such words could not thus pass away.[1] It was indeed true that the power of fishing for men was an acknowledgment and a reward of previous discipleship. It was true that such discipleship prepared the heart to receive such power. But also, it was true that in following Christ the ordained Apostles became ever increasingly successful as fishers of men. Without this imitative energy, the hallowing grace which He had breathed forth upon their spirits might have lost its power like a natural faculty which has never been exercised; although the indelible character and stamp of ministry should remain traced for ever, as its note of condemnation, on the soul. The imitation of Christ as a law of the Christian life has been often treated of. We are now considering a distinct subject,—the imitation of Christ as the regulating principle of ministerial *force*. "Follow Me, and I will make you fishers of men."

Fishers of men! Let us dwell, dear brethren, on that word, for it describes our work. We may underrate,— we cannot easily form an exaggerated estimate whether of its nobleness or of its difficulty. Man, we know, is an animal, yet endowed with a reasonable soul. His lower nature excels, while it links him to, all the strata of natural

---

[1] St. Mark xiii. 31.

life which are ranged beneath him. By his higher he is associated with that world of spiritual intelligences of which he is the lowest and the feeblest inhabitant. With a being thus composite, his heart is the frontier-boundary of two worlds,—the world of matter and the world of spirit. Each of the great divisions of existence claims him as belonging to it. Study the organism of his body, the laws which he obeys at birth, in growth, at death,—analyse his food, unravel and describe the mechanism of his movements, draw out and exhibit the chemical elements of his future decomposition;—and he will appear as nothing but the highest and most complex form of material and transient life. But look, on the other hand, at his spiritual nature; study its manifold resources and wellnigh boundless capacities; mark the strength, the subtlety, the daring, the impetuosity of its associated even though undeveloped powers; and you see before you that which never can die—nay, that which may and will become, according to the law of its development, even as an angel in heaven, or as a devil in hell. Such is man, the personal union of two natures in the midst of God's creation; on the one side crawling on the earth, on the other seeking the heavens; here linked to what is perishable and limited, there to the Infinite and the Eternal; by one set of impulses tending to descend altogether to the level of his animal existence, as if he were nothing better than a creature of sense and time, by another to rise upwards to the full height and tether of his spiritual capacities, and to seek amidst the ranks of angels and archangels the Face, the adoration, the possession of his God.

Such, brethren, are we ourselves; such is the being with which, as Christ's servants, we have to treat. All our work centres around this point—the conversion and sanctification of man. For this—since it more than aught else promotes our Master's glory—for this great end we preach, and visit, and build schools, and open missions, and erect reformatories, and build and beautify churches, and fill them with the voice of prayer and the grace and presence of Sacraments. We must then consider how complex and various are the influences which bear in upon the heart of man from opposite quarters. We must endeavour to estimate, as we can with a certain measure of accuracy, the forces of man's lower nature. We must allow for, since we cannot accurately investigate, the more mysterious forces, good and evil, which affect his higher. We cannot but observe that without and apart from Christ the balance of man's being, since the Fall, has been fatally over-weighted on the side of its animal and material propensions. A philosopher might here or there, in his proud isolation, affect the life of his higher nature; but he could not escape from those strong and fearful sins of the spirit, which make its partial emancipation from matter a doubtful blessing, if not an additional misery. And Paganism, as seen in the populations which it formed and nurtured, lived necessarily the life of sense. For without grace the flesh is more than a match for the spirit, and the powers of the angel are condemned, as a matter of course, to minister to the lusts and indulgence of the brute. Our Lord, we know, in His mercy and His love has restored the equilibrium, partly by opening upon the eye of the soul a true sense of its lofty destiny, and partly by the consecration of the lower nature through its union with His own Everlasting Godhead. "The law of the spirit of life in Christ Jesus makes free from the law of sin and death."[1] Still, allowing for and remembering this unspeakable and blessed truth, the problem before us His ministers is still a fearful one. We need not look far abroad to conclude that the forces ranged against us,

[1] Rom. viii. 2.

whether they be "flesh and blood," or "the principalities and powers and rulers of this world's darkness,"[1] are such as to make us, with good reason, anxious respecting the all-important issue. How far the higher nature may be reached through the lower, what are the influences to which the soul is most sensitively open, how Truth can best make a lasting home in the heart, and win empire over the passions of man,—these and other like questions force themselves upon us. And it will help us, I venture to think, in our difficulty, if we observe how Our Lord, in the days of His flesh, dealt with the being with whom we have to deal; if we endeavour to discover His moral attitude, and motive, and spirit, and method of approach and treatment in His intercourse with man, at that time when He, in His marvellous condescension, was engaged in the very work, a share of which (O wondrous thought!) He bequeaths, as on this day, even to us!

Of so vast a subject as the Ministerial Life of Our Lord we can but seize a few leading features. Here first observe—

1. Our Lord's ruling motive. This was stamped visibly upon His ministry. It was the glory and will of the Eternal Father. This indeed, we are permitted to know, was the principle of His Incarnation. "Sacrifice and offering Thou wouldest not, but a Body hast Thou prepared Me: Then said I, Lo, I come!"[2] Every Mystery of His Life, from His Birth in the manger to His Ascension into Heaven, was an act of homage to the glory of the Father. Our Lord, we may say without risk of exaggeration, never conceived a thought, nor formed a desire, nor uttered a word, unless in some way word, and desire, and thought might set forth His Father's glory. Witness His own words: "I seek not Mine own glory";[3] "I seek not Mine own Will, but the Will of the Father

---
[1] Eph. vi. 12. [2] Heb. x. 5-7; Ps. xl. 6, 7.
[3] St. John viii. 50.

Which hath sent Me";[1] "I receive not honour from men";[2] "He that speaketh of himself seeketh his own glory: but He That seeketh His glory That sent Him, the Same is true, and there is no unrighteousness in Him";[3] "I do always such things as please Him"; and at last, "I have glorified Thee on the earth: I have finished the work which Thou gavest Me to do."[4]

Let us observe this more in detail during His ministry. When Our Lord's doctrine drew on Him the admiration and the applause of men, He was careful to assure them that it came from heaven. "My doctrine is not Mine, but His That sent Me."[5] Let us remember that "in Him were hid all the treasures of wisdom and knowledge,"[6] and that even in His Boyhood, the Jewish Doctors "were astonished" at one Ray of His Intellectual Glory.[7] Yet how measured are His communications of knowledge, made, "as men were able to hear,"[8] in the interests of the simple and of the poor, and as if purposely to rebuke "display" of earthly learning in His ministers! When addressed as "Good Master," by one who wished to pay Him a compliment, He answered almost sharply, "Why callest thou Me good? there is none good but One, that is, God."[9] If His miracles made Him an object of popularity, He withdrew Himself from the applause of the crowd.[10] He desired the recipients of His mercy to see that they told no man.[11] He, the Eternal and Infinite Son of God, was content to pass for the son of the carpenter.[12] He imposed silence upon the devil who confessed Him to be What He really was.[13] He Who advanced to meet His enemies, when they sought His life,[14] fled when He knew that the people sought to make Him a king.[15]

---

[1] St. John v. 30.   [2] *Ibid.* 41.   [3] *Ibid.* vii. 18.   [4] *Ibid.* xvii. 4.
[5] St. John vii. 16.   [6] Col. ii. 3.   [7] St. Luke ii. 47.
[8] St. Mark iv. 33.   [9] *Ibid.* x. 17, 18.   [10] *Ibid.* i. 45; St. Luke v. 16.
[11] St. Mark i. 44, viii. 26; St. Luke viii. 56.   [12] St. Matt. xiii. 55.
[13] St. Mark i. 25, 34; iii. 11, 12.   [14] St. John xviii. 4.   [15] *Ibid.* vi. 15.

Be well assured, brethren, that you have here a principle of spiritual force. To the natural man the power of attractive speech, the opportunity of conferring benefits, a place and name in the words and hearts of men, is precious, as leading to personal gain of some kind or other.[1] It is an investment, so to say, which, as is thought, should yield its corresponding return. Few sensible men in the present day would enter the ministry for the sake of an income. But the other sins of the Pharisees are the sins of a teaching order; they are the sins into which it most naturally falls. The love of prominence, the love of influence, the love of popularity and of the praise of men, are the dangers of all priesthoods of all time. For often it is in truth very difficult to say where the pure motive shades off into the impure; and the real state of the case is probably unknown to us, until some failure in our work lets in upon solitude and disappointment a ray of light from heaven, and shows us how much self has appropriated of that which was all along half-meant for God. Yet men are really awed by a perfect disinterestedness, from its very unlikeness to what they see within themselves. It is a power which baffles their understandings, while it takes captive their imaginations and their hearts. Even amid the sin and turmoil of this world, disinterestedness is always power; and we have marked during the past year, how a nation could bend in enthusiastic devotion before a single name, because that name was at least believed to represent none of the self-seeking ambition of ordinary political and national effort.[2] So, although Our Lord declined the homage of the people, it was thrust upon Him; the multitude so hung upon His Lips that they had scarcely room to stand,[3] time to eat:[4] if He sought to conceal His fame, so much the more a great deal

[1] Acts viii. 18-23; Mal. i. 10. St. Mark iv. 1.
[2] The reference is apparently to Garibaldi.
[4] St. Mark iii. 20, vi. 31.

men published it;[1] if He enjoined silence respecting His miracles, "whithersoever He entered, villages or cities," the sick were laid out, and laid out only to be made whole. He "seeks not His own glory: but there is One That seeketh and judgeth."[3]

And if this was so with Him, the All-holy and Eternal, what with ourselves? If in our pulpits, our schools, our visiting, we seek men's praise, we must in the end find confusion. We dare not assume a glory which belongs to Another. Only at our utmost peril can we seek to make capital, and position, and a name out of the things of God. For in truth we have nothing, whether in nature or in grace, that we can call our own. If our Master "raises the needy from the earth, and lifteth up the poor out of the dunghill, that He may set us with the princes, even with the princes of His people,"[4] the glory and the work is His. We are only strong when in heart and deed we confess our utter weakness. We are only powerful, as the ministers of Christ, in such degree as, for His blessed sake, we can succeed in utterly forgetting ourselves. By following Him in His disinterestedness we may indeed become "fishers of men."

2. A second prominent feature in Our Lord's ministry is His tender love for souls, and His burning desire for their salvation. He came to seek and to save that which was lost.[5] He who would win man must begin by loving him. Our Lord indeed loved the souls of men so as to die for them. He loved the whole race, from its first parent to the latest generation; yet He entered with perfect sympathy into each instance of individual suffering. And it is good for us, brethren, to hang on His footsteps in the Gospel narrative: for verily to us, His ministers, that portion of His Divine Word is, in a

---

[1] St. Mark vii. 36. [2] *Ibid.* vi. 56. [3] St. John viii. 50.
[4] Ps. cxiii. 7, 8. [5] St. Luke xix. 10.

peculiar sense, "a lantern unto the feet and a light unto the paths."[1] "Seeing the multitudes," we read, "He was moved with compassion on them, because they fainted, and were scattered abroad, as sheep having no shepherd."[2] If the people are hungry, it is He Who feels at once compassion, and it issues in one of the greatest of His miracles.[3] If the centurion speaks to Him of his palsied servant, Our Lord offers at once to come and heal him.[4] If the afflicted ruler breaks in upon His discourse with the disciples of St. John, and pours forth the anguish of his bereavement at the Feet of the Great Consoler, Our Lord at once "arose and followed him."[5] If He meets a widow who has lost her only son, "He has compassion on her, and saith unto her, Woman, weep not."[6] If He seems for a moment harsh towards the Canaanite woman, it is only that He may stimulate and reward her greater faith.[7] Even on the way to Calvary He pauses, as if in forgetfulness of His own awful Passion, to console the women who followed Him weeping.[8] Even from His Cross, when His life was ebbing, and the Father's Face was hidden, and the sins of the world lay as a burden on His Soul, He consoled and provided for His Mother and His disciple.[9] These Acts and Words of Our Lord answer to those portions of ministerial work with which we easily become most familiar; since many will seek comfort at our hands under the sorrows of this life, who have no due value for the next. Follow we, then, the Saviour of the world in His tender and comprehensive sympathy, even though afar off, and at the cost of precious time and personal suffering, that we become, like Him, fishers of men. Mark we, too, how He seized every opportunity for converting those who were living in sin. If men asked Him

---

[1] Ps. cxix. 105. [2] St. Matt. ix. 36. [3] St. Mark vi. 34, 35.
[4] St. Matt. viii. 7. [5] Ibid. ix. 19. [6] St. Luke vii. 13.
[7] St. Matt. xv. 21 sqq. [8] St. Luke xxiii. 28. [9] St. John xix. 26, 27.

for temporal favours, He made of the earthly benefit a vehicle for a spiritual blessing. He touches the higher nature by healing the lower. He ministers to the suffering body that He may reach the unseen, wellnigh inaccessible spirit. The sick of the palsy is set down before Him lying on a bed; but our Lord's first words speak of the paralysis, not of the body, but of the soul; and the miraculous cure of the body is wrought as a warrant of the reality of the soul's absolution from sin.[1] Our Lord even accepted invitations to places where sinners were to be met, that He might heal their souls. He was content, for the sake of the perishing, to pass "as a man gluttonous and a wine-bibber, the friend of publicans and sinners."[2] He meekly reminded His critics that they that were whole "need not a physician, but they that are sick."[3] He even invited Himself to the house of the publican Zacchæus ("To-day I must abide at thine house") that He might bless and convert him.[4] Wearied with His journey, He rests at the well of Sychar; when a soul presents herself.[5] Even the much-needed rest must be interrupted that He may teach us, His ministers, how unceasing are our obligations to those who seek from us spiritual aid. He shows us, too, how from the trifles of daily life we may draw out materials for rousing souls from the sleep of sin. The water of that well imaged forth to the soul of that lost one the well of water—Christ's life-giving grace—springing up into everlasting life; till she desired that grace, and won it. It is of vital moment that we should mark this our Lord's readiness to receive sinners. The Magdalen presents herself most inopportunely, in the midst of a banquet; but our Lord, instead of putting her off to another occasion, at once accepts her, while Simon, His host, looks on her with an evil eye, as a public sinner.[6]

[1] St. Matt. ix. 2, 6. [2] Ibid. xi. 19. [3] Ibid. ix. 12.
[4] St. Luke xix. 5. [5] St. John iv. 6-26. [6] St. Luke vii. 36-50.

The thief on the cross, who shortly before had joined his fellow in their chorus of dying blasphemy, makes but one advance; the insult is at once forgiven: "To-day shalt thou be with Me in Paradise."[1] The woman taken in adultery, trembling and ashamed, is brought before Him; but He, Who knows that all have need of mercy, dismisses her accusers in silence and confusion, and adds, "Neither do I condemn thee; go and sin no more."[2] Perhaps Nicodemus experienced our Lord's condescension to weak souls as strikingly as did these others His tender gentleness in welcoming sinners. Nicodemus was learned, and knew that our Lord spake truth; but he was timid, he shrank from avowing his convictions and taking a part; he "came to Jesus by night."[3] Our Lord received him at his own time, and on his own terms; He did not compel a more courageous expression of conviction; He instructed the "master in Israel," and gained his affection. And it was Nicodemus who spoke boldly for the truth in the Council of the Pharisees;[4] it was Nicodemus who, at great personal risk, joined in embalming the Holy Body.[5] So again, when we are wearied with toiling in our schools, it may help us to remember that our Lord suffered little children to come unto Him, and forbade them not.[6] In training holy souls for heaven, we may note how our Lord corrected even the smaller defects which still clung to His disciples, as when they disputed among themselves which should be the greatest,[7] and when they forbade one casting out devils in His name because he followed them not.[8] So His approval of Mary sitting at His Feet might teach us that it is our duty to cherish in certain souls a life of contemplation.[9]

[1] St. Luke xxiii. 43.   [2] St. John viii. 11.   [3] St. John iii. 2.
[4] St. John vii. 50, 51.   [5] *Ibid.* xix. 39.
[6] St. Mark x. 14; St. Luke xviii. 16.
[7] St. Mark ix. 34, 35; St. Luke xxii. 24-27.   [8] St. Luke ix. 49, 50.
[9] St. Luke x. 39, 42.

His washing the feet of His disciples may encourage us to decline no labour, however irksome and humiliating, which may be necessary to assure to our people a profitable and worthy receiving of the Holy Communion.[1] Above all, His words, "The Lord hath anointed Me to preach the Gospel to the poor,"[2] must be the motto of our work. If we shrink from those whom we naturally dislike, if we indulge prejudices of family, or station, or refinement, or education, when we ought to be labouring equally for all, we shall find ample rebuke in the pages of the Gospel. We cannot suppose that impenitent Chorazin and Bethsaida were specially attractive to our Lord; yet we know that they were the scene of numberless miracles.[3] It is fatal for an ordained man to hold the faith of our Lord Jesus Christ with respect of places or respect of persons.[4] He is sent to all, by a Saviour Who loves all, and his strength lies in a hearty recognition of this feature of universality which ennobles his mission. By following our Lord's steps in His love for men, in His sensitive sympathy for all suffering, in His persevering seeking for lost sinners, in His readiness and tenderness in receiving them, in His condescension to the weak, and in His anxious training of the strong, we shall become, in our far-off measure, fishers of men. For mankind are open to such world-embracing love; it is a force the might of which they involuntarily recognise; it is as powerful in one age as another, in one society or civilisation as in another; it is always needful, as it is always welcome, to the mental and bodily sufferings of mankind; it gives the man who brings it influence with souls which he may and must turn to his Master's glory; it gives him this influence in the largest measure at the time when he most earnestly declines it.

[1] St. John xiii. 5.   [2] St. Luke iv. 18.
[3] St. Matt. xi. 21.   [4] St. James ii. 1.

3. Our Lord's Teaching is so vast a subject that we can note only one feature of it. The servant, we may observe in passing, too often must hear from a faithful conscience, the rebuke of Him Who sends him, "Why dost thou preach My law, and takest My covenant in thy mouth, whereas thou hatest to be reformed, and hast cast My words behind thee?"[1] But in the Divine Master doctrine was perfectly illustrated by example. "He was the first," St. Gregory observes, "perfectly to practise what He preached." "He began," says St. Luke, "to *do* as well as *teach*" at the opening of His ministry.[2] Much might be said of the fervency, of the simplicity, of the wisdom, of the manifold attractiveness to be noted in the discourses of our Divine Lord. But the point to which I invite your attention concerns neither the method nor the style of our Master's words, nor their consistency with His Life, important as is each of these considerations. Looking at the *matter* of His teaching, let us observe this dominant and most noteworthy characteristic; it was *definite*.

It is not difficult for educated persons, at their ease, with few cares, and in the strength and buoyancy of youth, to speak of religious truth as versatile and impalpable; to depreciate or ridicule the prophetical office of the Church of Christ; to insist on the equal claims of contradictory interpretations; to indulge in feats of ingenuity which make the sacred words of Divine Scripture mean anything or nothing; to hazard the false and humiliating paradox, that in the things of God faith befits only the infancy of mankind, and that doubt and speculation are the higher and more intellectual notes of maturer years and of a more advanced civilisation; and so at length to volatilise the Divine message, that, while God affirms that He has made a Revelation, they can bring themselves to believe that hardly any one nameable truth has been

[1] Ps. l. 16, 17. [2] Acts i. 1.

certainly revealed. But that broken-hearted, desponding sinner,—but that poverty-stricken, homeless wanderer,—nay, your educated man himself, when he comes to lie, face to face with eternity, upon his bed of death, needs something stronger and better than the residuary probabilities which may perchance have been suffered to escape from some crucible of a destructive criticism. He wants, in truth, to "plant his foot on some Rock beyond the sands of time"; he must be assured that what seems true to him is true in itself; he must have something to lean on, holier, diviner, more enduring than his own shifting consciousness.

Every good man must own the antecedent probability that a Revelation would have been given. Every earnest and thoughtful man feels it to be the merest trifling, if after admitting that a Revelation has been made, you add that it "tells us nothing certain, nothing that we do not know or cannot guess without it, nothing that comes absolutely from without," and so is distinct from our own untrustworthy impressions concerning it. Religion, whether true or false, cannot be a mere sentiment; she never has lived and never can live in this disembodied, airy, unsubstantial form to which Idealism would condemn her; she must have doctrines; she must speak with precision and authority; she must undertake the responsibility and bear the odium of asserting that which will be assuredly and energetically contradicted; or she will make no adequate response whatever to the deepest needs of man. But, you ask, has God made any such response? Undoubtedly He has. Our Lord's teaching was emphatically definite. Witness His Sermon on the Mount, where He contrasts the Judaic glosses on the law with the true morality which He brought from heaven, not contenting Himself with general undefined assertion, but descending into particular cases, and putting each form of moral error into sharp contrast with its antagonistic truth. Again, consider the peculiar imperativeness and detailed character of His instructions to His Apostles. Again, how clear and startling are His enunciations of Sacramental truth to Nicodemus in the third chapter of St. John's Gospel, and to the Jews in the sixth. Again, the very explicitness of His revelations respecting His Eternal Person is acknowledged by unbelieving critics, and even erected into an argument against the genuineness of that Gospel in which these revelations are principally contained. Even our Lord's detached sayings (to adapt an illustration from the infidel Strauss) lie on the surface of the Gospel narrative like boulder fragments of granite, which have been rent asunder from the parent rock,—so firm are they, so eloquent are they of certainty, and of a clear undoubting vision of absolute truth. Only consider that scene in the synagogue of Nazareth. He has read the prophecy concerning Himself from the roll of the prophet Esaias; and "closed the book, and delivered it again to the minister, and has sat down." And He began to say, "This day is this scripture fulfilled in your ears." Here you have a sharply defined commentary upon the words of Scripture; and how was it received? "All bare Him witness, and wondered at the gracious words that proceeded out of His Mouth."[1] They, forsooth, had had enough of probable, doubtful glosses from generations of Rabbinical commentators; and their great prophet had told them that a King was coming to reign in righteousness, and that His Reign would be marked by a religious certainty which would console them for the ages of hesitation and, relatively, of ignorance, which had preceded it. "The eyes of them that see shall not be dim; the ears of them that hear shall hearken; the heart of the rash shall understand knowledge, and the tongue of the stammerers shall be ready to speak."[2] And why? "Thy teachers

[1] St. Luke iv. 16-22.   [2] Isa. xxxii. 3, 4.

shall not be removed into a corner any more, but thine eyes shall see thy teachers; and thine ears shall hear a word behind thee, saying, This is the way, walk ye in it, when ye turn to the right hand, and when ye turn to the left."[1] And therefore when our Lord came we are told that His word was with power (ἐν ἐξουσίᾳ[2]); it was because He responded to the deep yearnings of mankind while He fulfilled the anticipations of prophecy; it was because He "taught as one having authority, and not as the Scribes."[3] I do not forget that much has been put forward as certain, even in the Name of Christ, which is unquestionably false. This is only to admit that error can caricature the features of truth, just as vice can mimic the fruits of good-living. Nor do I forget that Revelation leaves as less than absolutely certain some truth which it appears to intimate; that there is a margin round the Central Verities of faith, in which there is a lawful place and home for mere opinion. Nor, again, does our Lord's practice of teaching as men were able to bear His disclosures of truth[4] (so touching an illustration this of His thoughtful tenderness), in any way militate against the fact that He required faith in what He taught at last, as being absolutely certain. "He that believeth in Him is not condemned; but he that believeth not is condemned already, because he hath not believed on the Name of the Only-begotten Son of God."[5] If this were so, it was not harshness or want of charity to point out the consequences of wilful error; rather was it the highest mercy to tell men what such consequences were.

In this same spirit the teaching of the early Church was always definite: her enemies have accused her of crystallising faith into dogmas when she was in reality defending positive truth against a disintegrating scepticism; she was

[1] Isa. xxx. 20, 21. [2] St. Luke iv. 32. [3] St. Matt. vii. 29.
[4] St. Mark iv. 33. [5] St. John iii. 18, 36; St. Mark xvi. 16.

true to the essential spirit of our Lord, and to the highest interests of His Gospel, when she maintained the symbol *Homoousion* against the versatile but unhappy Arius, or, as afterwards, the *Theotokos* against the miserable Nestorius. For what was this but to carry out those words of the great Apostle, "If we or an angel from heaven preach unto you any other Gospel than that which we have preached unto you, let him be accursed"?[1] What was this but to remember the spirit of our Lord's Prayer, "Sanctify them through thy *truth*,"[2] or of His declaration, "The *truth* shall make you free"?[3] Once, brethren, without that *truth*, and we have lost the great instrument as well as the justification of our work—the one great means of bringing men to Christ. He has surrounded us in His mercy with ample means of learning the truth, if we will but believe that there is a truth to be learnt. And it is not for us to speak of the eternal Gospel with the hesitating, criticising, suspicious accent that might befit a commentator on some cunningly devised fable[4] of Pagan lore. Let us not forget that the emissaries of error, ever watchful and active, stand by to make the most of our shortcomings. Certainly, if in the long run we would win souls, we must reflect our Master's tone of certainty and definiteness. Multitudes are weary of mere speculation; they have spent their lives in ever learning and never coming to the knowledge of the truth.[5] It is for us to point to our Divine Lord, as the Church proclaims Him, in His Person, His Natures, His Office, and His Work, "as an hiding-place from the wind, and a covert from the tempest; as rivers of water in a dry place, and as the shadow of a great rock in a weary land."[6]

4. Once more, the Gospel narrative introduces us not merely to the outward characteristics of Our Lord's

[1] Gal. i. 8, 9.   [2] St. John xvii. 17.   [3] *Ibid.* viii. 32.
[4] 2 St. Pet. i. 16.   [5] 2 Tim. iii. 7.   [6] Isa. xxxii. 2.

ministry, but to the more awful sanctuary of the Inner Life of His Human Soul. Every man lives two lives: an outward life which is visible to and felt by others, and an inner life which is open to the Eye of God. As the soul of the body, so the inner life is the animating, quickening principle of the outward life. The outward life may, for a time and under circumstances, be maintained in apparent independence of the life within. In a hypocrite it is as the soil which overlies the volcano, the treacherous cinder only separates you from the smouldering fire beneath. In a good man it is characterised by more or less of that reserve which is the true garb of conscientiousness. Virtue, we know, fears to be seen, lest the fresh hues of her beauty should be imperilled by exposure. The inner life is, however, a force which must make itself felt (especially in a clergyman) on the life without. It is a fountain, whose jet as it plays upon the surface of clerical effort, must freshen or pollute all around. "Out of the abundance of the heart the mouth speaketh."[1] Now the Gospel permits us to penetrate below the outward activities of speech and miracle, to observe, from time to time, as if by glimpses, the Inner Life of our Holy Lord. In Him we see that Life continuing under all outward circumstances, unchanged and unruffled. We catch glimpses of It in the several notices of His dispositions, His affections, His judgments, His regularity and system, as, *e.g.*, in the record of His calmness before His judges, and other like details of which we read in the Gospels. Already in considering our Lord's devotion to the glory of the Eternal Father, we have encountered a leading feature of His Inward Life, as well as a principle of His outward Ministry. But especially let us observe how this Life was sustained by prayer. Before the turning-points of

[1] St. Matt. xii. 34.

His ministry, such as the calling of the Apostles and the Passion, He engaged in special earnest prayer. In the press of His ministry, we read that "in the morning, rising up a great while before day, He went out and departed into a solitary place, and there prayed."[1] Again, before the calling of the Apostles "He went out into a mountain to pray, and continued all night in prayer to God."[2] Again, in His Agony, that He might teach us how to continue instant in prayer, He repeated the selfsame words three times with increasing earnestness.[3] How touchingly did He, when foreseeing the trials of His Apostle, remind St. Peter, "I have prayed for thee, that thy faith fail not."[4] Most of all, in the upper chamber He poured forth to His Father that most wonderful prayer which is recorded in St. John xvii., which reads as if it were a recorded fragment of His Intercession in heaven, although we know that it was uttered on earth. In that mighty Offering of our great High Priest, His ministers may discover the strength, the substance, the model of their own feeble but constant intercessions. If outward ministries are not to become heartless and formal, if the soul is to escape dryness and dearth, if we are to meet inevitable suffering and disappointment, we must be men of prayer; men, too, I would add, of meditation on our Lord's Life, whereby the past is rendered present to the soul, and thus rescued from the neglect which is apt to attach to a mere historical record, however sacred its origin. Thus, and by other means on which time does not permit me to dwell, may we feed the sources of the inner life. God knows that we need such sustenance. For our people have the Bible in their hands, and they recognise, even where they cannot describe, the true mien and outline of

---

[1] St. Mark i. 35.   [2] St. Luke vi. 12.
[3] St. Matt. xxvi. 44.   [4] St. Luke xxii. 32.

prophets and apostles. They are not satisfied by a claim to steer the bark of Peter, when the men who handle the Gospel nets are unlike Peter in their whole spirit and bearing. They are keenly alive to the power of holiness: and holiness is not a thing of impulse and eccentricity, it is the product of a regular, measured growth; there is an organic connection between its several stages, a regular graduated ascent, marked by successive conquests and expansions, which begin with the fontal Regeneration or some subsequent conversion, and lead up steadily to the opening heavens and to the place in glory. And of this growth the Life of our Lord's Human Soul is at once the model and the principle. "Let this Mind be in you which was also in Christ Jesus,"[1]—something of His humility, of His meekness, of His fortitude, of His keen-sighted prudence, of His perfect obedience, of His awful purity, of His separateness from earthly aims and motives,—for it is possible. It is possible, for He has promised again and again to aid us in growing up unto the measure of the stature of the fulness that is in Him. And to have the Mind of Christ is to bring to bear upon the complex, mysterious nature of man, a force which cannot but be owned and felt; it is to justify to men the supernatural ordinances and divine mission of the Church; above all, it is in the deepest sense to follow our Great Master, and, like Him, to become fishers of men.

You will have perceived, my brethren, that I have only drawn attention to a subject with which, in such narrow limits, it is impossible more fully to deal. But enough will have been said if, at this solemn hour, one soul resolves, by the grace of God, to make nothing less than the Life of Christ the rule and pattern of ministerial attainment. "I have given you," He says, "an Example,

[1] Phil. ii. 5.

that ye should do as I have done unto you."[1] Men talk of low and high standards, just as if there existed allowable varieties, and as if each variety might equally be right. In Scripture now, and at the bar of God hereafter, it will be seen that there is no standard but ONE. Each minister of God on whom we fix our gaze, from Xavier and Henry Martyn upwards to St. Athanasius and St. Paul, will bid us with the latter look onward and higher for the real measure of apostolic perfection: "Be ye imitators ($\mu\iota\mu\eta\tau\alpha\acute{\iota}$) of me, even as I also am of Christ."[2] But He Who stands above them all receives as of right the homage of an imitation which can mount no higher, nor find a more absolutely perfect model. "Thou Only art holy; Thou Only art the Lord; Thou Only, O Christ, with the Holy Ghost, art Most High in the Glory of God the Father." To each of us, dear brethren, there comes this day a voice out of the more excellent glory, as of old the first command was repeated as a parting admonition to St. Peter on the shore of the lake of Galilee, 'Follow thou Me;[3]—My devotion to the glory of Him Who sent Me; My tenderness for all and each of the sons of men with whom I dealt; My doctrine, so clear and precise in its final enunciation, yet so adapted in its delivery to the weak capacities of those who heard it; My inward Life of prayer and self-dedication, and obedience to the leading of the Eternal Spirit,—as these were the power and instruments of My first Apostles, so may they, if ye will, be yours.' May the Holy overshadowing Spirit enable each to hear and obey that gracious whispering during the solemn hours on which we are entering; may we penetrate by faith beyond the outward veil which meets the eye of the body in this Cathedral, and with the deepest inner reverence of our prostrate spirits, may we behold Christ

[1] St. John xiii. 15.   [2] 1 Cor. xi. 1.   [3] St. John xxi. 22.

Jesus, our Living and Present Lord, moving among us with Hand and Eye, to discern and bless; even as the Apostle beheld in vision at Patmos, in the midst of the seven candlesticks, "One like unto the Son of Man, clothed with a garment down to the Foot . . . . and with a Countenance as the sun shining in his strength."[1] At this awful crisis of our destinies, may He support and brighten us by resting our minds on Himself, the true Model as well as the Hope of our ministerial calling, the abiding Riches of the glory of our future inheritance among the saints.[2]

[1] Rev. i. 13, 16.   [2] Eph. i. 18.

SERMON IV.

THE WHOLE COUNSEL OF GOD.[1]

ACTS xx. 27.

I have not shunned to declare unto you the whole counsel of God.

HERE is one of those passages in the New Testament, which make a forcible and direct appeal to the heart and conscience of every man who has undertaken or is undertaking to serve God in Holy Orders. The words occur in that parting charge to the Presbyters of the Church of Ephesus, which on the eve of his going up to Jerusalem, at the close of what is termed his third Missionary journey, the great Apostle delivered on the strand at Miletus. They are such words as escape men at the turning-points of life, at entering upon or taking leave of great responsibilities—compressed, fervid utterances of the deepest thought and of the strongest currents of feeling—of thought and feeling which for the moment will not be pent up and restrained within the barriers of ordinary habit, or of studied reserve. Even a saint may, nay, at certain times, he must speak of himself: and so the great Apostle glances hastily at the labours and sufferings which had marked his sojourn at Ephesus.[1] Then he points anxiously to the lowering future: he tells his hearers the precise limits of his supernatural knowledge. The exact form of each of the many trials before him he did not know; but he knew generally, that in

[1] Preached at the Ordination of the Bishop of Salisbury, in the Abbey Church of St. Mary, Sherborne, on the Second Sunday in Lent, February 21, 1864.   [2] Vers. 18-21.

every city bonds and afflictions awaited him, and in particular, that he and they to whom he spake would meet again in this world no more.[1] Under the pressing urgency of this conviction, he predicts the coming sorrows of the Church of Ephesus—the Church indeed of St. Timothy and of St. John, but also the Church of men who denied the central truth of the Resurrection;[2] the Church of Hymenæus, and Philetus and Alexander; the Church of the Nicolaitans, whose morals were hateful (we are told in the Apocalypse) to the Lord Jesus;[3] the Church, as it might seem from St. John's first Epistle, of some of the earliest heretics, who denied the real Union of Godhead and Manhood in our Lord and Saviour.[4] Indeed, only a few years later, we see in the two Epistles to Timothy the clear traces of an organised opposition to Christian truth at Ephesus, so formidable in its various intellectual activities, that the stern energy of the Apostle's language in the speech before us is only understood when read by the light of a struggle, unlike to, and in some respects more serious than, any other within the limits of the Apostolical Age.

Casting his eye over this troubled future, St. Paul utters a prophecy of mournful solemnity. "I know this, that after my departing shall grievous wolves enter in among you, not sparing the flock. Also of your own selves shall men arise, speaking perverse things to draw away disciples after them."[5] He exhorts them to watch: he commends them tenderly to God: but he also recalls to them the full measure of their personal responsibility. His ministry had put them in entire possession of the truth as it had come from heaven: and, if they fell into the snares which lay thick around their future path, they could not, when facing the knowledge and the justice of

---

[1] Vers. 22, 25.   [2] 1 Tim. i. 20; 2 Tim. ii. 17, 18.
[3] Rev. ii. 6.   [4] 1 St. John iv. 2, 3.   [5] Acts xx. 29, 30.

God, attempt to shelter themselves under the plea of ignorance. "I take you to record this day, that I am pure from the blood of all men. For I have not shunned to declare unto you, all the counsel of God."[1]

The whole counsel of God! Such is the Apostle's expression for that fixed body of Truth, which we of this day name more commonly the Gospel, the Revelation of Christ, the Faith of Christians. St. Paul says, that he had declared the whole mind—that is, the whole revealed mind—of God. Observe, of God. His language excludes that conception of religious truth which makes it merely the product of the truest, purest, deepest thoughts of the highest and largest minds among the sons of men. "Flesh and blood" had not revealed to St. Peter the dignity and the claims of Jesus.[2] "Flesh and blood" added nothing to that Revelation of His Son which the Eternal Father had made to the soul of St. Paul.[3] Resting on a Divine Authority, and being human only so far as was necessary if it was to close with the intellect and the heart of man,—human in its condescensions and human in its sympathy, but in its truth and essence Divine—the Gospel was for St. Paul unlike any other object-matter that entered into his thought. It was sundered by a broad line of demarcation from all else that seemed like it on this side or on that; it did not shade off into any either of the higher philosophies or of the less sensual idolatries of the time. So absolutely and exclusively true did he deem this Gospel-truth to be, that could an Angel from heaven have been conceived as preaching any other, the Apostle would unhesitatingly have held him "accursed."[4]

The whole counsel of God! It was God's word, not man's; it was neither the result of a thoughtful speculation, nor yet an approximate guess, nor yet a cunningly devised fable. Being God's word, it was as a *whole* worthy

---

[1] Acts xx. 26, 27.   [2] St. Matt. xvi. 17.   [3] Gal. i. 16.   [4] *Ibid.* i. 8.

of the best thought and love that His creature could give it. That ministry of three months in the great Ephesian synagogue,[1] and then the two years which followed of laborious teaching in the School of the Rhetorician Tyrannus,[2] and last, but not least, the wide publicity, the general attention,[3] and the active hatred of heathen foes which culminated in the Riot of the Amphitheatre,[4] had enabled the Apostle to put forward the Gospel, the whole area of its Doctrine, the many sides on which it attracted, and awed, and subdued the soul of man—in unabridged unmutilated completeness. " All they which dwelt in Asia (*i.e.* Asia Minor) heard the word of the Lord Jesus, both Jews and Greeks."

This solemn and momentous day may be the very crisis of their destiny to those of us who are waiting to receive a Commission from heaven at the Altar of this noble Minster. And the words of the Apostle may serve us well, as a guide to our thoughts, our aspirations, our resolves. These time-honoured walls cannot but recall to a stranger some of the most cherished memories of the Anglo-Saxon Church;[5] while in their renewed beauty they speak not less persuasively of the renovated life of the modern Church of England. Can we forget to-day that wellnigh eight centuries have passed since here at Sherborne the Commission of Christ was handed on by a predecessor of our Chief Pastor to those who in the early ages of our national history sought to serve God within the precincts of the Sanctuary? How vast, we feel, is the life of a Church, when contrasted with the fleeting existence of her members: yet how insignificant, when we place it side by side with the Being of her Everlasting Lord! His Person, His Word, the Laws of His Kingdom

---

[1] Acts xix. 8.   [2] *Ibid.* xix. 9, 10.
[3] Acts xix. 10, 17, 20.   [4] *Ibid.* xix. 23-41.
[5] Cf. *Handbook to the Abbey Church of St. Mary, Sherborne*, by the Rev. E. Harston, pp. 32-38.

and of His Service, the results of His doctrine upon the soul of man, are at this hour what they were at the first, what they will be to the end of time. And if instead of losing ourselves in vague reflection, we would give a practical turn to our (it may be) somewhat eager tide of thought and feeling, let us fix our attention on this primal, this simple duty of an ordained man—the declaration of the whole counsel of God. When St. Paul asserts that he has not "shunned" to declare it, the English word, and yet more strongly[1] the original for which it stands, must remind us that there are many motives and hindrances calculated to keep a man back from doing that which must be done, if he fears his God, if he cares for his own soul, if he has any true love for the souls of those to whom of his own free will he undertakes to minister.

I.

Now one cause of failure in this primary duty would seem to lie in a lack of religious knowledge. It is much more easy to be deficient in essential knowledge of religious truth than we are apt to assume. I do not contemplate the extreme case of ignorance, whether this or that doctrine does or does not lie within the limits of Revealed Truth. For it would be simply immoral in a Christian Teacher not to have learnt the frontier and outline of that sacred deposit of the Faith which our Lord and Saviour has committed to His Church to hold fast and to hand on to the end of time. But far short of this extreme shortcoming, may we not too easily acquiesce in an ignorance which is scarcely less fatal to souls? May we not lapse into a habit of thinking and speaking of the doctrines of the Gospel, as if they were like soldiers in a

---

[1] ὑπεστειλάμην, cf. Meyer *in loc.* Dr. Wordsworth sees in it a nautical metaphor, which might have been suggested by the scene before the speaker.

regiment,—so many units, each adding something no doubt to the collective bulk and area of doctrine, while yet in no way essential to its organic completeness, and therefore each capable of being withdrawn, without inflicting any more serious injury upon the entire truth than that of diminished size? Do we not hear persons talk of the articles of the Creed in this way,—as if each article was a perfectly separate and new truth,—as if each was, I might almost say, a new and gratuitous infliction upon the reluctant intellect of man,—as if each was round and perfect in itself, and had no relations whatever to any truth beyond it?

Yet what does such language really prove but defective knowledge in those (be they who they may) who use it? They "know" the doctrines of the faith only as so many separate propositions. Of the Great Whole, which lies beyond the words,—the several sides of which the words do at best but imperfectly represent,—of the Body and Substance of the Faith, they know little or nothing. They fail to perceive the connexion, the interdependence, the organic unity of all truth that rests on the authority of God. Their view is too superficial to enable them to do justice to that marvellous adjustment of truth to truth, of faculty to object, of result to cause, which is a direct and obvious perception to souls who gaze prayerfully and steadily at the complete Revelation of Christ. These really shortsighted persons do not miss a revealed doctrine which is withdrawn; nor are they offended when a human speculation is elevated to co-ordinate rank with the certainties of Faith. It seems to them to be merely a question between more or less belief; between a larger or a smaller creed; between, as they would speak, a greater or a less number of dogmas. But in reality each truth touches, implies, has relations to, truths right and left of it; and these relations are so intimate and so vital, that no truth can be withdrawn, and leave conterminous truths intact. The Faith is, if I may say so with reverence, so marvellously compacted, so instinct with a pervading life, as to resemble a natural organism, I had almost said a living creature. Just as St. James says of the moral law, that he who offends in one point is guilty of all,[1] because of the unity of the impaired principle; and as St. Paul teaches, that in the body of the Church, if one limb or member suffer, all the members suffer with it,[2] in virtue of an internal and necessary sympathy; so in the Creed, no one truth can be misrepresented, strained, dislocated, much less withdrawn, without a certain, and frequently an ascertainable injury resulting to other truths which are supposed to be still unquestioned and intact. For there are nerves and arteries which link the very extremities of Revealed Doctrine to its brain and heart; and the wound which a strain or an amputation may inflict, must in its effects extend far beyond the particular doctrine which is the immediate seat and scene of the injury.

This power of perceiving and exhibiting the deeper internal relations and grounds of Christian Doctrine might seem to correspond to that "word of knowledge" (λόγος γνώσεως) which in his catalogue of the gifts of the Spirit St. Paul distinguishes from the "word of wisdom" (λόγος σοφίας)—the faculty of stating the truths and mysteries of the faith in clear and precise language.[3] It is to be won partly by the culture and exercise of the sanctified intellect in study, partly, nay rather specially, by prayer

[1] St. James ii. 10. [2] 1 Cor. xii. 26, 27.
[3] σοφία nämlich ist die höhere christliche Weisheit (1 Cor. ii. 6) an und für sich, so dass Rede, welche die Lehrstücke (Mysterien) derselben ausspricht, klar macht, anwendet, u. s. w., λόγος σοφίας ist. Damit ist aber die tiefdringende Erkenntniss dieser Lehrstücke, die speculative Erfassung und Einsicht und Verarbeitung ihres Zusammenhangs, ihrer Gründe, ihrer tiefern Ideen, ihrer Beweise, ihrer Ziele, u. s. w. noch nicht gesetzt; eine Rede aber, welche sicht damit beschäftigt, ist λόγος γνώσεως. Meyer in 1 Cor. xii. 8.

for illumination and a habit of meditation on Scripture and the Creeds. There are eminent exercises of this gift within the limits of inspiration. St. Paul's demonstration of the fatal antagonism of the practice of circumcision to true belief in our Lord's redemptive work, in the Epistle to the Galatians, will naturally occur to us. Of uninspired instances I may refer to that masterly and well-known account of the connection between the doctrine of the Sacraments and the doctrine of the Incarnation, which the English Church owes to the mind, and which she studies in the language of the great Hooker.

When a man possesses this gift of knowledge—of "knowledge" in the technical sense of St. Paul—he will teach the whole truth not by an effort or mechanically, but in virtue of an instinct. He will be carried forward, from principle to application, from centre to circumference, from the heart and brain of doctrine to its utmost extremities ; because he sees, he cannot but see, its evident, its organic unity ; because to mutilate it would be to him scarcely anything short of a moral and intellectual agony. A living faith, informed by study, and quickened and stimulated by prayer, can hardly be guilty of accidental, never of culpable reticence ; it cannot but "declare the whole counsel of God."

II.

A second hindrance is lack of courage. To speak for God to man,—for the Just and Holy God to man, sinful and wilful in his sin—requires nerve and courage. To represent God as He is—as Just no less than Merciful, as punishing sin no less certainly than rewarding faith and holiness—this, to be done well and honestly, requires courage. Moses before Pharaoh, Samuel before Saul, Micaiah before Ahab, Jeremiah before the Princes of Judah, St. John the Baptist before Herod Antipas, St.

Stephen before the Sanhedrim, St. Paul before Felix and Agrippa, and (in a sense altogether peculiar and unrivalled) our Divine Lord before the Jewish Priest and the Roman Magistrate—these represent the attitude and the fortunes of truth at the bar of human nature. Human nature indeed is wretched, and it craves for comfort—that, my clerical brethren, that is our opportunity;[1] but it is also proud, and it resents humiliations—ay, and it is strong, and likely, in its own fashion and way, to express its roused resentment. Of old they understood this well, who went forth uplifting the cross, while yet baring their breasts to death. They knew that the patient to whom they were carrying the medicine that would cure him would often refuse the draught, and would punish the physician who dared to offer it. But they loved man, and they loved and feared their God too sincerely and too well, to infuse new ingredients, or to withdraw any of the bitter but needful elements of cure. They accepted civil and social proscription; they endured moral and physical agony; they embraced, one after another, with cheerful hearts, the very warrants and instruments of their death,—because they had counted the cost, and had measured too well the greatness of their task, and the glories of their anticipated eternity, to shrink sensitively back at the first symptoms of opposition, or of difficulty. St. Paul might have foreseen the conduct of Demetrius, and the tumult in the amphitheatre; but this was no serious reason for considering the worship of Diana as a sort of modified or imperfect revelation, or as anything short of a hateful lie.[2] He did not shrink from declaring the whole counsel of God.

---

[1] 2 Cor. i. 4.
[2] St. Paul's speech at Athens recognises that element of natural Religion which is at the bottom of all superstitions, however debased. What the Apostle really thought of the Paganism of the Ancient World as a whole is best understood from such passages as Rom. i. 23-32.

If I yet feared men, says the Apostle, I should not be the servant of Christ.[1] The man who is not in very deed emancipated from bondage to any human fear cannot do justice either to the needs of his fellow-men or the Rights of God. He cannot be loyal to Truth. There are petty oppositions, petty persecutions, indirect yet powerful influences, which will stay a man's hand, and silence his tongue, even in this age and land of civil freedom; unless his conscience be quick and his will strong, through a constant sight of One Who is the Lord and the Subject of that Truth which He proclaims. He will abridge, soften down, mutilate his message, unless he have penetrated the certainty that the fear of man bringeth a snare[2]—to all indeed who would serve God in sincerity of purpose,—to none, with such fatal and destructive results, as to the man who undertakes to serve Him in the Christian Priesthood.

III.

The want of spirituality of heart and soul is a third cause of defective representation of doctrine. To speak for God to the souls of men, a man must himself, in his inmost soul, have consciously stood face to face with that truth of which he speaks.[3] He must speak *of God* as one who has known at once His dread awfulness and His tender love; *of sin*, as that which he feels to be the one master-evil, and with which as such he has struggled in good truth within his secret self; *of Christ*, His Person, His propitiatory and atoning Death, His life-giving Sacraments, as of the Person and Acts of a dear Friend, loved with the heart's warmest and best affection, while yet adored with the deepest homage and by the chiefest powers of his prostrate spirit; *of Eternity* as of that for

---

[1] Gal. i. 10.   [2] Prov. xxix. 25.
[3] 1 St. John i. 1-3.

which he is himself making daily solemn preparation; *of prayer, and the care of conscience* and the culture of purity and truth within, as of things of which he knows something by trial and exercise, perhaps even something more by failure. Himself a redeemed sinner speaking to sinners who need or who have found their Redeemer, he will speak in earnest. The issues of endless life or endless death may hang upon his words; but his strength must lie in the profound conviction that he is but the instrument and organ of One Whose livery he wears before the eyes of men, and without Whom he can do nothing. Christian Preaching may be defined either as Speaking for God, or as Speaking to souls; but whichever definition a man keeps most prominently before him, he must aim in the pulpit at making a spiritual as distinct from a merely literary effort. Above him is the Father of Spirits, dwelling in light which no man can approach unto. Before him is the human soul, strong, subtle, intricate, with untold capabilities for good and evil, for joy and agony. Surely he cannot but keep close to those great truths which warm the heart and nerve the will, and raise the whole spiritual being from sin to holiness, from death to life, from the miseries and degradations of mere nature to the sanctities and magnificence of grace. But if the preacher should himself stand outside the spiritual life; if prayer, communion with God, discipline of the will, culture of the affections,—if these things should seem to him but an extravagance or a fanaticism, and if the Faith of the Church be only lodged in his understanding, as an important fact in the history of opinion, or as the bare result of an arithmetical calculation; then it is not difficult to see how he will presently fail, as a matter of course, to declare the whole counsel of God. His thought will drift naturally away from the central and most solemn truths to the literary embellishments which surround the faith;

he will toy with questions of geography, or history, or custom, or scene, or dress; he will reproduce with vivid power the personages and events of long-past ages, it may be with the talent of a master-artist; he will give to the human side of Religion the best of his time and of his toil. In doing this he may, after the world's measure, be doing good work; but let us not deceive ourselves—he will not be saving souls. Souls are saved by men who themselves count all things but dung that they may win Christ, and be found in Him;[1] and who, even if they be men of refined taste and of cultivated intellect, know well how to subordinate the embellishments of Truth to its vital and soul-subduing certainties. Especially if a man should take refuge in the literary aspects of Scripture, because he is not sufficiently assured of its leading truths to reproduce them with the accent—the accent which the people understand so perfectly—of simple unfaltering conviction; then the contrast between his graceful but relatively useless disquisitions, and the glorious Creed of the Church of God—which in its integrity alone responds to the profound yearnings of the soul—will be painful in proportion to the opportunities which he has missed, and to the powers which he has abused.

IV.

Once more: here, as in the whole field of ministerial labour, let a man work and pray for the grace of an unselfish spirit. Let him endeavour to strangle the love of self by the love of God and the love of man. For without charity, though a man should speak with the tongues of men or of angels, he will do nought for the real good of his hearers, or for the glory of his Lord. Selfishness will spoil everything. How often are not we, the Representa-

[1] Phil. iii. 8.

tives of Christ, constrained to rebuke ourselves, humble ourselves, condemn ourselves, by the words which we speak from the Chair of Truth! Some there have been who have yielded to the fatal temptation of being, what they call, consistent. They tone down God's message to the miserable level of their own felt shortcomings. They make of the Gospel a Gospel of acquiescence in sin, rather than a Gospel of redemption from it; they profess to see in it a patronage of the flesh, and a recognition of the world, I had almost said, a co-partnership with the Evil One. Alas! who can doubt, that unless a man can speak, in simple sincerity, as for Christ and from Christ,—careless though his words should only reach his people at the manifest expense, nay, through the deep humiliation, the self-inflicted, self-adjudged penance of their Minister,—it must needs go hard with him hereafter in the day of account. Better it surely were never to speak at all, than to make the Lord of Purity and Light a seeming accomplice in the crime and darkness of His creature! Far better were silence than the advocacy of an impoverished —a mutilated—a false Gospel—a Gospel robbed of all that is mysterious, awful, supernatural, divine; because, forsooth, to preach the perfect Truth which came from heaven is unbecoming for one who lives, and who feels that he lives, as if it were not true! Even the double-hearted prophet, who knew that he had much to win by falsehood, could not but tell the Pagan king, who would fain have subsidised his inspirations, "Whatsoever the Lord telleth me, that will I speak."[1] And can we, beneath the Cross of Christ, so pander to self, as to "handle the word of God deceitfully"? Dare we say less than what we know to be Truth, because we know also that Truth in its fulness would be our condemnation?

Or take another illustration of the need of an un-

[1] Numb. xxii. 38; xxiii. 12, 26; xxiv. 13.

selfish spirit. It is possible, nay probable, that we may have what are called favourite doctrines, sections or sides of Truth through which God has in a special sense spoken to us, moved us, sanctified us, (as we trust) saved us. Of these, no doubt, we can speak with more power, because with more intimate perception of their bearing on the secret springs of life and death. But we also speak of such points with less of moral and intellectual effort than of others; and this greater facility is likely to be the real cause of our giving them an undue prominence in our cycle of teaching, while we endeavour to whisper to our consciences, and to persuade our friends, that these points are the essentials of the Gospel, and that all the rest is comparatively unnecessary. Thus men teach the Atonement, and ignore the Sacraments; or they teach the need of faith, and ignore the need of love and holiness; or they teach the beauty of our Lord's character, and forget His Propitiatory and Sacrificial Death; or, conversely, they insist upon the outward duties of religion, and do scant justice to the spiritual and internal forces of the soul. We must teach *all* that God has revealed, because He has revealed it, leaving it to Him to touch one soul by this, and another soul by that portion of His Revelation. Even within the limits of inspiration, St. Paul preached faith, and St. John love, and St. James practical energy, each giving prominence (but nothing more) to these several sides of the Christian life, while yet each preached it as a whole. No man of modesty and thoughtfulness would make the narrow circle of experiences that have passed within his own soul the absolute standard of the truths and powers which may act on others: and no duty is more difficult or more serious than that of detaching ourselves from the influence of "favourite doctrines," and, as far as may be, teaching the whole truth in its integrity to all to whom we owe it, as the gift of God. And the Proper Lessons and Epistles and Gospels of the Church Service enable us to correct our natural tendency towards a choice of texts and subjects which fall within our own more contracted area of thought and feeling: so that in making it a rule always to preach from the Services of the Day, or at least on a subject suggested by the season, we make provision against one of the chief temptations to teach something less than the whole counsel of God. Nothing, however, but a spirit of genuine self-sacrifice, nothing but a true love of the souls of men, can enable a man so to forego his own predilections, so to throw himself into the state of mind, and points of view, and peculiar difficulties, and narrower or broader horizons of his hearers, as to lose himself, and the little history of his own spirit, in the mighty work of proclaiming in its perfectness the Truth of God. We know how the great Apostle combined this perfect consideration for others, with an unflinching, chivalrous loyalty to the claims of Truth. "Though I be free from all men, yet have I made myself servant unto all, that I might gain the more. And unto the Jews I became as a Jew, that I might gain the Jews; to them that are under the Law as under the Law, that I might gain them that are under the Law; to them that are without law, as without law (being not without law to God, but under the Law to Christ), that I might gain them that are without law; to the weak became I as weak, that I might gain the weak; I am made all things to all men, that I might by all means save some."[1] How could self-sacrifice be more unsparing? By whom could the duty of declaring the whole counsel of God be more forcibly proclaimed, than by a man who gave up all else to enable him to discharge it?

[1] 1 Cor. ix. 19-22.

Under ordinary circumstances, my brethren, it might be natural at this point to leave the principles which have been insisted on to your mature reflections, and to the obvious force of their intrinsic truth. The duty before us is sufficiently plain; and the risk of wearying you might well lead me to pause, if it were indeed possible to do so. But I yet owe something to the promptings of conscience, and to the Rights of God. Nor would your judgment be harsh or unreasonable, if you should interpret my silence as to a matter of pressing and public anxiety, as something less easily to be pardoned than mere failure to satisfy the many claims of this great occasion. Such silence would in fact be nothing short of notorious treachery to the whole spirit and drift of those kindling words, which it has been my endeavour to recommend and illustrate.

At no age of the Church could the ambassadors of Christ have afforded to forget the Apostle's example of "not shunning to declare all the counsel of God." But never was the force of that example more needed than in our own day. Illustrations indeed press so urgently upon the mind, as it ranges over the recent history of the Church, that the preacher's embarrassment lies in the very liberty of his choice: but one illustration, I doubt not, will have occurred to many of us living at this time, and living, my Lord Bishop, under your Lordship's jurisdiction, in this your diocese of Salisbury, with painful but irrepressible prominence. My brethren, it would be an affectation, if I should profess to suppose you ignorant of a recent Judgment,[1] proceeding not indeed from a spiritual but from a temporal Court; which, although it professes, and that eagerly,[2] to avoid all attempts at formal deter-

---

[1] The reference is to the then recent Judgment in the case of Fendall *versus* Wilson.

[2] "With respect to the legal tests of doctrine in the Church of England, by the application of which we are to try the soundness or unsoundness of the

mination of doctrine, yet does unquestionably determine the *legal* sense and value of doctrinal formularies, and, as doing this, has and must have, practically and morally, no little weight with large classes of our countrymen. That Judgment would seem, among other points, to have ruled, that it is permissible in law for a clergyman to express a "hope" for the final restoration of the lost. No man can know anything of his own sinful heart who does not know how much there is within him which is ready to welcome such a permission; but the question is a question not of the inclinations of a sinful creature, but of the Revealed Will of a Holy God. May we, consistently with that Will, indulge that "hope"? Assuredly not. For nothing is more certain than that by the terms of the Christian revelation any such hope is delusive and vain, since it is opposed to the awful Truth, that they who die out of favour with God and are lost, are lost irrevocably, lost for ever. If Holy Scripture is still to be our Rule of Faith, Scripture, I submit, is decisive. If Hooker's well-known caution as to the interpretation of Scripture, "that where a literal interpretation will stand, the farthest from the letter is commonly the worst" is still to be kept in mind, that rule will preclude any serious doubt as to the real mind of Scripture in this solemn matter. Scripture is no less explicit as to the endlessness of the woe of the lost soul than as to the endlessness of the scene or instrument of its punishment. Isaiah speaks of the "everlasting burnings,"[1] Daniel of "everlasting contempt,"[2] our

passages libelled, we agree with the learned Judge in the Court below that the Judgment in the Gorham case is conclusive:—This Court has no jurisdiction or authority to settle matters of faith, or to determine what ought in any particular to be the Doctrine of the Church of England. Its duty extends only to the consideration of that which is by law established to be the Doctrine of the Church of England, upon the true and legal construction of her articles and formularies."—Judgment (*Guardian*, Feb. 10, 1864).

[1] מוֹקְדֵי עוֹלָם Isa. xxxiii. 14.   [2] דִּרְאוֹן עוֹלָם Dan. xii. 2.

Lord of "the everlasting fire" once and again,[1] St. Paul of "everlasting destruction" or ruin,[2] St. Jude of "a blackness of darkness which is reserved for ever."[3] Three times speaking of the penal woe of the lost, the Apostle of Love uses an expression of energetic redundancy and force: he says that it lasts "unto ages of ages."[4] Just as the elect will reign in heaven for ever and ever,[5] as holy souls desire that God may be glorified for ever and ever,[6] as Jesus Risen from His grave is alive "for evermore,"[7] as in His glory He shall reign for ever and ever,[8] as the very Life of God Himself is described by saying that "He liveth for ever and ever,"[9] so is this same measure applied to the punishment of the lost souls.[10] Are we to say that a period of limited duration is all that is meant to be ascribed in Scripture to the glory of the blessed in heaven, to the Glorified Life and Reign of Jesus, to the very self-existent Life of God Himself, in order to enable ourselves to rest in the conception of a Purgatory beyond the Final Judgment, as less shocking to our "consciousness" than the Belief in Hell? And if not, can we certainly determine that as applied to Hell this phrase has an altogether narrower sense than that which we ascribe to it in such passages as apply it to Heaven or to the Reign of Christ? Modern scepticism has tampered with the word "Eternal," just as it has emptied "Salvation," "Atonement," "Grace," —nay the very Name of God Himself—of their natural meaning. But "everlasting" means neither more nor less than that which lasts for ever. True indeed it is that the

[1] τὸ πῦρ τὸ αἰώνιον, St. Matt. xviii. 8, xxv. 41.
[2] ὄλεθρον αἰώνιον, 2 Thess. i. 9.
[3] Οἷς ὁ ζόφος τοῦ σκότους εἰς τὸν αἰῶνα τετήρηται, Jude 13.
[4] The smoke of their torment ascendeth up for ever and ever, εἰς αἰῶνας αἰώνων, Rev. xiv. 11; εἰς τοὺς αἰῶνας τῶν αἰώνων, Rev. xix. 3, and Rev. xx. 10. The language of Isaiah from which this is taken would certainly seem to refer to a more than temporal judgment on Edom and other nations. Isa. xxxiv. 9, 10.   [5] Rev. xxii. 5.   [6] 1 Tim. i. 17; Heb. xiii. 21, etc.
[7] Rev. i. 18.   [8] Ibid. xi. 15.   [9] Ibid. iv. 9, 10, v. 14, x. 6.   [10] Ubi sup.

The Whole Counsel of God. 137

Hebrew expression which, when applied to future time, answers to the English "for ever," does in particular instances mean something less than boundless duration. But this is the case only where a limitation is forced upon the word by the subject to which it is applied. Originally the word does imply indefinite,—the nearest approach, perhaps, which the human mind can make to infinite,— extent of continuance. Taken at its lowest range of meaning, it means an existence co-extensive with that to which it is applied.[1] In the New Testament, there is a substantive which varies with the various meanings of this Hebrew word;[2] but there is also an adjective derived from that substantive, which at least, as used in the New Testament, does not so vary,[3] but means what we English

---

[1] עוֹלָם, properly that which is *hidden*; as applied to future time, that which is lost to sight in the distance. Instances of the narrow range of the word may be found in Gen. ix. 12; Ex. xii. 14-17, xxvii. 21, xxviii. 43; Lev. x. 15, etc. Not however in such passages as Ps. xlv. 7, lxxii. 5, 17, lxxxix. 37, where Rationalists limit the word in deference to their own prejudices against the Messianic predictions. Nor again in salutations, 1 Kings i. 31; Neh. ii. 3; Dan. ii. 4, etc., since in these cases the true force of the expression is to be measured by the belief of the Jews in the immortality of the soul. Of what range of meaning the word is really capable will be best understood from a consideration of the following extract from Gesenius: "vera æternitatis notio in vocabulo nostro iis in locis inest, qui immortalem summi Numinis naturam spectant, quod, vocatur אֵל עוֹלָם Deus æternus, Gen. xxi. 33; Jer. xl. 28. חַי הָעוֹלָם in æternum vivens Dan. xii. 7 (cf. חָיָה לְעוֹלָם vivere in æternum, immortalem esse instar deorum [Dei] Gen. iii. 22; Job vii. 16), Cui tribuuntur זְרֹעוֹת עוֹלָם brachia æterna Deut. xxxiii. 27, et de Quo dicitur מֵעוֹלָם וְעַד עוֹלָם אַתָּה אֵל Ps. xc. 2, ab æternitate ad æternitatem, Tu es Deus. Ps. ciii. 17, cf. Ps. ix. 8, x. 16, xxix. 10, xciii. 2."— *Thesaurus* sub voc. עלם.

[2] αἰών. Although, as Bretschneider remarks, "partim Græcorum more usurpatur." Like עוֹלָם its original meaning was that of unlimited duration, and the narrower senses were imposed upon it subsequently. "Aristoteles alicubi scripsit αἰών dici quasi αἰὲν ὤν."—Vorstius, *Hebraism. N. T.* ii. 39.

[3] That in the LXX. αἰώνιος like αἰών, when applied to future time, varies in its meanings with the senses of עוֹלָם is clear from the passages given in Trommius, *s. v.* But, when the Gospel had "brought life and immortality

mean by "everlasting." And it is this last-named word which is used in the passages principally under discussion. If it should be precariously contended that this word implies positive endlessness of continuance, as little as it admits of any defined limitation of continuance, it may at least be observed, that as used in Scripture of the penal misery of the lost, the expression "eternal" is fixed in the sense of endless duration by two considerations. Where that word is applied to our home in Heaven, the hopes and longings of men gladly do justice to the natural force of human language. But it is noteworthy,[1]

to light" more distinctly, the use of the word αἰώνιος was limited (within the precincts of the New Testament) to the idea (taken at the lowest) of indefinite continuance. It is used seventy-one times in the N. T. It is an attribute of ζωή forty-four times. St. John never uses it in any other connection; and it occurs twenty-three times in his writings. In two cases only is it possible to argue fairly that the word *may* have a limited meaning. (1) Philemon 15, αἰώνιον αὐτὸν ἀπέχῃς, where however Bretschneider (Lex. Man. *in voc.*) construes the word "illum in sempiternum, scilicet, quia Christianus factus jam vitæ æternæ particeps erat." So (to omit others) Huther *in loc.* "Die christliche brüderliche Verbindung in die Ewigkeit reiche." (2) St. Jude 7, πυρὸς αἰωνίου δίκην, where Pol. Synops. *in loc.* observes that the natural construction of the whole passage is that "Eas urbes incensas instar exhibere ignis æterni, qui impios expectat." The remarks of Huther apply to our E. V.: πυρὸς αἰωνίου construiren De Wette, Arnaud mit den folgenden δίκην ὑπέχουσαι, weil dieses sonst zu entblösst stände: allein das Feuer, womit sie bestraft sind, konnte von Judas nicht wohl *das ewige Feuer* genannt werden; dies ist stehende Bezeichnung des Höllenfeuers, dem die im letzen Gerichte Verurtheilten überliefert werden; darum ist es besser πυρ. αἰων. mit δεῖγμα zu verbinden; jene Städte sind δίκην ὑπέχουσαι ein Exempel des Ewigen Feuers.—*Brief des Judas*, p. 217.

[1] αἰώνιον in N. T. dicitur omne quod est finis expers, maxime id, quod est post hujus vitæ mundique decursum eventurum. Huc pertinent omnia illa N. T. loca, in quibus formulæ: πῦρ αἰώνιον, κρίσις αἰώνιος, κρίμα αἰώνιον, κόλασις αἰώνιος, ζωή (δόξα, σωτηρία) αἰώνιος reperiuntur, v. c. Matt. xviii. 8, xix. 16, xxv. 41, 46. Marc. iii. 29. Rom. ii. 7. 2 Tim. ii. 10. Heb. v. 9. Quemadmodum enim formulis πῦρ αἰώνιον et sqq. pœnæ perpetuæ peccatorum, quas impii post hanc vitam luent, *sorsque eorum misera futura non interrupta* indicantur, ita opposita formula: ζωή αἰώνιος perennis felicitatis piorum post mortem status et conditio significatur, quæ 2 Cor. iv. 17. αἰώνιον βάρος δόξης, Luc. xvi. 9. σχηναὶ αἰώνιοι, Heb. ix. 15. αἰώνιος κληρονομία, et 2 Pet. i. 11. αἰώνιος βασιλεία τοῦ Θεοῦ appellatur. Schleusner, *Lexicon*, p. 67. So too Bretschneider (Lex. Man. *in v.*), who after quoting all the

The Whole Counsel of God. 139

that no stronger expressions are applied anywhere to the Eternal Life of the Blessed in Heaven, within the New Testament, than are also used to describe the endlessness of the pains of Hell:[1] and therefore the notion that of the two states Heaven only is endless, finds no support from the language of Scripture, but rests solely upon a human speculation external to it. On the other hand, "eternal" is not the only attribute applied in the New Testament to the state of punishment: the word is illustrated and defined by other terms which necessarily fix its true meaning. The Baptist speaks of the penal fire as "unquenchable."[2] Our Lord Himself adopts the word; He thrice said of the "worm" of a sinful conscience that "it dieth not," and that "the fire" of its punishment "is not quenched."[3] The prophet, whose language is quoted, had used a *future* tense,[4] the Divine Speaker, before whose Eyes the unseen world is spread out—on this side in all its unspeakable Beauty, on that in all its unutterable Woe—uses a *present*, as describing the fact yet more

---

passages in which the word αἰώνιος is applied to blessedness or woe, observes, 'Αἰώνιος in formulis ζωὴ αἰών. πῦρ αἰών. δόξα αἰών. κόλασις, ὄλεθρος, κρίμα, κρίσις αἰών. *sempiternum nunquam finiendum* indicare dubio caret, quum præmia æque ac pœnæ post resurrectionem sempiternæ quoque haberentur a Judæis. Vid. test. Aser. in Fab. Cod. Pseud. V. T. i. p. 693. potissimum Psalter. Salom. Ps. 3. vers. 13. 15, 16, ubi ἡ ἀπώλεια τοῦ ἁμαρτωλοῦ εἰς τὸν αἰῶνα; piorum ζωὴ αἰώνιος autem, οὐκ ἐκλείψει ἔτι. p.31.

[1] Commenting on the use of αἰώνιος in St. Matt. xxv. 41, 46, with reference to endless life and endless death, St. Augustine observes: "Si utrumque æternum, profectò aut utrumque cum fine diuturnum, aut utrumque sine fine perpetuum debet intelligi. Par pari enim relata sunt, hinc supplicium æternum, inde vita æterna. Dicere autem in hoc uno eodemque sensu, vita æterna sine fine erit, supplicium æternum finem habebit, multùm absurdum est. Unde, quia vita æterna sanctorum sine fine erit, supplicium quoque æternum quibus erit, finem procul dubio non habebit."—*De Civ. Dei*, xxi. 23. Even Hagenbach, who quotes this passage, observes: "It is superfluous to quote other Fathers, inasmuch as they all more or less agree."—*Hist. Doct.* vol. i. p. 387.

[2] πῦρ ἄσβεστον, St. Matt. iii. 12.

[3] εἰς τὸ πῦρ τὸ ἄσβεστον· ὅπου ὁ σκώληξ αὐτῶν οὐ τελευτᾷ, καὶ τὸ πῦρ οὐ σβέννυται, St. Mark ix. 43, 44, 46, 48. וְאִשָּׁם לֹא תִכְבֶּה, Isa. lxvi. 24.

vividly. If endless punishment could be described in human words, no words could exhaust the description more absolutely than the recorded words of Christ. They admit of no limitation; they are patient of no toning down or softening away; in the page of the Evangelist, they live for all time before the eyes of men, in all their vivid, awful power. If Jesus Christ has told us anything certain about the other world, we cannot doubt that the Penal fire must last for ever. But may the soul be withdrawn from the punishment? or may it be annihilated? Few Christians have dared to say "Yes" to the first of these questions; to the second, fewer still. For there are Words of Christ which seem expressly designed to prevent any misconception. He speaks of a "punishment no less than of a "fire," which is "everlasting."[1] And we are told, that as "he that believeth on the Son hath everlasting life," so "he that believeth not the Son shall not see life, but the wrath of God abideth on him."[2] "Abideth

[1] St. Matt. xxv. 41, 46. After noticing the classical distinction between κόλασις and τιμωρία (Ar. *Rhet.* i. 15, Plat. *Prot.* 323, e) Archbishop Trench observes (*Synon. N. T.* i. p. 28): "It would be a very serious error, however, to attempt to transfer this distinction in its entireness to the words as employed in the New Testament. The κόλασις αἰώνιος of Matt. xxv. 46, as it plainly itself declares, is no corrective and therefore temporary discipline; it can be no other than the ἀθάνατος τιμωρία (Josephus, *B. J.* ii. 8. 11), the ἀΐδιοι τιμωρίαι (Plato, *Ax.* 372, a), with which the Lord elsewhere threatens finally impenitent men (Mark ix. 43-48); for in proof that κόλασις had acquired in Hellenistic Greek this severer sense, and was used simply as punishment or torment, with no necessary underthought of the bettering through it of him who endured it, we have only to refer to such passages as the following: Josephus, *Ant.* xv. 2. 2; Philo, *De Agricul.* 9; Mart. Polycar. 2; 2 Macc. iv. 38; Wisd. of Sol. xix. 4. This much, indeed, of Aristotle's distinction still remains, and may be recognised in the sacred usage of the words, that in κόλασις the relation of the punishment to the punished, in τιμωρία to the punisher, is predominant."

[2] St. John iii. 36, ἡ ὀργὴ τοῦ Θεοῦ μένει ἐπ' αὐτόν. Compare the Psalmist's עַד־בֶּצַח לֹא יִרְאוּ אוֹר (xlix. 20) with the earlier part of this text. The true force of these words can only be set aside by the *a priori* and unwarrantable assumption that the endless life of the soul was truth unknown to the Hebrew Psalmists. Compare König, *Theologie der Psalmen*, p. 329 *sqq.*

on him";—then if he die in unbelief, he still *exists*, though in his woe—then he is *not delivered* from it. "Abideth on him": the piercing words seem to ring on from day to day, from year to year, from century to century, from cycle to cycle of measureless periods; we feel at this moment that eighteen centuries have not blunted their edge, or lessened their solemnity and power. If so (you reply), it were better never to have lived, than to live and be lost. Unquestionably. Our Lord states this truth with equal clearness. He said of one lost soul, of one who had been blessed with the high privilege of His Companionship, but who fell so deeply as to betray Him to His enemies for money, " Good it were for that man if he had never been born."[1] There are undoubtedly critics who treat these words as they might treat an exclamation in some heathen dramatist; as if the sentence had been uttered in a free rhetorical spirit, and with no thought of the meaning—the vast illimitable meaning—which they really contain and convey. But you can only thus empty the Words of Christ of their native power, if you will consent to forget that they are the Words of One Whose horizon was not bounded by the things of time. The Lord of Life and Death, fixing His Eye in deepest woe, yet with unfaltering precision, upon a creature whom He willed to save, yet who spurned His Salvation—thus rules in the fulness of His knowledge, in the tenderness of His Love, that non-existence had been better than an undying being, which in the abuse of its free-will His creature had made an unending misery. It cannot be maintained that the Words of Jesus are true, if at any conceivable point of a distant future any restoration to heaven is possible for Judas. For beyond that point, however distant, there would still stretch the vision of a still illimitable Eternity; in which the restored soul would find in the presence of

[1] St. Mark xiv. 21. Compare St. Mark iv. 29, and viii. 36, 37.

God, a "fulness of joy" which would redress the balance, and would speedily reduce a purgatory that had lasted even for ages to a scarcely perceptible speck in a past existence. Unless the human soul be not necessarily immortal, Judas lives: unless the Words of Christ be untrustworthy on the question of Life and Death, Judas lives in woe. There is no escape: the unspeakable awfulness of our Saviour's language is precisely *this*, that it does leave no room for any reversal of the doom of the betrayer—of the man whose epitaph was thus traced by the finger of Infinite Knowledge and of Infinite Love,— "Good were it for that man if he had never been born."

A few gifted minds such as Origen[1] have made shipwreck, from whatever causes, of this Article of the Christian Faith. But amidst the rare aberrations of genius, the belief of the Christian people has been such as might have been expected from the tenor of the Words of Christ. And it is particularly observable how in the early ages of the Faith, the martyrs standing before their heathen judges felt one after another that their choice lay between a transient pang of suffering and an endless

---

[1] The passages which best illustrate his deliberate opinion are in formal treatises (*De Prin.* i. 6, *Contr. Celsum*, v. 14, 15). In his popular teaching, he sometimes expresses opinions which seem to foreshadow the later doctrine of a purgatory before the Judgment (Hom. vi. in Exod. No. 4, Hom. iii. in Ps. xxxvi. No. 1, quoted by Lumper, 9, 595), or which at least say nothing inconsistent with it. He admitted, however, that his doctrine of a final ἀποκατάστασις (of men and devils) might be dangerous to the unconverted. "For most," he says, "it is enough to know that sinners will be punished. It would be inexpedient to say more: since there are persons whom the fear of Eternal Punishment scarcely restrains from giving themselves up to wickedness with all the evils that follow on it!"—*Contr. Cels.* vi. 26. He speaks of belief in eternal punishment as morally useful, although not true (Hom. in Jer. 19, tom. iii. p. 507, 508, ed. Migne), when commenting on Jer. xx. 7, thus admitting the adaptation of the Revealed Truth to the wants of the human soul. This conviction seems to have coloured his popular teaching. (Hom. 7, in Exod. *Opp.* ed. Migne, vol. ii. p. 347, where he quotes Isa. lxvi. 24.)

woe.[1] Not that the error which is connected with the name of Origen has been repudiated by no process less rude and irregular than the action of popular sentiment. Apparently during his lifetime, and certainly after his decease, the speculations of the great Alexandrian were condemned by councils of the Church;[2] and if equivocal language on the subject of endless punishment is to be discovered in a stray writer here and there by the student of Patristic Literature, he will almost invariably observe that its force is destroyed by language of an opposite drift, which the same writer has elsewhere employed. Nor is it pretended that there is any serious ground for doubt as to the Catholic Belief of the Church, as evidenced by the consent of her Representative

[1] Ruinart, *Acta Sincera.* Passio Stæ Felicitatis (p. 23), circa 150. Passio S. Maximi, circa 250 (p. 133). Maximus is described as a plebeian who was engaged in trade. When desired by the Proconsul to sacrifice, that he might escape the torture, he replied, "Hæc non sunt tormenta quæ pro nomine Domini nostri Jesu Christi inferuntur, sed sunt unctiones. Si enim recessero a Domini mei præceptis, quibus sum de Evangelio Ejus eruditus, vera et perpetua mihi manebunt tormenta." Other examples might be cited from Ruinart: they show what was the simple, unhesitating faith of the Early Church.

[2] Origen was silenced and deposed by two successive synods held during his lifetime. His leading tenets were condemned at Constantinople in 540. "The erroneous doctrines," says Archdeacon Churton, "which Origen had taught, or which others taught in his name, were condemned as heretical; and among them the doctrine of the future restitution of fallen spirits and of evil men. See this very fully proved by a Church historian, who has given it the fullest examination. *Natal. Alex. Hist. Eccl.* Sæc. iii. Diss. xvi. And this is admitted by the best informed inquirers of our own Church, as by those of foreign Churches. See Bishop Pearson, *Minor Works,* i. 413, and the able Life of Origen in the venerable Archdeacon of Westmoreland's *Biographies of the Early Church,* ii. 114, 133."—(*Guardian,* March 9, 1864.) To the objection that Origen was not condemned by any of the first four General Councils it has been well replied, "that each Council did the special work of its own emergency, and not other kinds of work; and that Origenism was not a pressing question in 325, 381, 431, or 451."—(W. B. in *Guardian,* March 16, 1864.) It is at least certain that the sixth General Council declares the fifth to have assembled for the purpose of condemning Origen and other persons, thereby indorsing the anathema of the Synod in Constantinople in 540. —(Routh, *Script. Eccl. Opusc.* ii. 232.)

Fathers.[1] But, let us note it well, they who to-day deny the truth in question, or who rashly express "hopes" that the Faith of Christendom may not be true, oppose themselves not merely to the decrees of Councils and to the consent of Fathers, nor yet merely to the "popular" belief of centuries, nor to the reign of a world-wide Tradition. Nor do they merely controvert a Hebrew Prophet or a Christian Apostle, and take up the position of those inconsequent Rationalists who, respecting nothing else in Holy Scripture, still profess to respect as Divine and Infallible the recorded Words of Christ. For it is face to face with Him that they stand in controversy:[2] it is His sentence, in Whose disclosures concerning the world beyond the tomb we Christians place our hopes for life and for death, that they arraign at the bar of what is at best a section of contemporary opinion. Our Lord and Saviour, with what would be generosity in a mere man, but with what in Him doubtless was provision against the known weakness of His creatures, has not bequeathed to His Servants or Representatives the responsibility—nay the odium—of proclaiming those stern and awful certainties; He has Himself heralded, at one and the same time, the penalties and the benedictions of His Gospel; He has Himself unveiled the Eternal pit, in phrases and

[1] See Petavius *de Angelis*, lib. iii. c. 8. It will be observed that Petavius quotes language from Gregory of Nyssa, and Gregory Nazianzen, which may fairly outweigh those passages of doubtful import in their writings, to which appeal has recently been made.

[2] Observe the force of the following admission from a writer, of whose relations to the true faith of the Church of Christ no unfair estimate will be formed from the fact of his being one of the five authorities referred to with approbation by M. Renan, in his recent *Vie de Jésus* (Int. p. vii). M. Reuss has been citing St. Matt. xxv. 30, 41 *sqq.* and some similar passages : " Toutes ces peintures," he says, "sont claires et simples ; elles n'offrent rien d'équivoque ; il n'y a pas un mot qui trahisse une arrière-pensée, qui nous fasse entrevoir une signification cachée, qui les réduise à une valeur purement figurée et parabolique. Il est évident que les narrateurs qui nous servent ici de guides, ont pris tout cela au pied de la lettre et qu'il ne leur est pas resté une ombre de doute à cet égard."—Reuss, *Theol. Chrétienne*, tome i. p. 249, Deux^{me} edit.

words as urgent and positive as those whereby He has opened heaven to all believers; and fifty generations of Christians have believed and confessed that His Authority is final, and that to tamper with His Revelations is only more obviously foolish than it is perilously blasphemous.

Brethren! I seem to interpret to myself the thought of your hearts: men are won, you say, by the mercies rather than by the terrors of the Lord. Would it not be more accurate to say, with St. Augustine, that the terrors of the Lord drive us men to take refuge in His unspeakable mercies? Is it not a fact, familiar to every clergyman, is it not a matter of personal experience to some at least in this vast congregation, that the undefined, haunting fear of an endless woe does again and again guide unquiet souls to seek peace and safety in kneeling at the foot of the Cross, and in tasting of that Plenteous Redemption, which flows from the Wounds of Jesus? Are there not now resting in Paradise souls, who owe their predestined crowns and thrones to that first sharp pang which pierced their spirits, when, many years since, on earth, in the midst of a course of sin, they first realised the certain existence of an endless Hell? You urge that there are higher motives than terror for religious effort. Undoubtedly. It is better to love God for His own sake than to love Him for the sake of the blessings which He gives, or the woes from which He saves. But He Who made the human heart knew more perfectly what motives are really needed to act upon it than the theorists who proclaim what they would propose as the revision of His work. He knew that more men are moved by fear than by love: and that man may be educated to love fearlessly, if he begins by cultivating that fear which is the beginning of moral and spiritual wisdom. Certainly we cannot exaggerate the mercies of our redeeming Lord: they are simply infinite. But side by side with them lie also His judgments, unexplored and infinite; so that the "great deep" is their symbol in the world of nature; and His judgments are equally with His mercies an integral part of the Truth of His Revelation, nay, of His Being: they are equally a part of His "whole Counsel" as it has been made known to us men; and it is our business, as clergy, to proclaim them. To do so, many of us solemnly pledge ourselves this day before God and man. We owe it, my brethren of the laity, to our God; we owe it to Jesus Teaching and to Jesus Crucified; we owe it to the terms of our commission, and to the claims of our consciences; but we owe it above all to your undying souls to tell you the plain, unmutilated truth. We dare not, like the serpent in Paradise, whisper to you here, within the precincts of the Church of God, that you may cherish a "hope" that God's threats may after all be false. To tell you that in the future world the only alternative to Heaven is a Purgatory, might indeed earn for us, at the present crisis of thought in England, a momentary popularity. But if it were morally in our power to sacrifice one truth of the Creed, we could not thereby insure the rest. We could not stop at "expressing a hope" that the punishment of the wicked may not be final. On the one side, an Eternal Heaven might easily become both to the philologists and to the metaphysicians as problematical a thing as an Eternal Hell. On the other, that infinite Price which our Lord paid upon the Cross that He might save us from a boundless woe would soon be rejected as needless; and we should reduce His propitiatory Sacrifice to the level of a moral triumph. From that it were but a short step to the denial of His Godhead. For, as a perfect act of faith in a single truth has already, before perceiving it, grasped other truths by implication, so a deliberate rejection of a single truth entails the rejection, first in principle, and afterwards avowedly, of other truths beyond. Here is our danger. Fear you we may not: but you may shame our weakness by bidding us tell you the truth, or you may tempt us in speaking to you, to "prophesy smooth things," or at best to substitute the "hay, wood, and stubble" of the things of time for the unchangeable realities of the other world. If we dare not be honest with you; if through want of spirituality, from a selfish instinct that we should condemn ourselves in your eyes, we should shrink from a high and soul-controlling doctrine—woe, woe to us! One day we know, that, side by side with you, but with greater, far greater responsibilities than yours, which we have freely chosen to bear, we too, your ministers, must stand at the Judgment Seat of Christ. How shall we then make answer to the stern and terrible rebuke of our Master, how shall we endure to hear your deserved reproaches, your wail of remorse and agony, if now, through cowardly fear of man, or any false refinement, or weakly acquiescence in the polished unbelief of the hour, we hide from you one-half of our Master's message; justifying by our silence the taunt of His enemies, that in this age we fear to preach what He Himself announced as certain; or banding ourselves with them, in saying that He was at least in part mistaken, and that the men of to-day have improved His Gospel by eliminating its severities?

And you, my dear brethren, who now are pressing forward to receive your various powers from the consecrated hands through which to-day, as ever before and to the end of time, Christ our Lord reigning in His Church bestows them—bethink you, I pray, at this the most solemn crisis of your lives, of that great Day which cannot be distant, and which may be very near. Bethink you now, as you receive your talent of the account which you must then render for its due improvement. Pray that you may be fearless, as speaking for the Mighty

God; but pray too that you may be loving, and humble, as becomes sinners, who remember their own sins, while in God's name they dare to counsel their brethren. If we of the Clergy feel in our very hearts that we may be lost, as easily, nay rather, by reason of our greater opportunities, much more easily than other men; we shall speak of Hell, not as a threat which we flourish without measuring its awfulness, but as a fact, present to the eye of our spirits; we shall think and speak of it as of a common danger—just as of Heaven as of a common Hope, and a common Home. Let us by God's grace resolve to be true; let us pray God to make us true—true in our inmost selves—and true to that counsel of God, which it is our duty to proclaim to man. God indeed is severe and stern with the self-reliant; but for the self-distrustful and the prayerful He is a tender and most indulgent Master, Whose service is not less the highest joy than it is the highest freedom. Even on earth for every earnest, simple, truthful, unselfish spirit among the servants of the Church, there is a foretaste of the imperishable Reward above. It may be enjoyed, and that abundantly, in the cottages of the poor, in the pulpits of the Sanctuary, on the steps of the Altar. Stephen may still ennoble the lower grade of service by a sacrifice of self which opens heaven, and which Jesus owns as the first of martyrdoms. And there are mercies, blessings, crowns that fade not away [1]—for those who though afar off, yet by word and act faithfully witness to the justice and to the grace of their God, and who, standing beneath the Cross of the Redeemer of the world, wield, according to the measures of their ministry, the consolations of the keys of Peter, the powers of the sword of Paul.

---

[1] 1 St. Peter v. 4.

SERMON V.

THE SECRET OF CLERICAL POWER.[1]

Acts i. 8.

Ye shall receive power, after that the Holy Ghost is come upon you.

IT is very difficult for us to enter into the bewildering sense of desolation which the Apostles must have felt on the eve of the Ascension. Even before His Passion, our Lord had spoken of His going to the Father, and now that the event was imminent the Apostles were gradually facing the situation in which they would be placed by His departure. They had received a commission to make disciples of all the nations. But, looking to the actual circumstances of the world, they still seemed to lack wellnigh all the conditions of success. Before them were vast political bodies with the prestige of antiquity and the prestige of possession, and committed to the support of popular falsehoods. Before them were intellectual systems, elaborated by generations of thinkers, and commanding, if not the belief, yet certainly the respect of the educated classes. Before them were all the ambitions, all the lusts, all the luxuries, all the vested interests of a large and corrupt society. It may be that as yet they realised little in detail of their future work, of their coming sufferings. Yet a vague apprehension of unmeasured difficulties, of unsuspected obstacles, they must have had; they must have hoped that, ere He left them, our Lord would bring help and strength that might in

[1] Preached at the Ordination of the Bishop of Salisbury, in Salisbury Cathedral, on the Fifteenth Sunday after Trinity, September 24, 1865.

some sense redress the balance, even if it should not atone for His dreaded departure. Surely, they thought, it is for some such purpose that He has risen from His grave, and tarried among us. He is meditating some great blow, some striking deliverance; He has delayed it so long that He may the more conspicuously show strength with His arm and scatter the proud in the imagination of their hearts. Will He not now break the yoke of Roman oppression? Will He not now restore to Judæa a self-governing theocracy, an earthly Kingdom of Heaven, in which His first followers will sit visibly on His right hand and on His left? "Lord, wilt Thou at this time restore again the kingdom to Israel?"[1] In His reply, our Lord does not, as we might have expected, rebuke the outward, political, materialised conceptions of His work which His Apostles still entertained. He does not show how the Jewish commonwealth, which had forfeited its national existence for ever, was related to the Realm of the Incarnation only as shadow to substance. He glances in a few words of censure at the unspiritual curiosity which would, if it might, drag forth God's own secrets from beneath the veils of His providence: "It is not for you to know the times or the seasons, which the Father hath put in His own power."[2] But He at once passes from censure to promise and blessing. He graciously overlooks the form of their question; He addresses Himself to its motive, to the timid apprehensions which had prompted it. They were indeed to be strengthened for all that was before them: "Ye shall receive power, after that the Holy Ghost is come upon you."

I.

What, then, was this power thus promised to the Apostles? Power is a comprehensive term, and the

[1] Acts i. 6. [2] Ibid. i. 7.

specific form of power which was mainly intended can only be determined by reference to the actual history of the earliest Church of Christ.

What was this power which the Apostles were to receive? As a matter of fact, what "power" did they receive?

a. Was it, as they anticipated, political power? Certainly, my brethren, in the course of years the Church of Christ did acquire something very like the power of the sceptre. The prophecies of Isaiah seemed to intimate that this would be so: in the Evangelical prophet the Church is already represented as a spiritual empire, surrounded with the circumstances of temporal greatness.[1] But when did this form of power present itself? Not in her first years of missionary enterprise and of abundant martyrdom. Not when she first worshipped in the catacombs and bled in the amphitheatres. Not when her leaders and princes, like the first Apostles, were still and universally reckoned the "filth of the world, an offscouring of all things";[2] a spectacle of scorn and shame "to the world, to angels, and to men."[3] But when she was no longer composed of a despised minority, when by a long catalogue of labours and sufferings she had won her way to the understandings and to the hearts of multitudes, she forthwith acquired power in the State. Found in all the walks of life, in all the provinces of the great world-empire, and in regions beyond its frontiers; an intellectual force, when other thought was languishing or dying; a focus of high moral effort, when the world around was a very flood of revolting wickedness; a bond of the closest union, when all else was tending to social divergence and disruption of interests; she became a political force. Such she was long before Constantine associated the Cross with the Roman purple, nay, even, as it would appear, before the two last great persecutions.

[1] Isa. lx. 5, 6, 7, 13, 14.   [2] 1 Cor. iv. 13.   [3] *Ibid.* 9.

For high moral influence among multitudes of men carries with it political weight. Political power came to the Church, at first unbidden, and in many cases unwelcomed. It was a current charge against the primitive Christians that they neglected civil and political duties. But political power came to them from the nature of the case, and inevitably: the Gospel was necessarily a popular moral influence, and it could not be this on a great scale without tending to become a power in the State. Thus silently but surely a mighty revolution was wrought in the souls of men; and at last it was proclaimed in the outward forms of life and in the changed hands which administered government. The words of the *Magnificat* became history, and Christ, the Lion of the tribe of Judah, reigning in and triumphing with His Church, "put down the mighty from their seat, and exalted the humble and meek"[1]

Undoubtedly political power was given to the Church by the loving providence of our Lord, as an instrument whereby to promote man's highest good. But if such power was an opportunity often used for the highest purposes and with the happiest effect, it was also a temptation to worldly ambition, and even to worse sins, often yielded to with the most disastrous results. Who can doubt this after studying in the history of the great Western See such lives as, for example, those of a Julius II. or of a Leo X.? Who can doubt this, after an impartial consideration of the history of other portions of the Church nearer home, which have purchased a political status at the heavy cost of sacrificing spiritual energy and freedom? He Who said at the first, "My kingdom is not of this world," is perhaps bringing Christians everywhere back by the course of His providences to the fuller acknowledgment of this primal truth. On all sides the

[1] St. Luke i. 52.

Church is losing what she once possessed of political influence; on all sides the spiritual influences of the Gospel, which are indeed indestructible, are jealously warned to keep apart from the secular interests of human life. If political power had been of the essence of our Lord's promise to His Apostles, we might well lose heart; but there is no cause for despondency, if the power which the Apostles were to receive was of a higher and more enduring character.

Political power is after all but a clumsy instrument for achieving spiritual success. It imperils as much as it assists; it alienates as rapidly as it compels adhesion; and those spiritual institutions which have grasped the sword most tenaciously, illustrate, one after another, the warning of our Lord to St. Peter at the gate of Gethsemane: they perish, sooner or later, by the sword.

β. Was then the power in question intellectual power? The Gospel has undoubtedly lightened up man's understanding and fertilised his thought. Knowledge is of itself power; and knowledge on the highest and most interesting of all subjects is a very high form of power. For knowledge is the motive and warrant of action, and they whose eye ranges over two worlds occupy a more commanding position than they who see only one. A certain power of this description was undoubtedly a result of the gift of Pentecost. Our Lord had dwelt on the illuminating office of the Comforter: "He shall guide you into all truth."[1] And the first Apostles needed such an assistance, since they were utterly uneducated men, with the narrowest of mental horizons. How wonderfully, on the day of Pentecost itself, is the thought of St. Peter fertilised and expanded! The unlettered fisherman is suddenly the profound expositor of ancient prophecy, and within a short period his teaching brings him into collision

[1] St. John xvi. 13.

with the Sadducean leaders of educated sceptical opinion. And in later years how rich and how various are the intellectual gifts of the inspired Apostles of Christ! St. John speaks at once the language of the simplest devotion and of the profoundest philosophy. St. James teaches moral truth wellnigh in the language of an ancient prophet. Who can read his Epistle without feeling its keen sense of natural beauty, its vigorous and trenchant grasp of the secret tendencies and broad characteristics of human nature and of the practical side of Christianity? St. Peter, in his First Epistle, harmonises with marvellous comprehensiveness the practical tendencies of St. James and the dogmatic teaching of St. Paul. St. Paul, who owed something to his earlier education, counted it but loss for Christ;[1] and the vigorous dialectician of the Epistles to the Romans and the Galatians, the master of warning, of irony, of denunciation, of entreaty, whom we meet in the Epistles to the Corinthians, the entranced observer of sublime mysteries who speaks in the Epistle to the Ephesians, the defender of the faith against a subtle theosophy in the Epistle to the Colossians, the far-sighted administrator who organises the hierarchy and the religious communities and the discipline of the Church in the Pastoral Epistles, is an intellectual creation of Divine grace. And when we pass down into later ages, we find the promise of intellectual power fulfilled almost continuously in the annals of the Church. Take Origen's Treatise against Celsus, or St. Augustine's work on the Trinity or on the City of God, or the writings of Greek Fathers, of Athanasius, of Basil, of Gregory Nazianzen against the Arians and the Eunomians, or some of the astonishing productions of the scholastic period, such as the *Summa* of Aquinas, or the original works which attacks upon the faith have called forth among ourselves,

[1] Phil. iii. 7.

such as Bishop Butler's *Analogy* or the too-forgotten Treatises of Law, and Waterland, and Leslie, and Chandler, and say if this sense of the word has not been realised,— " Ye shall receive power."

But was this intellectual power, swaying the thoughts of educated men, the chief, or even a main, element of the promised gift? Surely not. The Gospel was meant for the whole human family; and the poor, in consideration of the hardness of their lot, had a first claim upon its preachers. The Church was to be, not as some early Gnostics seemed to desire, not as some contemporary rationalists have dreamed, a literary club, in which rival teachers were to discuss the claims of opposing theories; but a home, in which a fixed Revealed Truth should be clearly and simply brought home to the hearts and consciences of all.[1] Not many learned were called among the multitudes who first poured into the kingdom; and mere cultivated intellect is a sorry weapon wherewith to approach those who lack that cultivation which is necessary to understand it. The gift of Pentecost may indeed have included intellectual power; a living, active soul is a thinking as well as a loving soul; but the main essential gift itself was something beyond, something higher, something more universally acceptable, something more adapted to the soul of man, as man, something more capable of advancing the glory and of doing justice to the grace of God.

γ. Was this power then to be a faculty of working miracles? Our thoughts seem to gravitate naturally towards such a supposition. A certain limited power of this description, varying apparently with the spiritual state of the disciples themselves, had been granted to them during our Lord's ministry. At one time the disciples rejoice that the devils are subject to them;[2] at

[1] 1 Tim. iii. 15.   [2] St. Luke x. 17.

another they are powerless to relieve the lunatic at the foot of the Mount of Transfiguration.[1] But after the Ascension, and because of it, they were to do works even greater than those of their Divine Master. "Greater works than these shall he [that believeth] do, because I go to My Father."[2] The gift of miracles depended then on the Ascension in the same sense as did the gift of the promised Comforter; and it was natural to identify the two gifts, or to regard the former as a chief result or fruit of the latter. And immediately after Pentecost the Apostles are in possession of large and varied supernatural powers. It is important to observe the close connection in which the miracles of the Apostles stand throughout the narrative of the Acts with their missionary progress and success. The school of Paley may have laid a too exclusive rather than a too emphatic stress on the evidential force of miracle; but we witness at this day an immoderate reaction, which is disposed to ignore the value of miracles altogether. In the Acts of the Apostles, almost every step which is made by the advancing Gospel is preceded or accompanied by miraculous manifestations. The gift of tongues on the day of Pentecost itself,[3] the healing of the lame man in Solomon's porch,[4] the great wonders and miracles which Stephen the Deacon, "full of faith and power," is said to have done among the people,[5] the raising of Dorcas from the dead at Joppa,[6] the supernatural vision which preceded the conversion of Cornelius,[7] St. Peter's deliverance from prison by the angel,[8] St. Paul's healing the cripple at Lystra,[9] his exorcism of the damsel possessed with the spirit of divination at Philippi,[10] the handkerchiefs or aprons which were brought

[1] St. Mark ix. 28. [2] St. John xiv. 12. [3] Acts ii. 3-12.
[4] Acts iii. 7-11. [5] Ibid. vi. 8. [6] Ibid. ix. 40-42.
[7] Acts x. 9-48. [8] Ibid. xii. 7-16. [9] Ibid. xiv. 8-18.
[10] Acts xvi. 16-40.

from his body, and which healed the sick of their diseases at Ephesus,[1] his raising Eutychus from the dead at Troas,[2] his vision of our Lord at Corinth,[3] and of an angel during the Mediterranean storm,[4] his cure of the serpent's bite at Malta,[5] were all connected with important results to the spread of the faith. This indeed was not less the case with miracles of judgment than with miracles of mercy. The death of Ananias and Sapphira produced a keen sense of the awful presence of the Judge of hearts in His Church;[6] the blindness of Elymas the sorcerer was immediately followed by the conversion of the "deputy" Sergius Paulus.[7] The whole narrative of the Acts is penetrated by, encompassed with, the miraculous; the book becomes historically worthless, it falls absolutely to pieces, unless the full importance and reality of the Apostolical miracles be freely and truly acknowledged. Nor, whatever may be the lack of evidence for some later alleged miracles, is there any producible proof from Scripture that the miraculous power itself was destined to be withdrawn from the Church at the death of the Apostles, or at the end of the third century, or at the end of the sixth century, or at any subsequent period which may have been suggested by the supposed necessities of later controversy.

But was miracle of the essence of that power which the Apostles were to receive at Pentecost? Surely not. It was rather an evidence, an occasional accompaniment, an ornament of the central gift, than the gift itself. Miracle is by no means a resistless instrument for propagating a doctrine. Unbelief has many methods for escaping its force. Where it cannot insinuate trickery, it has no scruple about hinting at the agency of Beelzebub.[8] The

---

[1] Acts xix. 11, 12.   [2] Ibid. xx. 9-12.   [3] Ibid. xviii. 9-11.
[4] Acts xxvii. 23, 24.   [5] Ibid. xxviii. 3-10.   [6] Ibid. v. 5, 10, 11.
[7] Acts xiii. 10, 11, 12.   [8] St. Mark iii. 22; St. Luke xi. 15.

state of mind which resists the historical and prophetical evidences of Revelation is likely to deal somewhat summarily with a natural wonder, however well attested, in the domain of sense. Our Lord Himself tells us that this is so: "If they hear not Moses and the prophets, neither will they be persuaded, though one rose from the dead."[1] And the text seems decisively to point, if to miracle, yet also to something else, to something more constantly available, more nearly irresistible, more calculated to reassure the Apostles in that hour of their faintness and desolation of spirit. "Ye shall receive power."

δ. Nor did the power consist in the ministerial commission itself; in the authorisation to preach the Word and to administer the Sacraments. Undoubtedly, in a profound sense of the term, that commission, with its several elementary portions, is a power unlike any other which God has given to His creatures here below. But our Lord had already solemnly and fully commissioned His Apostles. Before speaking the words of our text, He had laid on the chosen eleven the full weight of the ministerial office. Not on a single occasion, and, as in a modern Ordination, through the medium of one very condensed and pregnant form, had He conveyed to them the essential and constitutive powers of the Christian Priesthood. The Apostles were ordained, so to speak, piecemeal. The several powers with which they were intrusted were laid upon them by a series of acts at considerable intervals, as they were gradually strengthened to undertake the accumulating burden. The various acts of this gradual ordination of the Apostles were grouped around the Cross, even as now Ordination in the Church is a part of the Eucharistic Service. On the eve of the Passion, in the supper-room, they received the momentous power of consecrating the Redeemer's Body and Blood.[2] Thus

[1] St. Luke xvi. 31.   [2] *Ibid.* xxii. 19, 20; 1 Cor. xi. 24, 25.

provision was made for the worship and growth of Christian souls to the end of time. The power of remitting and retaining sins was given by our Risen Lord in the upper room with closed doors, on the evening of the day of the Resurrection.[1] In this way Jesus provided a remedy for the wounds which sin would leave on the souls of His redeemed.[2] The full commission and command to make disciples of all the nations, baptizing them in the Name of the most Holy Trinity,[3] more immediately preceded the Ascension itself. The perpetual extension of the Gospel, and the self-perpetuating power of the Apostolical ministry, were thus proclaimed by our Divine Saviour. When then He said, "Ye shall receive power," these functional powers of the priesthood and apostolate had already been actually given; and the Holy Ghost had been bestowed in such sense as to convey to the Apostles the ministerial faculty or character. The Apostles were in full possession of all powers necessary to feed and teach the Lord's people, but it would seem that until the day of Pentecost these powers were like undeveloped faculties, latent in the souls of the Apostles, but unexercised. Something else was needed, some vivifying heavenly force which should quicken and stimulate these hidden energies, and, like the rain or the sunshine upon the dormant vitality of the seed or the shoot, should provoke them into an outburst of energetic life.

ε. Once more then let it be asked, Wherein did this power which the Apostles were to receive consist? Creating political ascendency, yet utterly distinct from it; fertilising intellectual power, yet differing in its essence from the activity of mere vigorous unsanctified intellect; working moral miracles, (it may be) gifted to work physical wonders, yet certainly in itself more persuasive than the miracle it was empowered to produce; intimately

[1] St. John xx. 22, 23. [2] 1 Cor. v. 3-5; 2 Cor. ii. 7. [3] St. Matt. xxviii. 19.

allied with, and the natural accompaniment of distinct ministerial faculties, yet not necessarily so; what is this higher, this highest power, this gift of gifts, this transforming influence, which was to countersign as if from heaven what had previously been given by the Incarnate Lord on earth, and was to form out of unlettered and irresolute peasants the evangelists of the world? My brethren, it was spiritual, it was personal, it was moral power. And spiritual power may be felt rather than described or analysed. It resides in or it permeates a man's whole circle of activities; it cannot be localised, it cannot be identified exclusively with one of them. It is felt in solemn statements of doctrine, and also in the informal utterances of casual intercourse; it is felt in action no less than in language, in trivial acts not less than in heroic ventures, or in yet more heroic resignation; it is traced perchance in the very expression of the countenance, yet the countenance is too coarse an organ to do it justice; it just asserts its presence, but its presence is too volatile, too immaterial, to admit of being seized, and measured, and brought by art or by language fairly within the compass of our comprehension. It is an unearthly beauty, whose native home is in a higher world, yet which tarries among men from age to age, since the time when the Son of God left us His example, and gave us His Spirit. It is nothing else than His spiritual presence, mantling upon His servants; they live in Him; they lose in Him something of their proper personality; they are absorbed into, they are transfigured by, a Life altogether higher than their own: His Voice blends with theirs, His Eye seems to lighten theirs with its sweetness and its penetration; His Hand gives gentleness and decision to their acts; His Heart communicates a ray of its Divine charity to their life of narrower and more stagnant affection; His Soul commingles with theirs, and their life of thought, and feeling, and resolve is irradiated and braced by His. "If a man love Me, he will keep My words, and My Father will love him, and We will come unto him, and make Our abode with him."[1] "It is not ye that speak, but the Spirit of My Father Which speaketh in you."[2] "He that heareth you heareth Me; and he that despiseth you despiseth Me."[3] "I live; yet not I, but Christ liveth in me."[4] "They glorified God in me."[5] The ministers of Christ reflected the glory of their invisible but present Lord. The face of Stephen in the moment of his triumph and of his anguish was as the face of an angel.[6] The very shadow of Peter was felt to possess an unearthly virtue.[7] The Galatians would have plucked out their eyes for the great missionary who first called them within the holy fold.[8] The Roman governor trembles, as the prisoner before him makes a simple statement of the elementary laws of truth and righteousness.[9]

This, and much else to the same purpose, dated from the Gift of Pentecost. A power was abroad in the world, and men were instinctively doing homage to its silent influence. Not that it was strictly confined to the ministers of Christ. God forbid. Every Christian who possesses a Divine Presence in his soul is a missionary to the world, and does his Master's work. And, alas! a man may be ordained, and may possess in their completeness, those ministerial functions which are essential to the life of souls and to the organic completeness of the Church, without possessing that personal spiritual influence which raises his ministerial acts, so far as he is himself concerned, above the level of a mechanical obedience. Certain it is, that such influence is offered as a distinct element, nay, as the most conspicuous element, of the Grace of

---

[1] St. John xiv. 23. [2] St. Matt. x. 20. [3] St. Luke x. 16.
[4] Gal. ii. 20. [5] Ibid. i. 24. [6] Acts vi. 15.
[7] Acts v. 15. [8] Gal. iv. 15. [9] Acts xxiv. 25.

Ordination. It is the complement, the very crown and beauty, of the other great gifts which are received from Christ through the laying on of hands; only, unlike those gifts, it depends for its transmission upon the spiritual condition of the recipient. No question can be more pertinent or more practical than the inquiry, How we may hope to claim and to secure this precious, this indispensable endowment.

The grace, we know, is offered to all. "Ye shall receive power" is an inheritance of all the ages of the Church. But it is conditioned. It presupposes a certain receptivity in the applicant. And that receptivity consists in nothing so much as in directness and simplicity of purpose.

So it was with the Apostles: they received power, because they abandoned themselves perfectly to the call of God. Their self-oblation was not retarded or marred by thoughts of self, which lagged in the rear of their profession of a perfect service. God gives Himself to the soul in a degree proportioned to the completeness with which the soul yields itself to Him. "With the holy Thou shalt be holy; and with a perfect man Thou shalt be perfect; with the clean Thou shalt be clean; and" (oh! marvellous and terrible irony!) "with the froward Thou shalt learn frowardness."[1] It is only when the eye is single that the whole body of the Christian character is full of light, and to be full of moral light is to be full of moral power.[2] It is only when in Holy Orders we "give ourselves wholly to this one thing, and turn all our desires and studies this way,"[3] that in the highest sense of the term we can hope to receive a gift of spiritual power which shall win souls for Christ. This was the deepest work of the Holy Ghost in the Apostle of Jesus Christ. He did not merely place the Christian Creed

---

[1] Ps. xviii. 25, 26.   [2] St. Matt. vi. 22.   [3] Ordination of Priests.

The Secret of Clerical Power. 163

before the eye of their understandings. He wrote it upon their hearts, and forthwith each revealed dogma became a germ of moral power. "We love Him," so speaks an Apostle, "because He first loved us."[1] "He died for all, that they which live should not henceforth live unto themselves, but unto Him Which died for them, and rose again."[2] "Our old man is crucified with Christ, that the body of sin might be destroyed, that henceforth we should not serve sin."[3] "Hereby perceive we the love of God, because He laid down His life for us: and we ought to lay down our life for the brethren."[4] "We ought to obey God rather than men."[5] Charity, humility, purity, courage, disinterestedness, patience, calmness, gentleness— these were the graces which were thus taught in the school of the Holy Ghost. And charity is a power; humility is a power; purity is a power; courage is a power; disinterestedness is a power. These graces are powers by reason of their rarity as well as on account of their intrinsic force. Gibbon has told us that the unbelieving world fears the virtues of the clergy, while it at once welcomes and despises their vices. And from the age of the Apostles until now our Lord's work in the world has varied with the personal and spiritual elevation of us His representatives among men, to whom at the first He left, if we will, a legacy of moral power.

II.

The presence of this "power" may be more especially noted by two leading characteristics or symptoms.

(1) The first, Consistency. The whole life is of a piece. Thought, feeling, action, are in harmony. Within, there is no waste of strength; all the faculties move together; all are directed upon one End of ends; and

---
[1] 1 St. John iv. 19.   [2] 2 Cor. v. 15.   [3] Rom. vi. 6.
[4] 1 St. John iii. 16.   [5] Acts v. 29.

this concentration is the economy and the secret of force. Without, there is no distracting instability of action. There may be a change of scene, change of work, change of friends and of intellectual atmosphere; there may be an ever-widening horizon of soul, and a silent or avowed rejection of some imperfections or misapprehensions of earlier years. But throughout the man's life there runs a line of manifest, persistent continuity of purpose. The vessel may be driving before the gale, or she may be for a while becalmed, while her sails hang heavily against the mast, but observe her movements when you will, and her prow is ever turned towards the Eternal Shore.

Now consistency is among all men an element of power. It is especially so among Englishmen, because, whatever our national faults, God has given us, as a race, a natural love of honesty. Thus it often happens that men who stand outside truth yet sincerely admire its vivifying power in the lives of others. They "do not agree with so-and-so, but they like a man to be consistent." There is, of course, a pride of consistency—of consistency in intellectual error or in moral evil; but every virtue has its counterfeit, and a virtue is not less a virtue because the devil has caricatured or degraded it. In a clergyman, consistency is of especial value. He theoretically represents intrepid adherence to faith amid feeble and vacillating convictions. He theoretically represents determined homage in practical matters to duty and principle, when other wills are weak, and the presence of temptation or of false public opinion is strong. He theoretically represents a practice of the duties, the sacrifices, the self-denials, the heroic efforts, which are doubtless absurd if religion is only a graceful sentiment; but which are natural and obvious, if we are indeed living on the brink of another world which is to last for ever. And the more unwaveringly he is true to his ideal, the more complete is his adherence to principle, the more coherent are all the aspects of his life, the more certainly will he be a power. His faith and love can afford to dispense with political or social sanctions; he needs not high natural gifts of mind, or manifest powers of miracle; he is a power with or without these. Men who do not believe, or who advocate or affect laxity of life, feel in their secret souls an awe in his presence; they perceive that there is a majesty and force in the life of a sincere servant of God; they revere long before they dream of imitation. For, as they know, a really consistent life is not to fallen man, as such, a natural human life: it witnesses to the presence in the soul of a superhuman force. It is a ray of His Beauty Who as the ages pass before Him knows no change; Who is What He has ever been, what He ever must be—the Same yesterday, to-day, and for ever; always Strong, always Wise, always Merciful, always Majestic, always Incomprehensible, always Holy, always Just.

Who would dare to say that consistency—strict, absolute consistency—is easy? Who, indeed, that has been for some years wearing the livery of Jesus Christ can but look back on accumulated errors, weaknesses, disloyalties, sins, marring the harmony and therefore impairing the force of his ministerial life? And consistency is not to be achieved by a dramatic attempt to practise it. It cannot be compassed by throwing ourselves in imagination outside ourselves, and thinking how our lives will look in the social landscape and to the popular eye. Consistency is created from within: it is the product of direct, simple homage to truth. The Majesty of God, the Justice of God, the Lovingkindness of God, the Omnipresence of God, the atoning and sacrificial Death of Jesus Christ, the power of the Eternal Spirit, the power and grace of the Christian Sacraments,—these truths really dwelt on, one by one, really mastered, really received into the secret soul, might work in the practical life the triumph of consistency. If they fail to do so, it is because we do not simply, heartily receive them, or because we allow ourselves, as we say, with an affectation of engaging frankness, to act from mixed motives, that is to say, to neutralise the influences of Divine truth by the influences of its antagonists in human society. Especially observe that rationalism forfeits, by the very law of its life, this power which arises from moral consistency. Holding, as it does, all truth more or less in solution, it never can submit itself to any, so as to translate the power of a received truth into actual life, and it is therefore condemned by the Wisdom and by the Love of God to a moral impotence. But faith has only to detach herself from the earthly influences around her, and she will forthwith remove mountains. Mountains of ignorance, mountains of prejudice, mountains of sin, mountains of self-sufficiency, mountains of unbelief; they would be removed, easily and speedily, if this grace of consistency —so freely granted to us by the Divine Spirit of our indulgent Master, so easily forfeited by disloyalty to His voice and to His truth—were but more earnestly cherished by us His ministers.

(2) The presence of this power is moreover evidenced by Sympathy. By sympathy I do not merely mean fellow-feeling with those who suffer acute pain or who experience extraordinary pleasure. Sympathy is the power of entering with intelligence and tenderness into the inner life and circumstances of others, although they are removed from us by distance, by station, by occupations, by blood. Sympathy is in this sense a very great gift. Most men live—" each in his hidden sphere of joy or woe "—with only a partial interest in those who are similarly circumstanced, and with no interest at all in

those who are otherwise. The young do not enter into the life of old age; and the old cannot comprehend the youthful spirits which they once enjoyed. Thinkers do not understand practical men, nor practical men the ways and motives of thinkers. Englishmen do not comprehend Frenchmen, nor Frenchmen Englishmen. The different classes of society are enigmas to each other. Nay, often the different members of the same family are mutually incapable of understanding the tastes and pursuits which they severally have. Men who meet each other daily, and who hold regular intercourse with each other, yet live in different worlds of thought and feeling, and each is often content to remain in tranquil ignorance of any other world than his own. Sympathy, then, generally requires the stimulus of a powerful motive to develop it. We are apt to assume that it is a matter of character and disposition. This is not often the case: mere nature leaves man a self-seeking, self-contemplating animal, with little or no interest in his brother man. Nature at best yields in some favoured cases the raw material of sympathy, but education is not alone sufficient to perfect it. Education may make men large-minded; but a cold intelligence directed like the ray of a polar sun upon a human life is a very different thing from sympathy. Genuine sympathy is beyond all else the creation of a religious conviction. When man's life is seen in the light of eternity and in the light of the Cross; when the unmeasured capacities of every human soul for happiness and for woe are realised, each human life is invested forthwith with genuine and extraordinary interest. All that is not evil in man's intelligence and his heart is interesting because it is human; it is interesting to the Christian who feels the awfulness and the blessedness of human life *per se*. This sympathy resided in its perfection in our Incarnate Lord. Of His earlier servants perhaps St. Paul is the most conspicuous example of its complete development; read his Epistles, and you will note that sympathy is his characteristic gift; mark the circumstances of his ministerial and missionary action, and you will be convinced that sympathy is a leading element of his spiritual power.

Without sympathy, religious influence is scarcely possible. "If you wish me to weep," said the heathen poet, "you must first grieve yourself." We may not deal with men as units composing a mass, or as machines, or as anything else or less than separate centres of life. Each human being is worth the most careful study and attention, and to get at his real nature is impossible unless you will note and consult its individualising peculiarities. He has forms of thought, under-currents and streams of affection, warps and weaknesses of will; he is a creature of habit, and habit has crystallised around him in forms which you can observe and count upon. You can attract him by a sympathy of which he will acknowledge the delicacy and the force, but unless you do so you will not touch his real self. Unless you do so, you and he may have public official relations with each other, but you will live in two different worlds. You might as well at once speak two different languages and pass your lives in different hemispheres. Yet to sympathise perfectly even with one man is no easy matter, especially when sympathy is a moral effort and not a thoughtless impulse, when it has a purpose, when it draws a line between good and evil, and holds its impetuosity well in check. And to sympathise with a class, with a parish, with men and women, of many ages and stations, and degrees of culture and degrees of goodness, to rejoice with them that do rejoice, and to weep with them that weep, to have in the eye and on the lip the ever-ready shade of expression which marks the keen perception of the soul within: this is a great, a most precious gift; it is a work of the Holy Spirit; it is a power supernaturally communicated from the world-embracing Heart of Jesus to the heart of the servant who reflects His charity while he carries His commission.

III.

"Ye shall receive power." Dear brethren, at this momentous hour, fold to your inmost hearts this promise of our gracious Master. See in these His words a *ground of confidence*. Who are we men that, left to ourselves, we should dare to speak of Him and for Him to our fellow-sinners? How unpardonable were the impertinence of my daring to address this congregation this morning from this pulpit, unless I were supported by the conviction that I have my Master's authority for doing so, and that He is pledged to strengthen those who bear His message! Ay, brethren, we need not scruple to be bold in His strength. No clerical duty would be tolerable to a man of modesty and sense who supposed himself to be acting in his own strength, and putting forth his own ideas; no clerical duty can give any anxiety to those who know that they are sent by Jesus Christ Himself, and who are sure that He will make good His word for all who in simple sincerity place themselves at His disposal.

"Ye shall receive power." See here a stimulus to *continuous effort*. You believe that you receive a gift from Heaven; you dare not bury it, however gracefully and decently, out of sight; you are a trustee, and you are bound to make the most of the fund which you administer in the interest of others. There is a mighty motive to conscientious work in the belief that you are intrusted with a delegated endowment, and you do well often to recur to it. The time will surely come when you will fall back upon the sense of possessing this gift of power as a source of refreshment and of life. It may often be your duty to engage in the holiest services when your heart is cold; to expound the Word of God when it says nothing to you, and you fear that your words, if they are to have force at all, must be an insincere transcript of your languid thought; to visit the poor, the sorrow-stricken, the dying, when within you there is no voice to utter more than the chilling formalities, which mean, and which pass for, worse than nothing; to hold to faith, to duty, to principle, when the tide of popular feeling around you, and your own feeble will within, points to surrender and to betrayal even of very sacred interests. At these times it will help you to remember that you have received power. Be sure that it is really there. Stir up the dormant gift that is in you through the laying on of hands. Rekindle, by faith in the reality of your Orders, the fervour with which you received His Blessing from the Pierced Hands of Jesus.

Once more, see in these words a preservative *against the snare of spiritual self-conceit*. It may be God's good pleasure to pour a special blessing on your work, to give you an access to the intelligence and to the conscience of men which He denies to others. And you may be tempted for a moment to forget that you have nothing that you have not received, and that you did not create the instrument with which you consciously wield empire over the hearts of your brethren. You may be tempted to convert the gifts of grace into some paltry equivalent of financial or social capital; to seek, on the strength of heavenly capacities, mere professional advancement, or, while avoiding this coarser temptation, to revel secretly in the perilous sense of a spiritual ascendency. What is this but to rob the Fountain of all Grace of His rights and of His honour, and to dim the very finest gold of His kingdom with the soil and baseness of an earthly instinct? Believe simply that the Gift is His, and you will be saved from claiming or treating it as your own. How encouraging, how stimulating, how chastening is this gracious promise! "Ye shall receive power." O Merciful and Almighty Redeemer, ever present in Thy Church beneath, as on Thy Throne in heaven; make good Thy word in this our hour of expectation and of weakness: that each one of Thy servants here gathered may be in spirit and power a prophet of Thee the Highest, to go before Thy Face to prepare Thy ways, to give knowledge of salvation unto Thy people for the remission of their sins, through the tender mercy of our God; whereby Thou, the Dayspring from on high, hast visited us, to give light to them that sit in darkness and in the shadow of death, and to guide our feet into the way of peace.[1]

[1] St. Luke i. 76-79.

SERMON VI.

FATALISM AND THE LIVING GOD.[1]

PSALM viii. 4.

What is man, that Thou art mindful of him?

DAVID here touches upon a thought, which is among the very deepest that can take shape in the mind of man, yet which in this or some kindred form must occur, and that frequently, to any man who really thinks at all. David, as it seems, is still a wandering shepherd: he is keeping his flock at night on the hills near Bethlehem. He looks up at the bright starlit sky of the East, and he bethinks himself of the interval that parts the Creator of all those worlds from the race of mankind, from his own insignificant personal life.

> "I will consider the heavens,
> Even the work of Thy fingers,
> The moon and the stars
> Which Thou hast ordained:
> What is man,
> That Thou art mindful of him?
> And the son of man,
> That Thou visitest him?"

David does not raise the question whether it is possible for so Magnificent a Being as God to take care and notice of so puny a creature as man. No Psalmist of Israel had any doubt about that. Read David's Psalms, read the songs of Asaph and of later composers, and mark how

[1] Preached at the Ordination of the Bishop of Salisbury, in Salisbury Cathedral, on the Seventeenth Sunday after Trinity, September 23, 1866.

deeply they are all and each persuaded of the truth of that relation of God to His creatures which we call His Providence. Observe, for instance, the tenor of some Psalms which have occurred in the daily services of the last week. In the hundred-and-fourth Psalm God's Providence is traced in its bearing on the whole natural world, on the atmospheric influences around us, on the plants and trees which beautify the earth, on the lower creatures, on the beasts of prey, on the monsters of the deep. Elsewhere, as in the hundred-and-fifth Psalm, the Providence of God is exhibited in its relation to the history of Israel. The covenant made with the patriarchs, the imprisonment and elevation of Joseph, the sojourn of Jacob and his sons in Egypt, the deliverance of Israel from Egypt by the ministry of Moses at the Exodus, are reviewed as so many illustrations of God's constant and protecting care. Or again, in the hundred-and-sixth Psalm, God's Providence is set forth in its alternate phases of judgment and mercy: the sins of Israel in the wilderness, the provocation at the Red Sea, the lust for the quails, the public jealousy of the authority of Moses, the worship of the idol-calf, the murmuring in the tents, the idolatry of Baal-peor, the angering at the waters of strife, the culpable leniency towards and intimacy with the Canaanites, leading to the Moloch sacrifices, are successively traced in their several relations to the Mind of God, expressing Itself, now in punishment, now in forgiveness. Perhaps God's Providence is nowhere pictured so vividly in the Psalter as in the hundred-and-seventh Psalm, which apparently describes the vicissitudes of various parties of the Jews, when returning to the Holy City after the dispersion occasioned by the Babylonish captivity. God it was Who had led some hungry and despairing wanderers home from Egypt across the pathless wilderness.[1] God it was Who had delivered another

[1] Ps. cvii. 4-7.

band of prisoners that lay in darkness and the shadow of death, in the dungeons of Babylon: He it was Who had Himself broken the gates of brass, and smitten the bars of iron in sunder.[1] God it was Who had taken pity upon a party of sick exiles, enfeebled probably by forced labours or by uncongenial climates, so that their soul abhorred all manner of meat, and they were even hard at death's door.[2] It was He that had calmed the stormy Mediterranean, on whose waves a ship's company returning to Palestine had "mounted up to heaven, and gone down to the depths," so "that their soul melted away because of the trouble." God had brought them to the haven where they would be.[3] God too would again restore to the impoverished land its ancient blessings:[4] but His providential care must be duly and constantly acknowledged.[5] It would be impossible to exhaust this great subject in connection with the Psalter; every Psalmist, almost every Psalm, in some way, does homage to God's Providence: and David, as the chief of Psalmists, if possible, more than others. Whether David is referring to his own early history, or making plans for the future of Israel, or going forth to war against the heathen; whether he feels himself surrounded by dark conspiracies, or is triumphing over foes who have threatened his destruction; whether he is rejoicing in the bounties poured around him, or writhing under a sense of his own guilt and ingratitude; —of one truth he is always sure, that the living, the personal God is mindful of His servant, keeping him as the apple of an eye, hiding him under the shadow of those eternal wings, guiding him with counsel, that He may after that receive him into glory. The God of David is David's hope and fortress, his castle and Deliverer, his Defender, in Whom he resolves persistently to trust.

[1] Ps. cvii. 10-14. [2] Ibid. 17-20. [3] Ibid. 23-30.
[4] Ps. cvii. 35-42. [5] Ibid. 43.

Fatalism and the Living God. 175

David's God is not merely above, He is around and within His worshipper. He sits indeed upon the throne of judgment, clouds and darkness are round about Him, and He is greatly to be feared in the council of the the saints; but He is also about David's path and about his bed, and spying out all his ways; He is mingling, as if with the intimate sympathy of a human friend, in the household cares, in the personal and spiritual joys and griefs of the sweet Psalmist of Israel.

David, then, does not inquire whether God is or is not mindful of mankind. He is sure of God's mindfulness, but it excites his marvel as he reflects on it. The posture of his thought in this Psalm is not one of scepticism, but of believing wonder. Yet his words may fairly suggest to our minds the general subject of God's providential action, although the subject altogether outruns the words. We have here a matter of such intrinsic and capital importance that, even on so solemn and exceptional an occasion as the present, it may be held to be entitled to our special consideration.

The Collects of the Church during the weeks through which we have lately been passing dwell on various sides and aspects of the Providence of God. In one Collect, God's never-failing Providence is asserted to govern all things in heaven and earth; and, therefore, we ask Him to put away from us all hurtful things, and to give us those things which be profitable for us.[1] Again, the general action of God's Providence is described in the statements, that God "declareth His Almighty power most chiefly in showing mercy and pity,"[2] and that "He is more ready to hear than we to pray, and is wont to give more than either we desire or deserve."[3] A specific form

---
[1] Collect for 8th Sunday after Trinity.
[2] Collect for 11th Sunday after Trinity.
[3] Collect for 12th Sunday after Trinity.

of that action, bearing upon the kingdom of the Redemption, is a "perpetual mercy," which is invoked that it may "keep" the Church of God;[1] or again, it is a continual "pity," ready to "cleanse and defend" her.[2] Without God's Presence the frailty of man cannot but fall;[3] without His succour the Church herself cannot continue in safety.[4] Of this Providential action, " grace," that is, not any mere barren favour,—a thing inconceivable on the part of the All-Good God,—but an actual power working in us, in other words, the direct energy of the Holy Ghost applying to the Redeemed the Human Nature and the Merits of Christ, is the highest possible expression. And on this day we pray that "grace" may be given to us in both its forms; in its lesser prevenient form, by which it courts, as it were, the obedience of our wills; and in its full co-operative or efficacious form, in which it braces and nerves us during the struggle and process of action, "furthering us," as we act, "with a continual help" from heaven. We pray to-day that this "grace of God may always prevent and follow us, and make us continually to be given to all good works.[5] Such a prayer obviously implies the very highest assertion of the doctrine of a Divine Providence. It implies a Providence which sustains us no less than It protects us; a Providence which touches the inmost life of the soul, while It guards and tends the outward life of the body.

The Church Services, then, of the current season might alone guide us to the truth suggested by the Psalmist; but there is, as it seems to me, an independent reason for some attempt to touch upon it at the present time. During the past year we have been witnesses of, it may

[1] Collect for 15th Sunday after Trinity.
[2] Collect for 16th Sunday after Trinity.
[3] Collect for 15th Sunday after Trinity.
[4] Collect for 16th Sunday after Trinity.
[5] Collect for 17th Sunday after Trinity.

be that some of us have been at least indirectly sufferers by, a series of occurrences calculated necessarily to arrest public attention, and to stir the deeper thoughts of men. A murrain upon our cattle, a pestilence carrying death into our homes, a great continental war, threatening at one time to become absolutely European in its range, and a political ferment more serious than has been known for many years in England, have already marked the present year. And even now a plague of rain and waters at the harvest season threatens our poor with high prices, if not with actual famine, during the coming winter. Circumstances such as these brace the faith of a people, or they draw forth into the sunlight the latent scepticism which is preying upon its life. And the public comments upon such events as these show in what currents the thoughts of men are now running. Do they not appeal, my brethren, very solemnly to us, as to the watchmen who stand, or who are presently to stand, upon the towers of the Holy City of God, that we may note the varying signs of that night of this earthly life, which must precede the dawn of the Eternal Morning ? Must we not accurately observe, and, after our measure of grace, deal with, such features of contemporary opinion as bear upon the honour and the rights of God ? For there are times when souls, too, are visited or threatened by epidemic disorders; there are times when we see hanging over the thought of a class or of a nation some murky cloud charged with a prodigious fallacy, with a gigantic misconception; these are times when the very atmosphere of thought around us is impregnated with poison, and when nothing but the utmost precautions of faith can save men's souls alive. And if this language be deemed too emphatic to describe anything that may have been observed of late in England; at least, my brethren, I make bold to say, that the manner in which the great events of this year

M

have been discussed in many quarters, betrays the prevalence of a great spiritual disease. That disease is an insensibility to the action of God in His own world, and especially upon the destinies of man. A view of life and death, of success and of reverses, of physical occurrences, and of human activities, which professes to be complete without God, which leaves God out of the question, which perhaps ignores God with quiet deliberation, or which uses the name of God, if at all, from a sentimental feeling of propriety, rather than with the practical motive of tracing events up to their One First Cause; is not such a view as this a serious spiritual disease? is it not, when widely accepted, nothing less than a calamity of the very greatest magnitude? And yet this, or something of the kind at least, appears to be threatening us now and here in England. Two or three writers of genius and popularity among the most educated classes of Englishmen, represent lines of thought which have for some time been steadily making way, and which simply ignore altogether the Presence and the action of a living God. The influence of these writers is seen in the language of a much larger circle: it is observable in that great periodical literature which is now so powerful an agency in forming the convictions of the English people. And, if we look below the educated and half-educated classes, the broad results of this generally godless habit of mind, as distinct from the intellectual processes by which those results are reached, are distributed most widely even among the humblest classes of our countrymen. It would certainly be a mistake to suppose that the danger in question affects only the educated classes; since in the social system of England there is a perpetual infiltration of thought going on from class to class; and this, too, more rapidly now than at any former period of history. The consequence is that the substance of any prominent line or result of thought in a particular class soon becomes in a greater or less degree the common property of the people. The philosophical (so to term it) and the popular form of the habit of thought now before us have this broad feature in common,—that they both dispense with, if they do not deliberately exclude, the active government and interference of God in the affairs of the world and of man. And if for this general mental tendency we must, for convenience' sake, find some general name, we shall do it no particular injustice by calling it Fatalism. It is the substitution of a blind destiny of some kind or other for the loving intelligent action of a living Personal God.

Fatalism, then, is undoubtedly a formidable power; for, quite independently of any arguments which it may be able to produce, its strength rests mainly on that dull, brutal insensibility to spiritual truth, which marks the life of a great number of animalised men. In its more developed and consistent form, Fatalism denies that any Supreme Being exists. In its more ordinary form, it admits the existence of God, but it empties that sacred Name of all the meaning which it has for Christians, by denying to God any freedom of action. Fatalism is not one of those speculative errors that involve no practical results. Fatalism eats out the very heart and root of religion. The action of Fatalism upon the soul may be observed principally in two separate effects. First, it destroys all belief in the power of prayer. Who would pray to an impotent, dormant God? to a name, to a shadow, to a something banished by the decree of the fatalist thinkers to a distant heaven, even when they still consent to recognise in the place of Deity the existence of the shadow or of the name? *Cui bono?* What is the good of prayer if there is no Being in existence who is free to answer it? Prayer presupposes—not a god imprisoned by a network of fixed laws—but a God Who is able and willing to interfere actively, if He sees good, on behalf of His clients. Prayer is an elaborate waste of time, unless it be addressed to a living, working God; to a God Who is as free now as He was on the day of creation; to a God Who is the Master and not the slave of nature, that is to say, of the work of His hands. If prayer cannot really touch the Divine Will, if prayer is after all only a high sort of poetry, well devised to act upon the mind of the worshipper, but having no real weight and currency in heaven, practical men will cease to pray. They do cease to pray, when they become fatalists. And this leads us to observe a second effect of Fatalism:—it is in the long run destructive of virtue. Virtue, as the word implies, is the force of a free will rising against the pressure of passion and circumstances, and expressing itself in right action. But what place is there for virtue, if after all man is but a reed floating helplessly along upon the torrent of impulse and of circumstance, the prey and sport of a host of resistless forces and laws around him? Even if a fatalist believes it to be his interest on the whole to be virtuous, self-interest is after all no match for the vehemence and impetuosity of passion. Passion sooner or later in such a man must sweep all barriers before it, and when passion has done its perfect work of moral and mental degradation and ruin, the fatalist will whisper to himself that there is no such thing as making head against natural inclinations or outward events; he will argue that it is folly for a man to attempt to shape or to direct his course either with or without any aid from on high; he will maintain that a man is inevitably what he is, just as trees and beasts are inevitably what they are; man, he will hold, is not the moral handiwork and nursling of a Father's Will;

man is but the helpless product and plaything of a heartless, lifeless mechanism of the Universe.

We shall then, it may be, do something to the purpose, if without attempting to deal at all exhaustively with so vast a problem, we contrast some leading lines of fatalist thought with those facts of Christian truth to which they stand in most direct, energetic, and irreconcilable opposition.

I.

Fatalism points first of all to the visible Universe, to its vast system of "laws" and "forces" under which we human beings live, and of which we form a part. Look, says the fatalist, towards the heavens, or pass your eye over the surface of the earth, and everywhere you will find the presence of law, with its undeviating action, its strict, absolute, invariable rule. All moves, all lives, all grows, all wanes, all decays, all dies, in obedience to a fixed order. In the Middle Ages, we are assured, men might fail to see the truth and the meaning of this. Early civilisations, like children, may hear the angry voice of the Eternal Justice in the storm and in the thunder; or they may welcome the smile of an unseen Father's love in the flowers and in the sunshine. But we of the nineteenth century, whom science has taken by the hand, must resign the beautiful poetry of that primitive stage of thought. We are to hear in the thunder, we are to trace in the bright day, or in the flower-bed, only the energy of laws, of laws of electricity, of laws of light, of laws of vegetation. For us the earth must but yield the results of uniform forces, the range and action of which we are gradually exploring, arranging, systematising: for us (I quote the words of a fatalistic writer) the heavens can no more declare the glory of God, they only declare the glory of Newton and of La Place.

Both on earth and in heaven a vast machinery of forces is working, above us and around us, irresistibly, silently, eternally; and we men are at once the products and the slaves of its action. Our individual births, our bodily forms, the vicissitudes of our lives, and of our deaths, are all alike determined by inevitable laws, just as truly as are the movements of the heavenly bodies; and to suppose that we are each one of us the objects of a particular plan, or care, or foresight on the part of a Supreme Being, is said to be a superstition which should have been quite killed and buried out of sight, long before our reaching this advanced stage of the world's intellectual history.

So speaks openly, or where it dare not speak, so hints covertly, in this our day, in many a learned coterie, during many an after-dinner conversation, in many a magazine, in many a newspaper, the spirit of scientific Fatalism. Nor is this only the language of the learned. The same idea in a ruder form is very widely diffused, and few men altogether escape from its blighting breath. Are we not all of us at times, in an indirect manner, subject to this depressing influence? Has it not occurred to us that, supposing "Nature" to be of a truth the plastic creature of our Father in heaven, her smiles and her frowns ought to be in keeping with the alternations of the inward life of His children? It may have been that we were sad or sick even unto death, while the seasons pursued in tranquil unfeeling indifference their even march of still beauty or of majestic tumult. The sun which shone upon our joy of yore, shines to-day, it may be, with yet more scorching brilliancy upon our sorrow; and the face of earth and heaven seems to our bleeding hearts to meet us with the same glance of an unmoved irony, as we assist in our gladness at the bridal party, or stand in tears by the side of the open grave. Forgetting that "Nature" is God's voice to all His creatures, we have, perhaps, in our little selfish estimate of her mission, yielded for a moment to the dreadful thought that she is but the garb of a dark lifeless destiny, which hangs around and imprisons our personal life; and we have said to ourselves that, instead of being children fondled by the love of a tender Parent, we are in truth only the eccentric fruitage of some vital "force," that we are lying for a brief span hapless and uncared for, ready to be crushed by the cruel machinery of heartless and resistless law which gave us birth.

And yet if we will, we may prove to ourselves, by a very simple experiment, that this conception of a system of resistless law, absolutely killing out all the freedom of the life of Individual Will, is but a creation of our diseased imaginations. Why does a stone lie on the surface of the ground instead of flying off into space? Every boy will answer, that the stone is held down by the "law" of gravitation. But if I stoop down, and pick up the stone, I suspend, I violate, I defy that law. My will, then, is a force which, in the act of picking up the stone, sensibly asserts its right to set at defiance one of the most powerful and well-ascertained "laws of nature." My will is a power, it seems, of quite another order from the power of natural law. Within certain limits, and of its own mere motion and caprice, my will can break in upon this assumed invariability of nature which lies around it; my will can secure and enhance its consciousness of its own existence, by its masterful defiance of the observed "laws" of nature upon which it innovates. And surely if my feeble created will is capable of this, I am right in ascending in thought to a Will above me, to a Will Almighty, irresistible, supreme. Such a Will is the only conceivable explanation of the existence of my own. Such a Will must be infinitely superior to the reign of natural laws, since even my own weak will is within certain limits ascertainably superior to them. Now and then, for grave purposes, such a supreme majestic Will may be reasonably expected to assert Its existence. History says that It has done so by a series of events which entirely outrage our conception of natural law, and which we call miracles. Of course there have been many false miracles, but if all had been false, faith in miracles would have died out from among men long ago. The false miracles naturally result from, and they really imply the existence of true miracles. And true proven miracles have this general value, as distinct from the more particular ends of their being severally wrought; they make manifest before the eyes of men, the subsisting freedom of the living God. They show that God is not the slave of "nature," but that "nature" is the slave and creature of God. They show that, if "nature" ordinarily sets forth that harmony and order in which God delights, by observing "the law" which He has "given" "that it should not be broken"; yet that, upon occasion, a deliberate violation of natural order has an effect analogous to the insistence upon a forgotten legal right among men. Miracle simply asserts God's right to act with unfettered freedom in the world which He has made. A proved miracle, then, destroys the fatalistic inference from the presumed invariableness of natural law. If it is certain that Jesus Christ literally, and as a matter of historical fact, rose[1] from the grave, then it is certain also, that however regular, and in the main unvaried may be the Great Creator's modes of working; there He is behind that screen-work of orderly beauty which so arrests and impresses our imagination; there

[1] It is remarkable that the specific evidence for the Resurrection is rarely or never met, simply on its own merits, by infidel writers: they start with an *à priori* assumption of its impossibility, and then try to bring the evidence into harmony with the assumption. For a "famous" sample of this, see M. Renan's recent work, *Les Apôtres*, chapters 1, 2.

He is, in all His living liberty and power of action; able to interfere, and at times actually interfering, on behalf of the wellbeing of His creatures; mindful, practically and sensibly mindful, of the general and special needs of man.

But beyond the miracles recorded by history, there is a truth which, even more imperatively than miracles, shatters the fatalistic conception of nature as a system of strictly resistless laws. Miracles suggest, they lead our minds back and up to, that miracle of miracles, that wonder compared with which all else is easy and obvious; they lead us up to the fact of a creation out of nothing. Both the Jewish and the Christian faiths repose on a belief in One God, the Maker of heaven and earth. The Bible begins by telling us that in the beginning God created the heavens and the earth. Now here it is that the fatalistic thinkers divide into two classes,—those who deny the existence of God point-blank, and those who still profess to believe in Him, while they deny His freedom of action. For the statement that God did create the Universe out of nothing is either true or it is false. If it is false, then men are only using words which blind themselves and others in still professing to believe in the existence of God. If God did not create the Universe out of nothing, then He is not what we mean by God; He is not the One Self-existing, Self-sustaining Being. If He did not create all that is besides Himself, then something must have existed everlastingly alongside of Himself, and independent of Himself: He must have been accompanied by uncreated matter or by uncreated force, or by both, which, on the supposition, are just as self-existing as He is Himself. To identify this self-existing matter or force with the essence of God is to annihilate Him outright; since it is to deny the very first truth of His nature, namely, that He is a purely simple uncompounded spiritual Essence. And this is what is done by the most " advanced " fatalistic thinkers; they believe in the eternity of matter and in the eternity of force, and in the eternity of nothing whatever else except matter and force. According to this school, all the very highest forms of the life of thought and feeling among men are only so many results of the action of "force" upon "matter." Certainly the attribution of such an effect as the genius of Shakespeare, to such a cause as the action of a blind force upon a little chemical matter, is more entirely in contradiction with the whole range of our experience than any mystery of Divine revelation whatever; and yet this is the creed of that logical and extreme Fatalism which calls itself Materialism, and which denies that God exists at all. If God does really exist, then He must have created all that is; He must have summoned the material of the Universe into being out of nothing; He must have imposed form and order upon the material thus placed by Himself at His own disposal. In doing this He must have been free to have left it all undone, or else some force would be in existence which is superior to Himself. But if He created by such a free exercise of His will, surely it follows that He can interfere with His creation; unless He can be proved to have deliberately abdicated His right of interference in favour of some other power: unless He has delegated it to some impersonal viceroy, such as "nature" is assumed to be by the less "advanced" school of fatalistic theorists. Need I say that the supposition of such a delegation is as opposed to accurate philosophical thought, as it is to the statements of revealed truth? It is an awkward expedient, devised to reconcile a shadowy theism with a fatalistic conception of "nature." The order which may be observed in the natural world is undoubtedly a matter of fact, having its origin in that highest order which is the Life of the Creator. But the highest order is also the highest freedom; and the substantial truth which keeps the idea of "laws of nature" in its proper place in the mind of a Christian, and which prevents his exaggerating it into a denial of God's liberty of action, is the truth of a creation out of nothing. Deny creation, and in reason you must deny the existence of God. Admit creation, and in reason you must admit the perpetuated action and freedom of the living Creator. The laws of nature themselves are but an orderly manifestation of that action and freedom : they are, to speak more accurately, abstract ideas of our own minds, not having any substantial being or shape outside our minds, and arising within our minds upon our observing the beautiful regularity of God's ordinary working in the world around us. But this regularity exists from moment to moment only, because the Author of "nature" wills it to exist; and nothing can be less true than that the general order and symmetry of God's active care and providences towards men, is a proof that He is not "mindful" of man.

II.

But Fatalism falls back upon a second line of argument; it pleads man's insignificance when we look at his place in the Universe. Granted, it says, that God is a living and working Being; granted that He can and does in some sense act upon the work which His Hands have made; yet is it conceivable that so insignificant a creature as man should be the object of His especial care ? Such an illusion of human conceit, we are told, was pardonable in ages when the earth was seriously believed to be the centre of the Universe. But the Copernican system of the heavens has long superseded the Ptolemaic, and our present knowledge of the Universe would have excited the marvel of Copernicus himself. We now know that the planet on which we live is but one of the smallest satellites of one of the least important of the countless suns that throng infinite space. "The milky way alone contains more than twenty million suns, and the milky way is but an island in the great ocean of the Universe." At distances which the imagination cannot strain itself to picture, the most remote fields of space are filled with worlds, filled with solar systems, compared with which our own is insignificant. Is it conceivable then that this world and its inhabitants is really an object of particular care to the Infinite Creator? Or must not such an impression die out along with those narrow-conceptions of the Universe which were prevalent some centuries ago, and which were more truly in harmony with so exaggerated an estimate of the importance of the human race?

So argues Fatalism; but what does this argument really involve? It manifestly proceeds on a presumption that material bulk is that which merits and enlists the attention of the Supreme Being. Whereas nothing can be less true than that material size is a measure of the real importance of an object, even within the field of human observation. The smallest creature that partakes in organic life is really higher in the scale of being than the largest inorganic mass; a daisy is really a nobler thing, and has in it more of the vital force of God, than a granite mountain. The most extended regions of space are as nothing compared to the little body or to the little spot which is the seat or the scene of mind. Two-thirds of the earth's surface is water, yet no naturalist would seriously maintain that the earth was intended chiefly to be the abode of whales. Of the remaining third, much is uninhabitable by man; and yet how true is the thought which runs through the eighth Psalm, namely, that man is lord of "Nature," and God's viceroy over it, although he is, as to size, but as a vanishing point when compared with the great heavenly bodies! Man, though encased in his small body, is in himself a spirit able to compass a world: and the material size of this earth on which man lives has nothing whatever to do with its real claim upon the attention of its Creator. If it had, we might agree in the fatalistic conclusion; but we should perhaps have still to inquire how many quadrillions of cubic miles a planet must have in point of bulk in order to fit it for being the object of a special Providence, or still more for being the scene of an incarnation of the Supreme Being.

What is man, that Thou art mindful of him? The Bible answers this question by saying, that man is a being made in the image of God. Man is the highest point of visible created life; in man created life reaches its climax, as far as the world of sense is concerned. The lower gradations of life are summed up in him; he is mineral, vegetable, and animal, all in one. His body may be dissolved by chemistry into mineral matter; yet he grows and is nourished like the vegetable; he feels and he moves like the animal. He shares in the life of instinct and sensation common to the whole animal world; but the qualities which, in the animal world, are portioned out among different races of animals and individual creatures, are in man united into one compendious and majestic whole. But, further, man has that which severs him from all, even the most intelligent, of the lower creatures: he has not merely a sensitive but a reasonable soul. All the powers of his body and of his mind are subject to this the great governing power within him, the real centre and seat of his being. The reasonable soul is the sphere of that within each one of us which is shared by no other being, and which each of us names "I." In other words, it is the seat of personality. We become conscious of the existence of a personal life by two distinct processes; by conscious thought, and by acts of free will. Animals have sensations, but thought, reflective thought, never. Man not merely thinks, but he knows that he thinks; he not merely thinks, but he can put his thought into the physical shape of sound; he can use language. He thinks not only about himself and the necessities of his life, but he can ascend to general truths; he can enter into the collective mental life of his race; he can conceive in his mind such vast ideas as the idea of God and the idea of eternity. He can turn his thought in upon himself, and he can make his own existence a subject of his thought. In this he is utterly unlike any of the lower creatures, and he is a distinct likeness of the Self-contemplating God Who made him. Of man's likeness to God, his free will is another aspect. As man's thought is distinct from the sensation and feeling of the animals, so is man's free will distinct from animal instinct. Man's true acts proceed not from any blind impulse within him, not from any constraining attraction of natural objects around and without him, but from himself, from the consent of his own self-determining will. Every man has within himself a certain point or pivot of freedom which no outward force, no inward emotion, can violate or crush. A man may be influenced by inward motives and by outward circumstances; but the man himself in the inner sanctuary of his free self-governing will decides whether or not to obey these circumstances and motives; they do not will for him, and they cannot oblige him to will against his will. His acts, in short, are his own free choice; and here again he is unlike any of the lower creatures, each and all of which are swayed irresistibly by inward instincts and by outward circumstances; here again, I say, man is like that Infinite, Self-existent, Self-determining Will to Which he owes his existence.

It is, then, sufficient to reply to the Psalmist's question, that man is demonstrably and essentially unlike any other being of which we have sensible experience. Thinking, and knowing that he thinks; willing, and being conscious of his freedom to will or not to will, man sees within himself a form of life which is distinct from and superior to those laws and processes of decay which touch the life of his body, and which carries within itself the secret suspicion of its own immortality. And this suspicion has been heightened—on the one hand by close reflection, on the other, as we Christians know, by revelation—into an absolute certainty. Man, then, in his likeness to God, may have higher claims upon the attention of the Great Creator than millions of suns of the vastest material bulk, but inhabited by no spiritual beings. It may or may not be the case, that our earth, although certainly not the material centre, is really the vital centre of the Universe; it may or may not be true that in other worlds, as according to one conjecture on the planet Mars, there are creatures with a life analogous to our own; it is unpractical to lavish suppositions upon a subject as to which certainty is out of our reach. But this at any rate is certain, that material bulk has nothing to do with eminence in the scale of being, since God Himself is not a huge mass of matter, but a strictly moral and spiritual Essence; and thus it is, that of all the orders of existence which fall under the observation of the senses, man is himself incomparably the highest, as being beyond all others in nearness and likeness to the strictly spiritual God.[1]

III.

But Fatalism will here reproduce the argument which it draws from the insignificance of man in a somewhat modified form. It will grant that God does govern

---

[1] See Dr. Luthardt's *Apologetische Vorträge über die Grundwahrheiten des Christenthums*, pp. 63-65 and 97-101.

and provide for mankind, but only in a general sense. We are told that God deals with great laws and with broad principles, and that it is unworthy of Him, on His throne in heaven, to trouble Himself with petty incidents immeasurably beneath Him, and seriously to go into the details of His government. The general progress of the human race, the great events of history, great inventions, great battles, great revolutions, great famines, earthquakes, pestilences,—these the modified Fatalism will admit to be under, or at least not quite beyond, God's notice and control. But that you and I should presume to think that the Infinite Creator of all those worlds is closely and earnestly interested in all the very humblest incidents of our separate lives; that we should claim His interest; that we should in prayer to Him associate His August Name not merely with the majestic evolutions of His Providence, having their sphere in the centuries, but with the petty joys and sorrows of our personal and domestic life, with our passing anxieties about ourselves and those around us;—this, according to the modified Fatalism, is to exaggerate our personal importance even to the very verge of the ridiculous, while it is to underrate altogether the lofty magnificence of the Great God.

And yet, my brethren, it might be conceded by this school of modified fatalists,—who are, it appears, too much engaged in vindicating the magnificence of God to allow themselves to pray to Him for special mercies,—it might be conceded even by these sensitive objectors, that the honour and greatness of God are sufficiently safe in the keeping of the greatest of the Prophets. When has modern thought mounted upwards more intelligently, more adoringly, towards the greatness of the Infinite God, than did the poetry of the inspired Isaiah? "Who is He," asks the Prophet, "that hath measured the waters in the hollow of His hand, and meted out heaven with the span, and comprehended the dust of the earth in a measure, and weighed the mountains in scales, and the hills in a balance? Who hath directed the Spirit of the Lord, or who hath been His counsellor? ... Behold, the nations are as a drop of a bucket, and are counted as the small dust of the balance: behold, He taketh up the isles as a very little thing. ... All nations before Him are as nothing; and they are counted to Him less than nothing, and vanity. To whom then will ye liken God? or what likeness will ye compare unto Him? ... Lift up your eyes on high, and behold Who hath created all these" (stars), "that bringeth out their host by number: He calleth them all by names, by the greatness of His might, ... not one faileth"[1] (to obey Him).

My brethren, the modified Fatalism itself will admit that it could not more entirely do justice to man's insignificance when compared with the majestic greatness of the Creator. Certainly Isaiah does not fear to look the magnificence of God well in the face: but what is the conclusion which this great Prophet draws from it? "Why sayest thou, O Jacob, and speakest thou, O Israel, My way is hid from the Lord, and my judgment is passed over from my God? Hast thou not known, hast thou not heard, that the everlasting God, the Lord, the Creator of the ends of the earth, fainteth not, neither is weary? ... They that wait upon the Lord shall renew their strength; they shall mount up with wings as eagles; they shall run, and not be weary; and they shall walk, and not faint."[2]

Isaiah then accepts the premise of the modified Fatalism, but he draws a very different conclusion from that of the Fatalist. "God is great," says the Fatalist; "and therefore He will not demean Himself to think of, and to care for us men." "God is great," says the Prophet, "and it

[1] Isa. xl. 12, 13, 15, 17, 18, 26.   [2] *Ibid.* 27-31.

is of the very essence of His greatness that He should 'have respect unto the lowly,' that He should look to and care for each of the puniest creatures of His Hand."

Is the Prophet's inference, think you, a forced or an extreme one? Must a true greatness then necessarily give itself airs, and like some earthly despot, affect, or honestly cultivate a sublime ignorance of all beneath itself, or of all the particular, as distinct from the general interests around it? Is it a dishonour to our Father in Heaven to suppose that His relations to His intelligent creatures are not strictly analogous to the relations which subsist between an Eastern Sultan, or Emperor, and the subject populations around his throne? Or do our truest and most perfect ideas of greatness point in a very opposite direction? What, for instance, is the test of true greatness in the human mind? Compare the mind which can only appreciate broad principles, the general line and bearing of a subject, with the mind which can combine with this grasp of principle a minute knowledge of detail. Which of the two is, I do not say the most practically useful, but the higher in the order of intelligence? Is a poet only or really great, who is so altogether absorbed in the study of the idea and scheme of his poem, as to be entirely careless about its metres, its rhythm, the justice and propriety of its expressions, verse by verse? Is an architect likely to achieve professional success, if he is incessantly occupied in drawing ground-plans and sections of magnificent buildings, but wholly indifferent to the detail of his plans, and so to the amount of labour and material which will be necessary to realise them? Should we not say that such an architect was intellectually deficient as well as practically untrustworthy? On the other hand, what is it that strikes us in the genius of a great sculptor or painter, of a Raffaelle, of a Michael Angelo? Surely this: that the artist can unite to so magnificent a general conception of his subject so careful and elaborate a treatment of its minutest features. Or how does the military genius, say of the First Napoleon, chiefly impress us? Is it not when we find him at one and the same moment planning a campaign which is to range across the Continent of Europe, and yet calculating with the skill of a retail vendor of provisions all the items of his commissariat, the rations of his soldiers, their clothes, their comforts in the camp as their movements in the field? Or in reading Burke, or when listening to one of the great speakers in our Houses of Parliament, must we not see genius in that surprising balance of thought which is maintained between the attractions of general principle and the attractions of minute detail? The orator is too accurate to be vague; yet he is too comprehensive to be petty. He impresses us and carries us with him, first by his felt grasp of and mastery over a great subject, and next by his power—not of condescending to, but—of sympathising with each of its subordinate elements; and we feel his greatness almost sensibly, when, even while the speaker is being carried most impetuously forward by a flash of thought which inspires him with unwonted fervour, he can yet deliberately choose those exact words which most perfectly express all the shades and undulations of his meaning.

Mental greatness, then, as we see it among men, seems to blend a comprehensiveness of view with a minute attention to detail; it is not overcome by the study of particular facts, but still less does it affect to disdain or to dispense with them. Mental greatness unites qualities of mind, which in men of more common mould are found apart: the really great mind perceives at a glance, and keeps its hold upon the two extremities of a chain of thought that connects the broadest of principles with the most minute of its illustrations. And if this be the gift of genius among men, is it altogether otherwise with the Source of genius, with the Eternal Mind of God? If true earthly statesmanship is not merely occupied with abstract principles of government, but has a quick eye to see, and a warm heart to feel for, the actual wants of the people in their daily lives, so that it may protect, and aid, and elevate them by a wise and provident legislation, is it otherwise with Him Whose Image may be traced in all that is really best in the thought of man?

Surely, if anything about Him is certain, it is *this*:—that in virtue of His Infinite Greatness, He unites the widest reach of thought to the most perfect concentration of it upon each detail of His creation; that nothing is so small as to escape the penetrating glance of His Omniscient Love; that literally not one sparrow can fall to the ground without His knowledge; and that, as a matter, not of hyperbole, but of strict fact, the very hairs of our head are all numbered. His knowledge of and care for detail is proportioned to His grasp of principle. Both are infinite. Thus His greatness it is, which makes Him attentive even to the least and lowest of His creatures; His greatness, so far from being an argument in favour of the fatalistic denial of a special Providence, is, when rightly considered, the very truth which imperatively obliges us to believe in it.

IV.

But the Fatalist has a last line of objection: he points to the history of man, to the state of the world, as we actually see it before us. You may argue *à priori*, he says, that God is thus mindful of man, because you say that He ought to be so, in virtue of the terms of His Nature. But see whether your anticipation is borne out by the facts. Do you then trace a clear providential plan in history? Is there no darkness, no confusion, no perplexity in the moral scheme of the annals of the world? What mean those sorrows, leading to no moral fruit that we can trace; those deeds of violence and of blood, followed as it seems by no adequate retribution, yet scattered so thickly throughout the arena of history, as almost to make up its main material? How do you explain those triumphs of injustice, those successes of the unscrupulous, those sudden, crushing misfortunes of the deserving, which meet us in the life of nations as in the life of individuals? Look at the human family scattered throughout the globe, with its vast and accumulating load of crime, with its yet larger burden of suffering, with its inheritance of widespread, vital, uneradicated errors. Do you suppose, he continues, that this vast mass of beings, pursuing each one of them its mysterious destiny, will really illustrate your doctrine of a Providential rule? Ah! you may hear the low deep murmurs of misfortune and of crime, rising from time to time above the din of human voices; you may hear the terrible insinuation, that if there be a God, He is the God of the rich; that if there be a Providence, it is a Providence devoted to the interests of the successful and of the fortunate; that for the mass of men the heaven overhead is but clouds and thick darkness; and that the last conclusion of the man who would look honestly and impartially at the facts of life must be a despair, dignified perhaps by some attempt to make it look like resignation. Even holy men for a moment have felt the pressure of the argument which is urged by Fatalism from the surface appearances of human life. "Lo, these are the ungodly," said one, "these prosper in the world, and these have riches in possession: then I said, Verily I have cleansed my heart in vain, and washed my hands in innocency."

Upon this difficulty let us make two observations.

First, that the world, as we see it, is the world as sin has made it. God did not make the world as it now is. God gave man moral freedom to obey or to disobey Him. This freedom was an essential part of man's dignity. Man has abused that freedom, and along with the resulting moral evil has come its shadow and its effect—mental and physical pain. If you say that God ought not to have risked so much, foreseeing, as He must have foreseen, the issue, you certainly carry the discussion into a region where no prudent man will follow you; few men who believe in God at all will venture to suggest that they personally could have improved upon the handiwork or plans of the Creator. If, however, you can learn that although sin and pain have abounded, they have abounded that in the end grace and joy might much more abound: you will not be disposed to charge God with the abuse which His free creature has made of His bounty, nor will you suggest that the freedom which has been abused had better have been denied.

And a second observation is this : that the past history of man, and the present aspect of the world, are only a very small fragment of a mighty drama. We do not see enough to form a final conclusion on the strength of what we see. Who would think of passing judgment on the merit and plot of one of Shakespeare's plays, after he had read only a scene or a couple of scenes of the first act? And in this world, and now, we follow only a little, a very little, of the mighty drama of human destiny. We see, indeed, enough to be quite certain that we do not see all: we know for certain that the perplexities of the part which we see will be unravelled by the discoveries of the part which we do not see. Dreary and wretched indeed would this life be, if it were our all, if there were no land of reward and retribution beyond the tomb. Here we are, after all, like private soldiers mingling in the fray of a vast battle; we only suspect, we cannot certainly explain in all its detail, the plan of our Commander. The clash of arms, the fury of the charge, the roar of the artillery, the dust, the smoke, the cries of the wounded and of the dying around us, render it impossible that we should make out clearly, now and here, the meaning and drift of each movement, of each advance, of each retreat. We are too immersed in the struggle to form an estimate of its bearings, as we might if we stood aside and looked down on the combatants from some neighbouring height. Still we may guess at, or be informed of the plans of our Captain, if we cannot unfalteringly trace them. And we know Whom we have believed; we know that He sees His way through the difficulties which to us appear insuperable; we are sure that our confidence in Him may be for a while baffled, but cannot in the end prove to have been misplaced. Although even millions of years should pass before we see the full justification of His foresight, we doubt not that He is leading us on to victory, and that the battle of truth and justice and love which He wages against error and wrong and selfishness can ultimately have but one issue, and will not have been fought in vain.

There are dark mysteries (I do not deny it) which hang like clouds around the life of man—mysteries which, like the transmission from sire to son, or through entire races, of bodily sufferings or of moral taints and dispositions to evil, seem, as we gaze at them, to darken for a while the Face of our God. Yet beyond these clouds we may trace, if we will, written in the heavens in letters of fire, the words, "God is love." God is a Moral Being. He is Morality in its highest and sublimest form: in other words, He is Love. If God has ever revealed Himself, He has revealed Himself not as a gigantic material machine, not as an intellect of crushing power, but as a Heart of boundless love. God is Love, but love is not always intelligible : love has its reserves, no less than its disclosures ; love has its periods of silence, as well as its interchange of affection from heart to heart. God is Love, and therefore these dark thoughts about Him, which Fatalism would suggest, are a wrong and an ingratitude. God is Love ; and, therefore, whether I can trace it or not, I am sure that there is a fundamental harmony in all His works, and that the passions, the agitations, the crimes, the agonies which are to be witnessed in the world, are not a chaos of unregulated accidents, not a mere wilderness of sterile misery, but parts of one all-embracing and Divine plan, which is hidden now, but will be seen in its fulness hereafter. Ah! how often in past ages did men long to behold some sensible proof of this truth, which underlies all that causes such perplexity to human thought, which, once mastered, makes all tolerable, and which will fully explain all hereafter—this blessed truth, that God is Love. For ages men longed for some sign, some satisfaction, some rending of the heavens, some enrichment of the earth. Entire generations of men despondingly confessed with David, "Thy way is in the sea, and Thy paths in the great waters, and Thy footsteps are not known."[1] Entire generations of men cried out with Job, "Oh that I knew where I might find Him, that I might come even unto His seat."[2] Entire generations of men confidently pleaded, with Isaiah, "Drop down, ye heavens, from above, and let the skies pour down righteousness : let the earth open, and let it bring forth salvation."[3]

And those longings, those plaints, those aspirations have been answered. For Christians, the Life of Jesus Christ is at once the standing proof and the central fact of Divine Providence. Our earth has witnessed One Life,

[1] Ps. lxxvii. 19.   [2] Job xxiii. 3.   [3] Isa. xlv. 8.

of Which love was the informing soul, the principle of Its every word and act; and He Who led that Life proclaimed Himself an actual Incarnation of God, and asserted that in seeing Him men had seen the Father.[1] God then has really been mindful of man, mindful of man's dignity, and mindful of man's misery and degradation; since He has set His seal upon the one, and He has relieved the other even by the Incarnation of His Blessed Son. In the Incarnation we contemplate the Divine Providence, not as an abstract quality, but in a concrete embodiment, and beneath the Features of a Man. God has not merely thought about us, He has not merely cared for us, He has not merely protected and sustained and guided us by His invisible hand; He has put on a visible Form, that He might inflict the fact of His Providence upon our dull earthly senses of hearing and of sight; He has shattered with tender but resistless force the fatalistic pleas, which would draw a veil between Himself and the souls of His creatures. When Jesus fed the famishing multitudes, when Jesus calmed the angry waves, when Jesus raised from its tomb the putrid corpse, above all, when at the dawn of morning Jesus Himself sprang from the grave, wherein the selfish hate of man had laid Him, He annihilated the dark suspicion, that the laws of nature, observable around us, are a network of tyrannical forces, which cramp the liberty of our God, and against which we men fretfully dash ourselves in vain. Deny Christ's Resurrection, and you do not merely break altogether with even the most shadowy species of Christianity: you invalidate the laws of historical evidence. Admit Christ's Resurrection, and you admit a fact which guards for ever in your thought the sacred truth of God's liberty of action, against the tyranny of that false conception which would destroy the freedom both of God and

[1] St. John xiv. 9.

man. Nor is this all : for it is impossible with the eye upon a Life of such manifest beauty, and enhanced by such miracles as that of Jesus of Nazareth, to yield to the idea that man is too puny a being, and that he inhabits too insignificant a world, to attract the attention of the great Creator. The Life of Jesus, passed in one little province of the East, passed among the lowest orders of society, begun in a manger, and crushed out of Him on a public gibbet,—yet withal illuminated, as even His enemies could not but own, with a light that was not of this world, and guarded and restored to him by a power, which the world could neither resist nor gainsay,—the Life of Jesus rebukes the idea that man is too microscopically small to be noticed by God. If Bethlehem was not the least among the thousands of Judah, by reason of the Governor Who should thence proceed to rule God's people Israel, neither is this our earth, though it be one of the smallest planets of one of the least important suns, less than the greatest of the heavenly bodies in that it has really been the scene of an Incarnation of the great Creator. And when our Incarnate Saviour made Himself a Member of a human family, and drew around Him special friends whom He admitted to various degrees of intimacy, and shed His gifts of healing, of consolation, of enfranchisement from moral and bodily evil, first upon one, and then upon another, of the human sufferers who thronged around Him; He represented palpably before the eyes of men, the action of God's particular Providence upon each separate human life; He taught us that our Father deals with us not through any delegated mechanical medium of general laws, but (even though He seems to act unvaryingly) with all the tenderness of a strictly personal relationship, maintained with each one of His creatures. Ay, the Life of Jesus meant yet more than this. When He had reached the lowest depth of His humiliation; when with His bleeding Brow,

His Eyes reddened with tears, His Ears filled with insults and blasphemies, His Hands and Feet pierced and torn, His Life-blood slowly ebbing away, He hung upon the cross in all the shame and agony of His dying hour; He really rose high above the perplexed and tangled maze of man's life and man's history, as the revelation of the hidden Providence of God. Surely in that supreme moment He rebukes the argument against God's Providence, which is based on the unequal distribution of human sorrow in the world. He is the perfect Saint, and yet He is the Greatest of sufferers. He is "fairer than the children of men, full of grace are His Lips"; and yet "His Visage is so marred more than any man, and His Form more than the sons of men." Oh! you who dream that your lot is exceptionally hard; that you suffer while the enemies of God prosper; that you suffer, and none around you comprehends your inner load of unmentioned sorrow; that you suffer, and Heaven itself seems deaf to your appeal for one, only one glance of compassion; look you to the Cross of the Man of sorrows for an explanation, and for a consecration of your woe. Rising above the crowd that surges beneath Him, and that represents the sins and the sorrows of the world, Jesus Crucified is the crowning revelation of the Justice, of the Holiness, and of the Love of that Infinite Being Who has given us life, and Who is never really nearer to us than when our fainting hearts would deem Him most absent. "God so loved the world," He so loved thee, thou solitary downcast sufferer, "that He" thus "gave" to humiliation and to death "His only-begotten Son," that whosoever should read in that Gift of Gifts the secret blessing of sorrow, as well as the true remedy for sin; in other words, "that whosoever believeth in Him should not perish, but have," even now and here, "everlasting life."[1]

Solemn, indeed, is this moment, my brethren, for you

[1] St. John iii. 16.

who stand on the steps of the altar of Christ, ready presently to vow yourselves to His more perfect service for life and until death, ready to receive from His pierced Hands the commission of the Diaconate, or the more awful powers of the Priesthood. It is no slight responsibility to venture to suggest to you the prayer, the aspiration, the resolution, which at this, the crisis of your destinies, might fitly be offered in the sanctuary of your secret souls to your God and Saviour. And yet, I am bold to bid you pray our gracious Master to make of you, each one, soldiers and heralds of His Providence. Determine here and now, pray now and here, as you never prayed before, that both in your secret lives, and in the world of outward activities, you may be servants—loyal, intelligent, devoted servants—of the living, working, loving God. See, first of all, that you recognise His Providence, the light of His eye, the action of His hand, in the mystery of your own personal lives. Each of those opportunities which have been yours, perhaps yours alone ; each of those perceptions of truth, of those upliftings of heart, of those strengthenings of will, which you, in solitary converse with your inmost self, can count in the past; each friend, each book, each Sacrament that has helped you onward and upward; each sorrow that has brought you on your knees, and made sin hateful to you, or crushed self, or something of self, out of you ; think them over; thank Him to whom you owe them ; and take courage. Adore His Providence in taking you—even you—as of old He took David from following the flocks, away from those lines of life in which there is, from the very nature of the case, more of earth and less of heaven than in the life of an ordained man,—in taking you to feed Jacob His people, and Israel His inheritance. If He has in very deed brought you hither (and may He forbid that it could have been otherwise!) by the guidance of His blessed Spirit ; you know already too much of Him ever to tamper with this or that philosophy, by which His erring creatures would fain imagine that they can banish Him from His own world; you know Him too well not to strive against that earthly dependence on sense and sight which fails ever to trace His Hand behind the veil, as the Hand of the Omnipresent, All-working God. Say to Him, Thou, Lord, hast taught me from my youth up until now: therefore will I tell of Thy wondrous works.[1] And then, to-morrow, go forth from the inner chamber of your consecrated spirits, all illuminated by this clearer vision of His Providence, to claim for Him His rights before those who know Him not, or who know Him but in part, or who are in a fair way to forget Him. Not merely in the pulpit, but in those manifold opportunities for the interchange of thought which are so dear to Christ's true servants, banish from your own vocabulary, and discountenance in others, those Pagan abstractions, "chance," "luck," "fortune," "nature," by which men would overlay and disguise from themselves His action in His own world. Point to the Living God in the province of sense, in the storm and in the sunshine, in abundance and in famine, in sickness and in health, in life and in death. Point to the Living God in the sphere of redemptive grace; in the words of Scripture, that very voice of God now as when it first was written; in the Cross, that great discovery of the Heart of God yearning over the sin and the woes of man; in the work of the Blessed Spirit, guiding, sanctifying, governing the Church and its living members; in the Sacraments, specially in the Blessed Eucharist, wherein, under the form of Bread and Wine, the living and eternal Christ is, as we know, present with us to the end of time, as a Providence of Love and Bounty, making us partakers of His Nature and of His Life.

And above all things, let us, the ministers of Christ,

[1] Ps. lxxi. 17.

remember that the loving Providence of our good God is never so effectively preached as when it is preached by imitation. Go to yon heart-broken sufferer, and tell him in a perfunctory way, as if you were repeating your official lesson, that he must cast all his care upon God, since God careth for him, and the blessed words will but seem to blister his sore and open wound. But be to him like the Providence of heaven, a Providence in act as well as a Providence in language; give him your time, your thought, your prayers, your substance, if need be; give him above all, and in all, your true, penetrating, unaffected sympathy; and he will bless your presence as a ray of the very Face of God. It must cost us something to be like Him, Who did not merely preach that God is mindful of man, but Who gave His Life-blood in attestation of the truth which He announced. It must cost us something, if we are to follow His precept of rising so perfectly above the petty selfishnesses of life as to be true children of our All-Provident Father in heaven, Who maketh His sun to shine upon the evil and the good, and sendeth His rain upon the just and upon the unjust. But with His love in our hearts we, too, may dare to tell the world of our day that God is really mindful of man, and to be certain that, after whatever discouragements, in the end our report will be listened to. With His love in our hearts, we may, by our works, our sacrifices, our prayers, no less than by our words, so reflect upon earth the Providence of God as to hasten the coming of that Blessed Day when the dark phantom of Fatalism shall have fled, never again to darken the sky of human thought, when the Life of that Being Who never slumbereth nor sleepeth, shall be owned by all His glorified creatures, thrilling around them, thrilling through them, in all Its undimmed and unfailing splendour.

SERMON VII.

THE MORAL VALUE OF A MISSION FROM CHRIST.[1]

St. John xv. 16.

Ye have not chosen Me, but I have chosen you, and ordained you, that ye should go and bring forth fruit, and that your fruit should remain.

LIKE many other sayings of our Lord, especially in His last discourse, these words have a double application. They are addressed to the Eleven as being disciples of Christ, but also as being the first Christian missionaries. The life of discipleship in the Eleven was practically inseparable from the ministerial life; but it is obvious that Christ chooses and places Christians in His Church whom He does not call to, or invest with, any specifically clerical mission. If, then, to-day we look only to the ministerial bearing of these words, this will not be supposed to imply any forgetfulness of the fact that every living Christian soul must read in them the true, authoritative explanation of its deepest history. To all Christians it is said, " Ye have not chosen Me, but I have chosen you, and ordained you, that ye should go and bring forth fruit, and that your fruit should remain."

At the same time, let it be noted that the purport of the text is mainly, although not exclusively, ministerial. It was addressed to the Eleven alone. It was addressed to them during those solemn hours, unrivalled in the moral history of the world, which passed between the

[1] Preached at the Ordination of the Bishop of Oxford, in the Cathedral Church of Christ, on the Fourth Sunday in Advent, December 22, 1867.

institution of the Eucharist and the Agony. It was addressed to them, as the context shows, in the capacity of missionaries, who had been chosen by Christ, who were soon to learn from the Comforter a heavenly lesson, and to be braced by Him with heavenly strength, and then to go forth into the wide world, that through toil and endurance they might bring forth fruit for the Master at whose bidding they went—fruit, as He said, that should remain. And, thus considered, the words convey our Lord's own judgment as to the source of ministerial power, and as to the object with which such power is given into the hands of men. "Ye have not chosen Me, but I have chosen you, and ordained you"—and wherefore? "That ye might go and bring forth fruit, and that your fruit should remain."

"Ye have not chosen Me." No empty antithesis to what follows—no admitted, purposeless truism, we may be sure, is here. The words evidently guard against, if they do not condemn, a misapprehension on the part of the Apostles. True, of course, it was, and beyond controversy, that they had not chosen Him. They had not met, after the fashion of some Jewish disciples of the time, to elect a popular rabbi, who might teach his pupils with an authority derived from their free vote in his favour. One by one, Christ had chosen them (ἐξελεξάμην) out of the great mass of their countrymen, to follow Him; and then, by a second act, He had associated them with His own blessed work by appointing them (ἔθηκα) to be His envoys and representatives. It could not be denied: He had called them from the toll-house or from the lake-side, and they had simply obeyed. But on the other hand, they had persevered in following Him, even until now, when all, as it seemed, was so dark around Him and them. Was not this perseverance, nay, was not the original act of obedience itself, of the nature of a choice? In form He had called and they had obeyed: but might not the reality have been that their obedience was an election? Was He not their Master so long only as they willed to serve Him? Were not the obligations which bound them to Him reciprocal? If they perseveringly followed Him now, in this hour of trial and darkness, might there not be even a balance of obligation in their favour?

"Ye have not chosen Me, but I have chosen you." Even in full view of Gethsemane, He will not consent to misinterpret the past, or to modify His claim. True, He does not deny their moral liberty. They had been free to set His original call at naught. They were free to desert, to betray Him. He had not forced self-sacrifice upon the rich young man, or perseverance upon Judas. As moral agents, with good and evil, truth and its opposite, before them, they were free; and in their freedom they had chosen and persevered in truth and goodness. But in a deeper sense, so far as they were saintly, they were not free; the yearning after goodness and truth within them was not free; and it conquered their whole being and led them captive. And whence came that yearning? His choice, it seems, is not a thing of yesterday: His choice embraces in its range the whole mystery of their several predestinations. His Eternal Person explains and illuminates His words. They had obeyed His call; they had persevered in obedience, because the dispositions, the desires, the secret sympathies within them, had been implanted by Himself. His choice had been beforehand with them; His love had been deeper than, and prior to, theirs. And as He had thus really chosen them, by giving them the capacity and the will to choose, without suspending their freedom; so He had placed them as plants in His vineyard, that they might bring forth fruit. If they loved Him, it was because He first had loved them. Looking to their act of obedience alone, they had, it might be said, freely chosen Him. Looking to the vast moral history of which that act was the consummate expression, a history penetrated from first to last by the activities of His Providence and His Grace, His words express a literal truth—" Ye have not chosen Me, but I have chosen you."

So indeed it is in every age of the Church of Christ: so it is at this hour. We speak of Holy Orders as of a profession, which for sufficient reasons a man chooses in preference to medicine, or to law, or to some other walk in life. And this language is justifiable, if it be taken to represent that final determination of the will by which a man resolves to present himself for ordination. Such choice is strictly within our power to make or to refuse. But in a deeper sense, none whom Christ will crown hereafter has really been able to do otherwise than obey Christ's call. He has been the object of a choice rather than its author. As a moral agent, with good and evil, a higher and a lower aim before him, he has, of course, been free, if he would, to choose the evil and to refuse the good. But as a Christian, making the most of the light given him, he has not been free. He has yielded to a mysterious attraction which has drawn him on. He has been guided, it may be, partly by the force of family circumstances, partly by natural tastes and sympathies, partly by the direction and results of education, partly by the influence of minds with which he has come in contact. He has followed, too, the guidance of an inward light, growing stronger in his soul as the years have passed on; a light which has discovered him in all his native misery to himself, face to face with the Eternal Love which has redeemed him, and which now bids him own and glorify It. And thus, what was at first a vague hope became more and more a purpose, and what had been for years only a general, indefinite purpose, ripened at length, in the strength of prayer, into a formal resolution, solemnly taken beneath the eye of the Redeemer. It was not that he heard a sensible voice behind him; it was not that there was a moment in his life when the physical and the moral in him seemed to blend, he knew not how,—a moment from which he dates a new spiritual sensation, the power and nature of which are beyond analysis. These things may be in the Church of God; but they are not common; they are not the rule. Yet when he is asked, "Dost thou believe that thou art called by the will of our Lord Jesus Christ to this office of Priest or Deacon in His Church?" it is the verdict of his whole moral being that he can answer confidently, yet humbly, "I trust so." In such a manner (the order of development may vary, its main features are invariable) Christ completes the inward, subjective side of His choice. But if the process stopped here, it would be necessarily imperfect. The strong aspiration of the soul must be countersigned by the objective reality of the Apostolical Commission. It comes to us, that commission, across the centuries, through the unbroken line of the Episcopate, through the sacred Twelve, straight from the hands and lips of Christ. As He said eighteen centuries ago, "Receive ye the Holy Ghost: whose soever sins ye remit, they are remitted unto them, and whose soever sins ye retain, they are retained," so presently in this Cathedral shall we listen to the echo of His creative word, sanctioning, completing the long, patient travail of His Spirit in souls which have heard His call, by the indelible stamp of His authoritative commission. The complete scope of His announcement will presently be manifest: "Ye have not chosen Me, but I have chosen you, and ordained you, that ye should go and bring forth much fruit."

The choice of His ministers by Christ is fully manifested only in the sanction of the inward call by the Apostolic authority. Without the inward call, an episcopal ordination can make a ministerial machine, through which life may flow to others, while itself is dead. Without the due episcopal ordination, an inward call is but as the budding of a tree which lacks the requisite conditions of climate or of soil to produce its proper flower or fruit. Such calls are among the mysteries of the spiritual world; they are spiritual parallels to the vast and mysterious waste of nature. They are found in the outskirts of, or even beyond, the kingdom of Grace, where the full meed of spiritual rain or sunshine is wanting. We mourn as we witness the efforts around us, produced by these anomalies—efforts earnest and devoted, yet, withal, spasmodic and incomplete,—achieving, undoubtedly, a large measure of well-intentioned disorder, but destined surely, as the years pass on, to wither and die back into weakness and inaction.

The reality of the inward vocation to the ministry follows upon a perception of the true nature of the soul, and of the power and work of the Spirit of Christ. It can only be disputed by a desperate Pelagianism, which, in our day, is shading off more and more consistently into sheer materialism. The reality of the Apostolic commission, conveyed by the episcopate, presupposes a Divine authority in the promise and words of Christ, and admits of a moral demonstration as complete and satisfactory as any parallel fact of history. Whether in the case of the other branches of the Universal Church, or in the case of our English Church since the sixteenth century, it can only be impugned by arguments which, if applied consistently, would be fatal to the authority of at least two or three books of the New Testament. And in truth, the temper of these latter days has been somewhat impatient of the large historical and psychological considerations which warrant our belief in Christ's continued choice of His ministers. Men are disposed to limit the evidence of a doctrine to those moral results which they themselves can trace as due to its influence and action. "What is a man the better," we are asked, "for believing that he is chosen and ordained to the ministry by an unseen Being? Why can he not be content to suppose that it is with the ministry as with other professions in life? A man takes, for instance, to the study of the law or of medicine, or of politics, or of agriculture, without supposing that he is moved or authorised to do so by any supernatural agency. Why cannot the clergy do likewise? Surely there is an abundance of reasons which might induce well-disposed young men to undertake the duties of the clerical profession without the historical assumption of the reality of an apostolically transmitted commission, or the psychological assumption of the reality of an inward call. Would it not be more *honest*—that is the word employed—to content yourselves with these practical reasons, reinforced, as they are in the case of the clergy of the Church of England, by the official sanction of the State, and to leave the notions of a special supernatural virtue in the act of ordination, or of a real spiritual afflatus touching individual souls with a heaven-sent impulse, as belonging to days which are passing or have passed away?"

As regards the question of "honesty," it of course depends upon an anterior question of opinion or rather of fact. As we descend in the scale of beliefs, we find that the larger faiths above us wear a necessary semblance either of credulity or knavery. To the pure materialist nothing seems more foolish or "dishonest" than what he regards as the assumptions of spiritualism. A Condillac cannot understand the empiricism of a Locke; since Locke assumes two sources of knowledge, sensation and reflection, while Condillac can see in all mental processes, honestly examined, only modified sensations. The religion of nature thinks the supernatural "dishonest"; so does the Socinian the doctrine of Christ's literal Godhead; so does the disciple of Strauss the assertion of the infallibility of Scripture; so does the theory which treats the Church as a purely human association, a belief in the reality of the ministerial call and of the ministerial commission. This use of the word *honest* implies, not necessarily ill-will, but only a limited imagination on the part of the speaker. The speaker cannot imagine the possibility of a larger range of certainties than that which he himself recognises. If other men make reference to truths which he does not recognise, he cannot divest himself of the idea that they must be wilfully deceiving themselves, or others, or both at once.

So much for the question of honesty; but how about the moral advantages of the belief before us? Now, in reply to this question, I answer that belief in a real ministerial call and mission, received from Jesus Christ, is not a resultless ecclesiastical fancy. It is a moral power directly promoting ministerial work. It is a stimulus to exertion, of which, without it, a man would be incapable. It is a protection against an unwillingness to be personally prominent, which belongs to the highest type of the Christian character. It is, moreover, a source of true consolation under the ministerial disappointments, which are a matter of course in all careers, even in the most successful. "Ye have not chosen Me, but I have chosen you, and ordained you, that ye should go and bring forth fruit." Our Saviour's words directly connect a strictly moral result, which He calls "fruit," with His own choice and ordination of the disciples who will produce it.

I.

It is argued that ministerial work, of itself, is a natural attraction to a large class of benevolent minds, sufficiently powerful to need no such stimulus as that afforded by a heavenly call and mission. In other professions, we are reminded, the work itself and its legitimate rewards constitute a sufficient attraction. A man pleads a cause, or he attends a patient, or he advocates a legislative improvement, or he drains and fertilises his broad acres, without any stronger reason for doing so than is supplied by the intrinsic advantage arising to society and to himself from these several occupations. Why should it not be thus, it is asked, with the clergy also? Is not the enlightenment of the ignorant, is not the alleviation of those who mourn and suffer, is not, in short, the whole staple and cycle of clerical occupations, a sufficient reason for undertaking and discharging them? What can be more welcome and grateful to a benevolent mind than these large and varied opportunities of doing good? To do good is its own reward; but if any further reward is needed, is it not forthcoming? Not to hint at anything beyond the clouds, beyond the grave, is not the gratitude with which ministerial work is welcomed, if there were nothing else, an ample reason for engaging in it?

At first sight this representation is forcible and persuasive; but a little consideration will convince us that it is, upon the whole, at issue with facts. While it has such an air of common sense about it, its real weakness is, that it is too idealistic. It ignores the plain, hard fact, that a great deal of honest clerical work, of necessary, inevitable clerical work, brings with it no sort of present reward, and exposes the worker to much obloquy and distress. If indeed Christianity were a system of teaching in entire accordance with the instincts of our fallen human nature, the work of a clergyman would not necessarily provoke any opposition; but at the same time it is difficult to see how it would raise his fellow-creatures really in the moral scale. But as a matter of fact, Christianity is a constant rebuke to man, being such as he is; and its ministers therefore are, in exact proportion to their faithfulness, perpetually engaged in a struggle with opposing human wills. How runs the Apostolic commission to Timothy? "Reprove, rebuke, exhort with all longsuffering and doctrine."[1] It is not possible in practice to obey St. Paul, however tenderly, considerately, humbly, without at times rousing earnest, nay, fierce opposition.

Doubtless there are theories afloat on the subject of the clerical office, which would regard any like duties with these as unnecessary, if not as impertinent. For instance, a clergyman is sometimes described as being merely an official lecturer upon the text of Scripture, capable of imparting useful information once a week to persons who have not leisure to study Scripture for themselves. Sometimes, too, he is said to be only an official philanthropist, an accredited agent of the largest charitable society in the world, whose one business it is to stimulate charity and to organise schemes for the relief of want and pain. Doubtless—it is a noble privilege—we clergy are, by the terms of our office, instructors and philanthropists. But we are this, because we are more, because we have duties towards our fellow-men considered as immortal beings, duties for which we are fitted by a special mission and by a supernatural grace. The conversion, the building up of souls, one by one;—this is our real business. To this all else is subservient. A clerical life which is spent upon literature, even upon sacred literature, without a practical spiritual object, or upon material philanthropy, without that higher philanthropy which loves the human soul, is a wasted life. Possibly a Divine call and a Divine commission are not needed in order to master a certain amount of Biblical scholarship, or to direct a well-con-

[1] 2 Tim. iv. 2.

sidered effort for relieving poverty. But to deal with the human soul, with one human soul; to reveal it to itself; to reveal God to it; to lead it in the light of that revelation to the cross of Jesus Christ, that it may be washed in His Blood and renewed by His Spirit; to make it thus taste of the good Word of God and the powers of the world to come; to watch earnestly for it; to struggle in prayer for it; to take frequent thought and to labour for it; to translate into the daily work of life that ideal of thought and care embodied in the word Pastor,—of care and thought which guides and feeds the flock of Christ;—this does require a Divine stimulus, that a man may undertake and persevere in it. For it requires, beyond everything else, enthusiasm, fervour. We are told, indeed, that even the most abstract of the sciences cannot be efficiently taught without a certain enthusiasm on the part of the teacher, on the ground that the successful teacher must not merely exercise and inform the learner's intellect, but must contrive to rouse and invigorate his will. Much more true is this of religion, with regard to which the learner's will is often not merely sluggish, but warped and hostile. Now this necessary fervour is created by nothing so effectively as by that feeling of personal devotion to Jesus Christ which is natural to a man who believes that he has been really chosen and sent forth by Him. That He in His love and condescension should have singled out one of His servants to take special charge of His interests, and to forward His work, must be to that servant a source of moral impulse of the strongest and most lasting kind. This sense of attachment and responsibility to a living Person, which results from a belief in clerical mission, does really avail to create and maintain that vigorous fervour, which is the raw material that prudence and knowledge must fashion unto effective clerical action. The mere lecturer chooses his subject, and in time grows tired of it. The mere philanthropist organises his scheme: he is satisfied when it has succeeded; he is out of heart when it has failed. But—"Ye have not chosen Me, but I have chosen you, and ordained you, that ye should go and bring forth fruit, and that your fruit should remain."

II.

Again, belief in the reality of a Divine call and mission affords a real support and protection in the work to which it impels an ordained man. This support is required, not merely as a make-weight against the pressure of opposition, but to counteract the promptings of natural modesty, which shrinks from personal prominence and leadership. It is not merely required for the effective discharge of such grave and sacred duties as are involved in the celebration of the Holy Sacrament and in dealing with the consciences of men. It is specially required in the pulpit. A belief in his call and commission from Christ can alone make his pulpit ministrations tolerable to a man of common sense and modesty. The more a man knows of God, of the human soul, of the vast range of spiritual truth; the more he knows of the attainments, intellectual or moral, of those around him, and of his own far-reaching and radical shortcomings; the more must he shrink, if left to himself, from such a part as that of enforcing spiritual truths—even the truths of which he is most certain—upon a large assemblage of his fellow-men. He must feel that the aged may well despise his youth, that the learned may take the measure of his ignorance, and the self-disciplined of his moral inconsistencies, and the thoughtful of his superficiality. Apart from his recollection of the presence of the All-wise God, he is sensitively conscious of being face to face with a phalanx of critics, each of whom might fairly be his instructor. He knows that if his personal qualifications alone are to decide the question, his appearance in the pulpit as the spiritual educator of his fellow-men can only be regarded as an impertinence. Rarely, indeed, can it ever happen that a parish priest is absolutely, in all respects, moral and spiritual, as well as mental, the natural chief and leader of his flock; and when he becomes aware of his inferiority, in any one respect, to one of his hearers, he must perforce fall back in his conscience upon some justification for presuming to address them, higher than any which personal fitness affords.

Here it may be hinted that such a justification is supplied, in the case of the clergy of the Church of England, by the sanction of the State. The State, it is argued, comes to the aid of individual shortcomings with the gift of official dignity and position. If the individual, as such, has no title to speak to his fellow-men, on questions of spiritual truth, in the tone of authority, yet we are told that the individual, mantled with the prestige and authority of the Nation or the Crown, may claim that title. The State, considered as a rational whole, is said to have its religious as well as its civil and military representatives; and its clergy can need no higher sanction than that which suffices for its soldiers, its diplomatists, its police.

Now, to a certain number of peculiarly constituted minds in our day and generation, this may appear to be satisfactory. Nor do I wish to depreciate, even indirectly, the many blessings arising to the Church, as well as to the nation, over and above the mere material protection which the nation affords to the Church's property, from the fact of the union of Church and State. These blessings, indeed, may be over-estimated, and they are not without a heavy balance of attendant disadvantages; but they are certainly not to be remembered without gratitude, or parted with, if they must be parted with, without anxiety and reluctance. But it should never for one moment be forgotten that the sanction which the State gives to the Church is not a source of any spiritual authority. No spiritually-minded man can suppose, since the coming of our Lord, that mankind, organised in a civil capacity as the State, can really confer any properly religious sanction upon a spiritual society, acting and teaching in the Name of God. If, in certain parts of his great work, Hooker might seem to countenance some like supposition, this is because, in Hooker's days, the Church and State of England were strictly co-extensive; the State of the Ecclesiastical Polity is only the Church acting in a civil capacity, among a people which wholly belongs to it. It is impossible to argue from the circumstances of the Elizabethan age to those of the present day; nor is the general principle, that religion, whether recognised by the State or not, is not indebted to the State for its true authority among men, other than certain. "Everywhere, before the time of Jesus Christ," says M. Guizot, "the civil and the religious life of mankind were confounded with each other; they were mutually oppressive of each other. Religion or religions were institutions incorporate with the State, and ruled or repressed by the State, as its interests might dictate." In "the independence of religious society," proclaimed by the Gospel, M. Guizot is constrained to recognise a sublime innovation, a ray of the very light of God. This, he contends, was the true meaning of Christ's answer to the Pharisees and Herodians: "Render therefore unto Cæsar the things which be Cæsar's, and unto God the things which be God's." Human society was thenceforth to rest on a double basis; it was to rest upon obedience to the civil law, going hand in hand with the independence of a faith which had come from heaven.[1]

It follows that the sanction of the State, valuable as it

[1] Cf. Guizot, *Méditations sur l'Essence de la Religion Chrétienne* (Paris, 1864), pp. 306, 307.

is for civil and social reasons, cannot afford to the clergy that support in the discharge of strictly religious functions which their sense of personal weakness so eminently needs. The nation may invest her officers, her ambassadors, her statesmen, with a dignity and consideration, which really supports them because they represent and embody her action; and she may give, as in this country for so many ages she has given, welcome, countenance, temporal place and consideration, to the ministers of Christ. Spiritual power or mission she never has given, she never could give. Her relation towards spiritual power is exactly identical with her relation towards the gifts of natural genius. She may recognise and reward, she cannot create, either. " His Majesty," it was once said by a statesman who has since become famous in English history,—" his Majesty can make a Lord-Lieutenant, but it requires God Almighty to make an Author." And in like manner the State can give peerages and an income; but a true inward call to the priesthood and the commission which descends from the Apostles, are alike the gifts of Jesus Christ alone.

Therefore I say, a higher sanction is needed than that of the State for the public duties of a clergyman. And a clergyman finds it in his conviction of the reality of his call and of the validity of his orders. His individuality is thus merged in the majestic commission which he bears; and he acquires a healthy indifference to criticism, or rather a devotion to duty, which is too engrossing to be conscious that it is criticised at all. Of himself, he shrinks from prominence; all that is best, if I may so say, in his natural, as still more in his regenerate, man, conspires to bid him keep in the background among his fellows, and to hold his peace. But a necessity is laid upon him from heaven, which continually does violence to this inclination. The never-forgotten consciousness of the mission which he has received whispers to him, as of old to the prophet by the river of Chebar, that he may not, if he would, be silent. There may be many better men unordained than he; but still his responsibilities are not theirs. "And he said unto me, Son of man, go, get thee unto the house of Israel, and speak with My words unto them.... But the house of Israel will not hearken unto thee; for they will not hearken unto Me: for all the house of Israel are impudent and hardhearted. Behold, I have made thy face strong against their faces, and thy forehead strong against their foreheads. As an adamant harder than flint have I made thy forehead: fear them not, neither be dismayed at their looks.... Speak unto them and tell them, Thus saith the Lord God, whether they will hear, or whether they will forbear."[1]

III.

Once more, a belief in the truth of his call and commission affords true and solid consolation to a clergyman, under the disappointments which are inevitable in every ministry. It may seem thoughtless or heartless in a preacher, on such an occasion as this, to suggest that, of the many hopes which are gathered around this altar, some are certainly doomed to die away unrealised, or to be cut short by ruder blows. Yet to look this contingency in the face is only part of that wisdom which does not "build a house," or "make war with another king," without previously calculating its moral resources. After all, my brethren, we are the servants, not of success, but of Jesus Christ and His Blessed Will, whatever that may be; and we can bear to be told that it may be our appointed portion to be sanctified rather by failure than by victory. Still, when it comes, the failure of bright hopes is hard to bear; it is hard in proportion to the enthusiasm which

[1] Ezek. iii. 4. 7-9, 11.

first begat them. We enter upon active life; we are alive to the great needs, the great resources, the great opportunities around us; alive to the crying deficiencies and the gaping wounds of the Church our Mother; alive to the vast possibilities for active good which are within our reach; alive, not to our own natural strength, whether of wit or of will, but to the illuminating and invigorating force of the grace of Christ. We do not see, perhaps we do not suspect, the obstacles before us; and our immediate foreground is filled with ideals of ecclesiastical, and national, and social, and personal improvement, in realising which, as we humbly hope, we may have, at least, a hand. Yet failure and disappointment have constantly been the portion of those who, as we see, on looking back upon their lives, have really been master-builders among the workmen, through whom in past ages most has been contributed to the splendour and dimensions of the House of God. Moses leads Israel out of Egypt, and dies in view of that land of promise, from which he is excluded, in consequence of a personal fault. Samuel reforms the disorders of Israel, yet lives to witness the election and the downward course of Saul. Isaiah strengthens Hezekiah to resist Sennacherib, and dies amid the excesses and at the hands of his son. The career of Jeremiah opens with the hopeful reign of Josiah, with the destruction of idolatry, by the royal authority, throughout the kingdom. Jeremiah is conspired against by the populace of Jerusalem; he is in danger of his life at the hands of his townsmen of Anathoth; he is seized by a powerful party of priests and prophets, and hardly rescued; he is imprisoned by Zedekiah; he is smitten and tortured by Pashur; he is imprisoned again, on the charge of treason, by the besieged Jews; he is then carried down to Egypt with feigned marks of deference, but in reality, as it would seem, to his martyrdom. Jeremiah is the type of those who hope for much and are conspicuous, at least to the eye of man, in failure. In the distance, such failure has a splendour of its own; ages of veneration have traced around it a nimbus which diverts attention from the historic reality. At the time it is hard, very hard, to bear: it brings with it a world of new temptations, unexperienced before. It brings temptations to impatient words and to impatient action, or, worse still, to suppressed gloom which issues in chronic discontent with work or with life, or even in the gradual growth of an indifference to truth once held as most precious and sacred. He had felt the beginning of these temptations who cried—"Woe is me, my mother, that thou hast borne me a man of strife and a man of contention to the whole earth. . . . O Lord, Thou hast deceived me, and I was deceived: Thou art stronger than I, and hast prevailed: I am in derision daily, every one mocketh me. . . . Cursed be the day wherein I was born: let not the day wherein my mother bare me be blessed."[1] And another, in a later age, not, most assuredly, the least noble among the servants of Christ, although living under circumstances, and labouring for some ends, which are not ours—he, too, had known these sore temptations, and he had conquered them when he exclaimed—"I have loved righteousness and hated iniquity, therefore I die in exile."[2]

Doubtless there are general considerations of God's wisdom and goodness upon which the faith of a good man will fall back in all times of trial. But the confidence with which he does so must depend, in no slight degree, upon the question, whether he has himself invited these trials, or whether they have come upon him through contingencies which were practically beyond his control. A general who fails after volunteering to command, fails in

[1] Jer. xv. 10; xx. 7, 14.
[2] See "The Disappointed Prophet," in *Plain Sermons*, vol. v.

a totally distinct sense from the leader who accepts a post of great responsibility at the bidding of his sovereign. If Jeremiah is constant amid the temptations of failure, this is because he is not responsible for having attempted a work which was destined to fail by the Providence of God. He had prophesied, against his natural bent of character, and in obedience to a heavenly call and mission. The words of that first commission must have strengthened him even in his dying hour, forty years later, in a land of idolaters. "Then the word of the Lord came unto me, saying, Before I formed thee in the belly I knew thee; and before thou camest forth out of the womb I sanctified thee, and I ordained thee a prophet unto the nations. Then said I, Ah, Lord God! behold, I cannot speak: for I am a child. But the Lord said unto me, Say not, I am a child: for thou shalt go to all that I shall send thee, and whatsoever I command thee thou shalt speak."[1] With these convictions, a man can indeed do his duty, and leave results, be they what they may, to Him Who sent him forth.

But it may be rejoined: Granting that belief in the reality of a call and commission from Christ is an incentive, a support, and an encouragement to ministerial work in the way described, is it not true that this belief has also a dangerous side? Does it not tend to foster an exaggerated sense of self-importance in those who hold it? Does it not lead many a man to think more of himself than of his work, more of his order than of his mission, more of his place and position in the Church than of the honour of Jesus Christ?

Undoubtedly, all forms of the conviction that we are specially privileged or responsible have their dangers. To know this a man need not be in Holy Orders. Pharisaism and self-assertion in sacred things are older than the

[1] Jer. i. 4-7.

day of Pentecost, and are not confined to the Apostolical Churches of Christendom. The moral sense of personal predestination, of redemption, of sanctification, the exercised privilege of almsgiving, the known power of prayer, the felt delight in Scripture and in holy things, have all in turn been perverted by the human heart to augment the sense of personal importance.

So, too, it has been with the calling and gifts of the clergy. The clergy are but men, and their faults are conspicuously thrown out into relief by the sacredness of their office. But is self-importance the *natural* result of belief in the reality of the ministerial call and commission? Is it certain that a clergy, which should profess to have no authority or powers whatever beyond their lay brethren, and should nevertheless undertake to teach and feed Christ's people solely on the ground of individual personal merit, would be more entirely free from self-importance than are the clergy of the Church? Is not that which is personal, individual, proper to a man himself, more likely to minister to this sense of self-importance than that which he only enjoys in common with every member of a vast corporation, and which implies nothing that distinguishes him among his clerical brethren? Surely, in every true Christian soul the felt contrast between the high commission received, and the feeble, grovelling efforts of the personal life, is a perpetual warning against self-exaltation, a constant stimulant of that sense of sin and weakness which forbids the words and thoughts that belong to pride. "Unto me, who am less than the least of all saints, is this grace given, that I should preach among the Gentiles the unsearchable riches of Christ."[1] So wrote an Apostle to whom it was natural to speak of himself as the chief of sinners, and who yet surpasses all other writers in the New Testament in the vigour with

[1] Eph. iii. 8; compare 1 Tim. i. 12, 13.

which he magnifies the office which he had received from Christ.

But the precious words remain as a perpetual reminder of the purpose with which Christ our Lord commits to human hands the responsibilities of a Divine commission. "I have chosen you, and ordained you, that ye should go and bring forth fruit, and that your fruit should remain." If any in the Church of Christ have higher capacities, whether of nature or of grace, than others, these capacities are not a title to high thoughts of self or to lordly leisure; they constitute an obligation to proportionate humility and exertion. Far better is it never to have received the talent than to have received and wasted it. They indeed whose ministry brings forth no fruit are under the strongest of temptations to think and say that their ordination has given them no powers of doing so. They who abound in work for God and for souls, find in that work the evidence of a strength within them which is not their own, and which assures them of the reality of their heavenly mission.

And surely, if ever in Christian history, the clergy of the Church of Christ need that strength in our day and country. Whether we look to the world of thought or to the world of social human life, towards each of which we have duties; how vast is the work before us, how ample the opportunities, how great the necessity! Never before in this generation have we Englishmen felt civil society so shaken as by the political events of the last two months, (may it not be added?) as by the tragic revelations of the last fortnight.[1] It is a time when all who love their country would fain gather in duty and loyalty around her, that each should contribute whatever he may of hearty support to the throne and to the law. But what is at the root of the anxiety felt and expressed on all sides

[1] The reference is to the explosion at the Clerkenwell Prison.

of us? Is it only that there has been an assault here, a procession or a riot there, a deadly explosion in the heart of our metropolis? These things are grave enough; but their gravity consists not in themselves, but in that of which they are the symptoms. The recent violence may not be so tragical in its immediate results as the loss of a steamship or a railway accident; it is more alarming, because it points to a moral and social disease, which is of itself a terrible evil, and is likely to produce other similar catastrophes. If indeed there was only a question of race between ourselves and our Celtic fellow-subjects beyond St. George's Channel, or only a question of law and order between the Government and a disloyal association, it might be improper to allude to such a subject on this occasion. But it is felt and stated that our reasons for anxiety are wider and deeper; that old faith in principles has been generally weakened, and that old attachment to institutions has largely died out; that there is no great positive enthusiasm to oppose to the social solvents at work amongst us. It is felt and stated by keen observers, who have no clerical interest in stating what they feel, that there are rottennesses and sores in the moral structure of English society at this hour which render it less able to sustain the shock of possible war or revolution than was the England of thirty years ago. And if this be so, have not we of the clergy a great duty towards our country, lying in that very path of sacred work which we are bound to tread in virtue of the commission we have received from Christ? The more we can implant, restore, deepen faith; faith in fixed truth, faith in God, faith in duty; dread of sin as the one great and only evil, honour and obedience towards constituted authorities (yet this, in the spirit which becomes the "Evangelical tribunes of the people"), the better shall we strengthen those social bands which are the real strength of our country. The remotest hamlet contributes something, however indirectly, to the stability of the empire; and it contributes most when it is the scene of a ministry which, in the confidence and strength of a heavenly mission, brings forth much fruit in rescued and sanctified souls.

And in this diocese there are generally some, often many, candidates for ordination, who are admitted to the diaconate or to the priesthood as holders of a fellowship. Too often a college title is contrasted with a parochial one, as if a life spent within college walls here in Oxford afforded no opportunities for strictly clerical work. Yet how great is the need of men chosen and ordained by Jesus Christ, that they should go and bring forth fruit in such a field as that of this University, they best know who live here. Here, as elsewhere, sin is rife; here, as elsewhere, the eternal contest between good and evil rages uninterruptedly; here, souls are to be won by the same spiritual activities, by the same heart-subduing truths, as elsewhere. But here there are special anxieties which may well invite the earnest attention of those among Christ's servants who have opportunities of grappling with them. Elsewhere, attention may be concentrated upon controversies, which are not without grave importance, yet which certainly are less fundamental than those which have become wellnigh chronic here. Elsewhere, questions are raised between principles that have confronted each other for centuries, while both are within the Christian pale; between importance ascribed and importance denied to sacraments; between the advocacy and the repudiation of Church ceremonial. In these discussions, doubtless, much is really at stake; but surely less, far less, than in the controversies whispered of late years around these walls, which, for so many ages, have sheltered the faith and love of Christian students. Not merely whether the Death of Jesus have any atoning virtue; not merely whether Jesus be God, or only a sinful creature; but whether those theistic truths which Christianity found in the world, and sanctioned by repetition, be themselves true;—these are the questions in debate. Whether prayer has any efficacy with God; whether the conception of a Providence be more than a fond dream of human self-importance; whether to affirm the freedom of the human will be not to reject the last and most triumphant conclusion of the inductive philosophy; whether to assert positively the existence of God be not to place at the summit of human thought a dogmatic statement so vast and exacting as to be inconsistent with the needs of that highest culture which, it would seem, demands, as a condition of its perfect development, nothing less than a strictly universal scepticism;—these are points here agitated, and, in too many instances, decided in a manner which proves that the most fundamental Christian and theistic truth is engaged in nothing less than a struggle for its existence. Who can watch, even distantly, the oft-repeated spectacle of intellectual perplexity, struggle, anguish, and even despair, without praying the Lord of the Vineyard to choose and ordain among His servants, in this place, men who can bring effective help in our present deep necessities? For, from this centre of English intellectual life truth or falsehood alike radiate, with terrible swiftness, throughout our Church and country. What is here said in the ear, by a tutor, to a group of pupils, is soon, through the vast machinery by which educated thought finds expression, proclaimed, for good or evil, upon the housetops of the land. Surely, if the sense of a mission from Christ be needed anywhere, to give zeal, decision, encouragement, patience, it is needed in a clerical fellow of a college of our day in Oxford.

"And your fruit shall remain." If more be required to make us do Christ's work than the fact that He sends us, it is here. The work of human hands and human brains, done for and in this passing world, passes also. It is with thought as with manual labour; it is with greatness as with obscurity; it is with genius as with mediocrity. An earthly immortality is only relative, after all; and centuries, or decades of centuries, are as nothing in the history of an Universe. It may seem, too, to the servants of Christ, amid the steady monotony of their daily work and their incessant conflict with evil, that they are but as children writing on the sands of time their little alphabet, which must presently be effaced by the waters of the rising tide. Brethren, it is not so. The tide of human thought and life ebbs as well as flows; but the message which we write upon the mind of a generation would be indelible, even if it were not destined to be re-written by our successors. For spiritual fruit, even the humblest, is assured of preservation in the Eternal storehouse. Love, courage, truth, purity—these cannot die. As each soul passes from a pastor's care, enlightened, repentant, sanctified, to wait a while and then to enter upon its rest in that better world beyond the stars, it bears with it the spiritual result of sanctified toil, which are as immortal as itself. Happy and blessed are they who, whether in themselves or with others, labour for that which alone does not suffer from the moth and rust of time! Happy and blessed are the servants of a Master so bountiful and indulgent, Who, when He comes to take account of the produce of His vineyard, will crown, as we know full well, with eternal distinctions, not our poor efforts or merits, but His own fruitful and majestic gifts.

SERMON VIII.

CLERICAL MOTIVES.[1]

1 COR. xvi. 8, 9.

But I will tarry at Ephesus until Pentecost. For a great door and effectual is opened unto me, and there are many adversaries.

IT is in incidental passages like these that we obtain the deepest and most vivid insight into a writer's mind and character. Among uninspired writings it is not in formal compositions or official documents that that which marks personal character and life makes itself felt; few persons would indorse the paradox of a modern historian, that the character of Henry VIII. is to be studied most advantageously in the preambles to his Acts of Parliament. The great charm of private correspondence, and the only reason which in thousands of cases can explain its publication, is that it is a revelation of that which is always interesting—a revelation of character. In an official mood, or in a public capacity, two men of profoundly different characters will say exactly the same thing: the truth being that for the time all personal characteristics are dropped; it is the office, or the circumstances, or the necessity of the case which really speaks; it is not the man. In private correspondence you see the man more as he is: he writes with a running pen; he writes as he feels; his impulse, his enthusiasm, his passion, his hopes and fears, his

[1] Preached at the Ordination of the Bishop of Winchester, in St. Philip's, Battersea, on Trinity Sunday, May 26, 1872.

attractions and repulsions, are represented by turns; they are vehemently uttered, or they escape him in spite of himself: and, as you read him, you feel that you are in contact not with a system, or a treatise, or formal theory or composition of any kind, but with a soul,—with all its strength or weakness, with all its thoroughness or inconsistency, with all its inertness or life and resolution.

Now, it is one of the many attractions of St. Paul's Epistles, that while they embody the greatest and most authoritative statements of the central necessary dogmas of Christianity, they also abound in this personal and incidental element,—keeping the figure of the writer continually before us, and enabling us all, but especially those of us who have succeeded, in whatever measure and degree, to a share in his great office and work for Christ, to feel at home with him, as with a personal friend,— just as if eighteen centuries did not divide us, and He were working at our sides in London and Southwark, or we with him in the ancient cities of the Levant.

The passage before us will illustrate these observations: the Apostle reveals in this expression of his intention features of his ministerial character which are well worth our study on an occasion like the present. "I must tarry at Ephesus until Pentecost. For a great door and effectual is opened unto me, and there are many adversaries."

Here we have, first of all, the announcement of a decision, and, secondly, the reasons on which that decision is based.

I.

1. In the decision to remain at Ephesus until Pentecost, we may remark the Apostle's power of making up his mind in face of a strong counterbalancing motive.

Certainly there was enough to make St. Paul, so profoundly sympathetic as he was by nature, as well as in his life of grace, anxious to leave Ephesus for Corinth at a moment's notice when he traced these lines. The Epistle in which they occur is, in fact, a long catalogue of motives, each one of which must have exerted over such a mind as his a strenuous power.

Since his arrival at Ephesus, in this his third journey, St. Paul had paid, as Wieseler has shown, a flying visit to Corinth; he had returned in much sorrow and dejection of spirits. He had gone on account of unfavourable news as to the condition of the Corinthian Church; he had found matters even worse than he expected. In an Epistle which is lost to us, he had ordered that the profligate members of the Corinthian Church who had occasioned a great scandal should be excluded from its communion. The Corinthians appear to have replied by asking whether the Apostle really meant them to seclude themselves from all the business of life; after all, Corinth was only what all the world knew it was; and it was easy for them to imply that the Apostle was too enthusiastic a person to be really practical. And since then, some members of the household of Chloe, a Christian family of distinction at Corinth, had arrived in Ephesus. They, too, left with the Apostle the saddest impressions of the state of things at Corinth. The Church there, they said, was divided by fierce party spirit. The Christians who wished to retain or recover as much as they could of the ceremonial law of the Jews were there pleading the name of St. Peter in favour of their attempt to undermine the authority of St. Paul. The Christians who had found in the Alexandrian culture of Apollos a predominant philosophical and literary element which was either wanting in the Apostle as a disciple of Gamaliel, or altogether subordinated to the spiritual side of his teaching, objected to the Apostle as comparatively dull and uninteresting. Others again used the Apostle's own

Clerical Motives.   235

name, altogether against his will, as that of a party leader to whom they owed allegiance; while another section, ostentatiously disclaiming all party spirit, and appealing to the holiest of all names as that which alone marked them, would probably have carried party feeling to a higher pitch of narrow intolerance than any of the rest. There was also,—whether distinct from these parties, or nearly connected with that of Apollos, it is now difficult to say,—an active antinomian body, defending loose living on principle, denying the resurrection of the dead, and practically representing the Gospel as a more graceful kind of Epicureanism; and a member of this section it would have been who, without being excluded from the Church, was living in open incest with his stepmother, during the lifetime of his father. Then the heathen law-courts were occupied with vexatious suits brought by Christians against Christians; the Holy Communion was profaned by excesses which immediately preceded its reception; the gifts of the Holy Spirit were turned into occasions of vain personal display; and Christian women, forgetting their higher natural instincts, and even those customs of their country which embodied them, came forward unveiled to make speeches in public assemblies of the Church. It seemed as if the Greek temper, restless, brilliant, paradoxical, had carried all its clever levity, all its resources of *finesse* and intrigue, all its genius for controversy, all its distaste for personal self-discipline and improvement, into the very heart of the Church of Corinth: and the Apostle may well have felt that he ought, without delay, to be on the spot, where there was not merely so much good to do, but also so much mischief to correct and prevent.

It must have cost St. Paul much, with all his penetrating insight into the details of a great moral struggle, with all his ready and burning sympathy, to set the claims of

Corinth aside, even for six weeks. Still he did: though he knew that much might depend upon the delay. He knew—he must have known—that there was one voice to which all would listen, one heart to whose strong sympathies all, sooner or later, would respond, one determined will to which all would bend. His own presence at Corinth was of the first necessity for Corinth. But there was a higher necessity for him to be elsewhere. He struck the balance as in a Higher Presence. Indecision may be the characteristic of a weak character, with no strong enthusiasms in any direction; or it may be a morbid growth attaching itself to a character of the very highest order, in which the sensitiveness of conscience as to the claims of conflicting lines of duty continually arrests the fiat of the executive will. But, in either case, it is a fatal drawback in any who bear the commission of Christ. They have to work for a cause which never can be popular, in face of an opposition which can never sleep: and a lack of resolution is as surely taken advantage of by opponents as it is disheartening to friends. No doubt a decision as to the right course is sometimes a matter of the greatest difficulty. No doubt there are rash resolutions, wrong resolutions, obstinacy in maintaining what is rash and wrong; yet, for all that, we may not, we dare not, abdicate—we who serve Jesus Christ in a sense different from that of other men, above all others, dare not abdicate—the duty of decision. If rash resolutions are wrong, the absence of all resolution is not right. A man asserts his manhood, a Christian puts forth within him the power of the Indwelling Christ, when, feeling that God's Eye is upon him, and that he will one day stand before the Judgment-seat, he makes up his mind; when he takes impulses, passions, hopes, fears, enthusiasms, shrinkings, well in hand, and proclaims, amid the tumult and chaos within him, the sentence of that sovereign faculty which is his real self—the sentence of the will; after placing his will under the guidance of well-instructed conscience. St. Paul has told us in his Epistle to the Romans of his conflicts with that other law in his members which warred against the true law of his mind: but here we see him not battling with rebellious passion, not irresolutely parleying with counteracting motives, nor yet yielding to the mastery of resistless impulse. He is announcing calmly, deliberately, finally, a judgment: he has his purpose clearly formed, yet well in hand: he knows how far to give reins to it, and where to assign a limit. "I will tarry at Ephesus," he says, "until Pentecost."

II.

Upon what reasons is this decision grounded? Upon two. Of these, the first is the greatness of the opportunity offered by Ephesus. St. Paul calls the opportunity a door. He had but to enter, and all that was nearest and dearest to his apostolic heart was there before him. Nay, he feels the opportunity so keenly that he intensifies the metaphor, though at the risk of destroying it. It is not merely a great door, but, as he expresses it, effectual or energetic: it is as if the opportunity itself were instinct with the action that should make the most of it—so impossible does it appear to the Apostle not to make the most of it. It had not been always thus at Ephesus. Although St. Paul must have been cheered by the recent conversion of Apollos, which had followed on the labours of Aquila and Priscilla before his arrival: although it must have gladdened his heart to baptize those twelve disciples of the Baptist who, when he first met them, had not heard whether there was any Holy Ghost—there had been a weary time since. At Ephesus, as elsewhere, he made the great Jewish synagogue the starting-point of his missionary activity. Saturday after Saturday, for three long months, he argued and disputed, he preached, as we should say, a series of Conferences, on the true nature of the Kingdom of God. As a pupil of Gamaliel, he knew, as well as any man, how to approach the intellect and heart of his countrymen. He knew that the Kingdom of Messiah, as shadowed out in prophecy, as explained by the earlier and better tradition of the Synagogue, was a very different thing from the hard and dry political programme which was popular in all the synagogues of his own day. But he preached to hearers who did not mean to be convinced, although they were intelligent enough to do justice to the power of the preacher. They could not afford to treat him with silent neglect.

His teaching was publicly denounced in terms of contempt and insult; and then, as before at Corinth, he determined to separate, by a formal act, from all appearance of communion with the Jewish worship. He and his assembled in one of the apsidal lounges which were attached to the gymnasiums and public baths in the cities of the ancient world, and which was then frequented by Tyrannus, probably a teacher of rhetoric. There for two years he was to be found day after day, speaking to all who would listen, sometimes to his countrymen, who remembered what he had said in the synagogue, sometimes to the Pagan Greeks: and Ephesus was so great a centre, that this daily public preaching acted as an advertisement of the nature and claims of the Gospel throughout the whole province of proconsular Asia. Thence were founded many of the smaller churches which at the close of the Apostolic age covered the soil of Western Asia. There, too, were probably worked some of those remarkable miracles which are mentioned by the writer of the Acts; there would have been discussed again and again the disgrace and discomfiture of the seven sons of the

Jewish high priest, who had tried to use our Lord's Sacred Name as a spell in their attempted exorcisms; there would have been heard those public confessions of sinful and wasted lives which preceded the baptism of Pagan converts; there the costly books, filled with receipts for rare magical incantations, were publicly burned; it was felt that a new moral power had gone forth from the place, and that society, both Jewish and Pagan, was fermenting sensibly all around.

None would have known this better than St. Paul. "A great door—and effectual," he exclaimed—"is opened unto me." The old settled surface of Pagan and Jewish thought was heaving with agitation before his mind's eye. Men were asking what was really true, really worth living for, really worth dying for, if there was any such thing. There was a wish to base life, if it could be, upon a moral rock of some kind; there was an impatience of fiction, of all that was not real. These things were not the Gospel, but they were preparatory to it. The soil had to be broken up before the heavenly seed could be sown with any probability of growth.

Brethren, it is no slight part of our responsibility to make the most of every opening for doing our Master's work. Every ministerial life has such opportunities, sooner or later. We may work for some years amid the discouragements of the synagogue; but the school of Tyrannus comes at last. To fail to make the most of it may well happen—such is our weakness. But to fail to try to make the most of it, to make no efforts to understand it, to let it slip by us, or ourselves to glide by it down the stream of life as if there were nothing particular in it, as if it had no bearing either on our own highest good or on that of others, this implies the presence of some grave disease in our moral and spiritual constitution; nay, it is that deadly apathy for which the stern realities of spiritual life and death have no real meaning. St. Paul was constantly failing, to all appearance: "as dying, and behold we live." He was constantly succeeding, for this among other reasons, that he was always alive to the possibility of success.

2. A second reason for St. Paul's remaining at Ephesus until Pentecost was the difficulty of the situation. "There are," he said, "many adversaries." To begin with, of course, there were the Jews of the synagogue, who would not forget the circumstances which led to the secession to the school of Tyrannus. Then there would have been in such a city as Ephesus, a mass of inert wickedness, reduced to outward decorum by military and social forces, but always ready to rise in active opposition to the energies of truth and goodness, and always able to command the services of powerful representatives. St. Paul already discerned the coming storm. He did not imagine that the religion of the Crucified would make itself a permanent home in that gay, pleasure-seeking, easy-tempered, superstitious population without a struggle. Sooner or later it would come into conflict with classes who were deeply concerned to oppose it—ay,—to the death. Among them were the skilled workmen who made miniature copies of the inner shrine of the temple of Artemis, which were bought by visitors, and placed as ornaments on tables or elsewhere in the interior of wealthy houses. These men were interested in preventing the triumph of Christianity. They were bound to the worship of Diana by the double tie of old association and commercial enterprise: and such a combination of motives in favour of a very foolish or bad system (it is a matter of experience) is excessively strong. Then the working men throughout Asia Minor, at this period, were, as has been amply shown from inscriptions, enrolled in clubs and unions almost without exception; so that, when

the interests of a particular trade were threatened, nothing was easier than to organise resistance of a very serious kind. St. Paul may or may not have had his eye upon Demetrius the silversmith; but he must have known enough of the forces which were at work around him to anticipate some such scene as the riot in the theatre as at least very probable.

"There are many adversaries." Yes; but that was no reason for leaving Ephesus. Had the Divine Master listened to the persuasions of the disciples, who would have kept Him at a distance from Judæa, on the ground that the Jews sought to stone Him? Had the Christians whom Paul himself had persecuted to the death before his conversion shrunk from their place or their work because of his own cruel opposition? Was not opposition the rule, the condition—nay, more, was it not the stimulus and opportunity—of all true Christian work, true Christian virtue? What does virtue mean, but manly force put forth in accordance with the rule of right, put forth all the more steadily when it is encompassed by difficulties? Difficulty, as a heathen saw, is positively necessary to the full development of virtue: the soft atmosphere of unimpeded success fosters only and surely moral effeminacy, moral decay. And therefore St. Paul looked upon the many adversaries at Ephesus not merely as no drawback, but as a positive attraction. They roused within him,—not any natural spirit of brute combativeness,—but the higher spiritualised military temper, which he tells us in the Epistle to the Ephesians is part of the outfit of the general Christian character, which in the Pastoral Epistles he associates especially with those who have given themselves to the service of Jesus Christ. It was a good thing, since he was a soldier by profession—a good soldier of Jesus Christ—to be on the field and taking note of the strength of the enemy. Each opponent was a possible convert; but in the last resort, an impotent antagonist, come what might. " Who shall separate us from the love of Christ ? " " I am persuaded, that neither death, nor life, nor angels, nor principalities, nor powers, nor things present, nor things to come, nor height, nor depth, nor any other creature, shall be able to separate us from the love of God, which is in Christ Jesus our Lord."[1]

III.

This solemn occasion, brethren, in the main, speaks for itself. Words are often out of place when men's hearts are full; when there is much that flits before the eye of the soul that no words can compass. Those of us who are here as candidates for ordination this morning can understand St. Paul in the text. Like him, we have arrived at a conclusion. We have made up our minds in a matter which binds us for life, as he did as to the best way of spending six weeks. It is well. God help us now and hereafter to say: "I will pay Thee my vows, which I promised with my lips and spake with my heart, when I gave myself to Thee, Lord Jesus Christ." There may have been much to plead for other lines of life: we do not deny that God may be served by men who serve Him in secular employments, or that all secular employments may be hallowed by a religious motive. But, for us, we have taken our parts: we have considered the claims of Corinth and chosen Ephesus. We have put our hands to the plough, and may not look back. We want no Clerical Disabilities Act to relieve us from a voluntary and welcome service: we wear the uniform of the Captain of our salvation, and would wear no other for all that this world can give.

But " there are many adversaries." Certainly there are. A man who takes Orders in the present day does so

[1] Rom. viii. 35, 38, 39.

under very different circumstances from those which would have attended the act forty, or even twenty years ago. It is undeniably more difficult to meet a clergyman's responsibilities now than then. Much more is expected in the way of personal exertion and ministerial efficiency. The air is filled with many controversies, which may be approached in many ways, but which can only be safely handled in one. The Roman Church has never confronted us before on so serious a scale, in every rank of society: nonconformity and irreligion have never before so openly joined their forces against what remains to us of power to give a Christian education to the people. The future is pregnant with possibilities; who can say what will be the status of the Church of England thirty, twenty, ten years hence? Who can now look forward as did our fathers, as did some among ourselves, to a settled order of events which would outlast us, which would subsist unimpaired, almost unvaried, when we should have passed away? Out of those days of routine, of tranquil and assured repose, we have passed into a very different period, when all around us betrays a feverish impatience of what has been and what is; when change as change is spoken of as if it had an inherent, a sacramental virtue; when blasts of destructive thought sweep through the intellectual atmosphere, pulverising in numbers of souls the most venerable convictions; when, even within the Church, men have accustomed themselves to think patiently of—in some cases even to welcome—the public repudiation of the most sacred and authoritative landmarks of the central certainties of the Faith. It is a time, too, this, when moral and social ideas are not less challenged than doctrinal truths; when society is troubled by the terrible suspicion that it may have to reckon with forces more serious than any it has yet encountered since it rose out of the chaos of barbarous life. Beyond any other class of men, the clergy, who deal with the gravest problems in the world of thought, who are more directly and intimately interested than any other class of men in the material as well as the spiritual wellbeing of the people, must be sensitively alive to these grave circumstances; and, as a matter of fact, they do actually deter many men, who in other days would have taken Holy Orders, from doing so now. Do not let us regret it: it is better thus. The strength of a Church does not consist in the number of pages of a clerical directory, but in the sum-total of moral force which she has at command. It is well that we should look on the difficulties of our time as did St. Paul on his: they are as nothing for a man with an honest heart and a clear positive faith.

For, after all, why is it that we do take Orders? Is it not because we believe and are sure that eighteen centuries ago an event occurred, compared with which all that has happened since, all that can happen in this eventful day—happen what may—is utterly insignificant? Is it not because, like St. Paul at Ephesus, we believe that the Everlasting Son of God really entered into conditions of space and time, and died upon the cross for the sins of all men, and rose from the grave, and ascended, and has been pleading for us all ever since, and is doing so at this moment, and has sent us His Spirit, and given us His Sacraments? Is it not because we are convinced that if He has done so much for us—for each of us,—the least we can do is to yield Him a free and cheerful service, in such circumstances as He wills, in storm or sunshine, in battle or repose, in hopeful times or days of despondency, it matters little? Surely this is so, brethren, and, when we think of it, the present scene, the nearer horizon, the tangled web of ecclesiastical and political change, dwarfs down into its true proportions, and we see only Jesus Christ Crucified, and souls perishing all around for lack of knowledge or lack of grace, and our own one duty —the duty of our predecessors, the duty of the great Apostle—to bring each within our reach, by whatever moral or intellectual instruments, close to the Atoning Cross, to have a share in the sprinkling of the Cleansing Blood, to know something of that Power and Wisdom of God which is still a stumbling-block to the self-righteous, and foolishness to the self-opinionated. And for this blessed work—blessed in its results to others, blessed in its reflex effect upon all who earnestly undertake it in dependence on God's grace—we have at this day great opportunities. The difficulties of the time do not merely stimulate us: they unwillingly assist us. Our rivals in this work, if we must term them such, are not so formidable after all. Rome, by her own act, has recently condemned herself to the task of advocating the equal infallibility of a long line of self-contradicting Popes. Puritanism, in all its phases, is, while it still clutches the pietistic formulas of its earlier history with convulsive eagerness, more and more surely forfeiting its old vitality as it sinks into the pit of scepticism which its sturdy repudiation of external authority has too surely made.

And as for those forms of thought which are the implacable enemies of all who believe in a Living God, and who own the Name of Christ, they cannot in the long-run satisfy a being like man, who has the ineffaceable presentiment of his immortality ever within him, and for whom the ideas of moral right and judgment can never be resolved into mere sentiment. The movement all around is, in some ways, in our favour. We have a better chance of winning a hearing for our Divine Master than in days when thought was stagnant, and habit fixed, and men were what they were not unfrequently for no reason but the traditional one. Earthly theories cannot exercise the human mind on the great questions which surround us in this present state of existence, without affording to the Truth of Heaven an opportunity of triumph. They who are furthest from Truth often have profound, although as yet undeveloped, perhaps unrecognised, sympathies with it: the King of the New Covenant is Ruler even in the midst among His enemies. And the conditions of human life do not alter: men live, and suffer, and die, just as they did eighteen centuries ago, and the real significance of this short and mysterious passage which we call life is not obliterated by our material civilisation or our mental theories. God grant that, be the scene of our labours what it may, with simple hearts we may teach and act as men who know that they will die among dying men; that so our light anxieties—afflictions, if such await us—which are but for a moment, may lead us on to an exceeding and an eternal weight of glory, through the boundless grace and mercy of Jesus our Lord.

SERMON IX.

FAITH WITHOUT MIRACLES.[1]

ST. JOHN x. 41, 42.

And many resorted unto Him, and said, John did no miracle: but all things that John spake of this Man were true. And many believed on Him there.

THE Jews of Jerusalem had attempted to lay violent hands on our Lord at the Feast of Dedication, and He retired into the district beyond the Jordan. It was at the end of December, in the winter before His last Passover. The final conflict between Light and darkness which was witnessed on Calvary could not now be long delayed. But the hour had not yet come: and therefore, in the words of the Evangelist, "Jesus went away again beyond Jordan, unto the place where John at first baptized, and there He abode." There is a subtle charm in finding ourselves, as life and work are drawing towards the end, amid the scenes which witnessed our first hopes and efforts; and our Lord, with His true Humanity, would, we may be reverently sure, have shared in feelings which belong to the loftiest side of our common nature. But the district would not have been welcome to Him only from its connection with His earlier days. It was the place where John at first baptized. It was just a year before that the intrepid Baptist, after being imprisoned in the gloomy fortress of Machærus, on the border of the desert, had, partly for political reasons, partly for his intrepid adherence to moral truth, been

---

Preached at the Ordination of the Bishop of London, in St. Paul's, on Trinity Sunday, May 31, 1874.

laid in a martyr's grave; but though his voice was silenced, his work survived him. Certainly the "Scribes and Pharisees of Jerusalem had rejected the counsel of God against themselves, being not baptized of him"; but it was otherwise with the honest, earnest populations of the Jordan valley. Among these people the Baptist's preaching had made a deep impression; and particularly they had noted what he said about "One Who, coming after him, was preferred before him." The consequence was that when Jesus retired from the violent controversies of Jerusalem into this peaceful district, He found something more than welcome memories of the past and a hospitable reception. The seed which John had sown had not perished in a soil like that: it had struck root, and had grown; it had been watered no doubt by the oft-repeated story of the Baptist's wrongs, culminating in a cruel death—a story repeated and pondered on by affectionate hearts. Nothing fosters truth like the sufferings of its representatives. And so the seed had grown, first the blade, then the ear, then the full corn in the ear; and the fields were white already to harvest, when the Divine Reaper came on His way. His appearance finished a spiritual work which had been begun long before. "Many resorted unto Him and said, John did no miracle: but all things that John said concerning this Man are true. And many believed on Him there."

Now the language of these Jordan converts appears to suggest matter for fruitful consideration on an occasion like this, when we are about to witness the bestowal of a Divine Commission upon men who are undertaking spiritual work in the Church of God.

St. John's disciples state two things about the man to whom they owed their conversion to Jesus Christ: he did no miracle, yet all that he spake of Christ was true. Let us consider these points in order.

I.

That the Baptist should have performed no miracle, that he should have given no outward sign that he had come from God, must strike any who reflect upon the fact as remarkable. He was the heir of ages of miracle; and he spoke to a people which knew its own history, and might well have looked for miracles at hands like his. Spiritually speaking, he was in direct succession from Daniel, from Elisha, from Elijah most of all. Himself a prophet, he was himself also the subject of prophecy; the last prophet of the Hebrew Canon had distinctly announced him;[1] and at his birth a heavenly messenger had predicted that he would live and work in the spirit and power of Elijah.[2] What did this reference to the prophet of Carmel mean, if its subject was to have no share in the supernatural powers which awed the apostate court of Israel? In one respect, which our Lord glances at, the Baptist stood on a higher eminence than his great predecessor. "The prophets and the law prophesied *until* John."[3] He was closing the system in and for which Elijah had laboured; a system which had been inaugurated and maintained by miracle, and which it was natural to suppose would not be closed without some sign of corresponding meaning. Yet "John did no miracle."

Nor is the fact less remarkable if we consider the other side of the work which the Baptist had in hand. He stood on the frontier-line between two dispensations. He looked forward as well as backward; he told men to repent because a new spiritual organisation, which prophecy had glanced at, which Jewish Rabbis had guessed at, which was intimately bound up with the very heart and substance of the national hope, was now at hand. He

[1] Mal. iii. 1; iv. 5, 6. [2] St. Luke i. 17. [3] St. Matt. xi. 13.

announced what he called the "Kingdom of the Heavens"; and we, as we look back upon that which he announced, know that the kingdom which dates from the day of Pentecost was itself cradled in miracle. Its Author worked miracles; His Birth, His Death, His reappearance among men, His final departure from the scene of sense, were all accompanied by miracle; His Apostles, in His Name, worked miracles just as He did; and it might have been supposed that the forerunner of a system like this would have worked them too. The Jordan people felt the contrast between the works of Jesus and that of their first teacher when they said, "John did no miracle."

Nor can it be said that the time at which John lived was not of a character to make miracle probable. All the analogies of Israel's history pointed the other way. Miracles occur mainly in sacred history when a new truth has to be proclaimed for the first time; or when an apostate or immoral generation has to be recalled to the truth and holiness which it is in danger of forgetting; or when a revelation is wellnigh discredited and trodden out of men's daily thoughts by the stress and intolerance of heathen persecution. Egypt, Samaria, Babylon, are, so to speak, the natural scenes of Biblical miracle; Moses, Elijah, Daniel, the appropriate organs of miraculous power. Yet in the Baptist these several conditions seem to meet concurrently. The Baptist had to prepare the way for a new revelation. He had to do this by recalling men's minds in a corrupt and careless age to the first principles of the Jewish theocracy; his baptism, unlike that of Jesus Christ, was an acted sermon—it was an outward pledge of renewed fidelity to the moral truth which had come down from Moses and the prophets. Surely under these circumstances, if we are to go by historical analogies, we might have expected a miracle-worker. If at any pre-

Faith without Miracles.

vious time miracles had recommended or had upheld God's truth in the minds of men, we should have looked for them at the hands of the austere prophet of the wilderness who immediately preceded our Lord Jesus Christ. If the suggestions of the old history of Israel were to go for anything, the days of John the Baptist should have been—so we might think—a miracle-working epoch.

2. Yet in spite of this, "John did no miracle"; that is the first fact on which the Jordan converts lay stress. On the other hand—this is the second fact—he produced conviction. "All things that John spake of this Man were true." St. John had made heavy demands upon the faith of these converts. He had said that Jesus was altogether greater than himself, so much greater that he, John, was not worthy to unloose and hold His sandals when He entered a house or the temple—the duty of the lowest slaves![1] He had said that Jesus held in His hand the winnowing-fan of judgment, with which He was on the point of thoroughly purging the floor or territory of Palestine, separating the just and holy souls who would acknowledge His mission from the mass of corrupt and hypocritical chaff around.[2] He had said that Jesus would baptize, not merely, as he himself did, in water, which was to symbolise repentance, but also in the Holy Ghost, and in the fire, whether of God's Love or of His Justice.[3] He had, as reported by the fourth Evangelist, gone far beyond this. Jesus was the Lamb of God—not merely the perfectly innocent Sufferer, but the predestined Victim Whose death was to atone effectually for human sin.[4] Nay more, Jesus, although coming after St. John in the order of time, was before him, not merely in the order of eminence, but in that of real existence. "He was before me."[5] Clothed as

---

[1] St. Matt. iii. 11.   [2] *Ibid.* 12.   [3] *Ibid.* 11.   [4] St. John i. 29.
[5] St. John i. 30.

He was in flesh and blood, and younger in years than His forerunner, Jesus was yet indefinitely more ancient; His true existence reached back into an Eternity when as yet the Baptist was not.

These were tremendous assertions, yet the people of the Upper Jordan could say in after years, "All things that John spake of this Man are true." They looked hard at Jesus; they listened to Him; they watched Him; they felt that there was something about Him which altogether transcended their ordinary experience. John's language might well have seemed paradoxical: yet—face to face with the fact—they felt that it was sober, prosaic truth. They were plainly in presence of a superhuman Being of unspeakable holiness and of fathomless love, Whose Person, Whose self-sacrifice, Whose judgment of men, Whose baptism, was, or might well be, all that John predicted. "All things that John spake of this Man are true."

Yes! mark it well: John had been a full year at the least in his martyr grave, and the world had gone on its course, talking and thinking of topics of the day, and forgetting the victim of royal levity and female passion. And wellnigh three years had passed since John had been there; he was "out of sight"—in his prison first, and then in his grave, in the fortress away to the south; but he was not "out of mind." He lived, if not in bodily presence, yet by his words, and in the memory of those who had heard him. All those sayings of his, now that he was gone, lived in human hearts deep down beneath the daily speech and works of men; and they would have been forgotten in time if none had appeared to verify and claim them, or if, when He did appear, they had been felt to be distorted, or beside the mark, or exaggerated. As it was, when Jesus presented Himself, there was a common upheaving of convictions and hearts,

Faith without Miracles. 253

"This," men said, "this is the Man, this the Character, of Whom our loved and murdered master spoke to us of old." "All things that John spake to us of this Man are true."

3. How are we to account for the conviction thus produced in the minds of those people of the Jordan valley by the Baptist's ministry, when he dispensed altogether with the instrumentality of miracle?

Certainly we are not to account for it by saying that miracles are practically useless for the purpose of producing religious conviction. Holy Scripture and the common or general sense of human thought both forbid us to say that. Scripture says expressly that miracles are a great agent in producing faith in the mission of the worker. Jesus Christ, says St. Peter, was "a Man approved of God by miracles, and wonders, and signs, which God did by Him in the midst of the Jewish people."[1] The multitude followed Him, says the last Evangelist, "because they saw His miracles, which He did on them that were diseased."[2] Men argued, as they looked on, with the blind man, "How can a man that is a sinner do such miracles?"[3] or, more decisively, with Nicodemus, "No man can do these miracles that Thou doest, except God be with him."[4] And, therefore, when Jesus did the beginning of His miracles in Cana of Galilee, and manifested forth His glory, His disciples believed on Him;[5] and later on, "many believed in His Name, when they saw the miracles that He did."[6] And the Jewish authorities felt that Christ's miracles were on this account a formidable fact. "What do we?" they said, "for this Man worketh many miracles."[7] And when He had passed into His glory, and His Apostles undertook

---

[1] Acts ii. 22.
[2] St. John vi. 2.
[3] Ibid. ix. 16, 30-34.
[4] St. John iii. 2.
[5] Ibid. ii. 11.
[6] Ibid. ii. 23.
[7] St. John xi. 47.

to preach Him to the world, "God also bare them witness, both with signs and wonders, and with divers miracles, and with gifts of the Holy Ghost, according to His own will";[1] and these supernatural agencies, as we know, did as a matter of fact largely recommend to a reluctant world the faith which the Apostles preached.

The modern disposition to depreciate the evidential force of miracles is mainly due to two causes. It represents a reaction of religious thought from the system of Paley, who—without disrespect to a great and honoured name—may be thought to have made the case of Christianity depend too exclusively upon the Apostolic conviction of the reality of the greatest Christian miracle; through not having taken collateral lines of evidence sufficiently into account. But it is also due to a profound, although not always avowed, disbelief in the reality of any miracles at all—a disbelief which is due to an assumption that the generally unvarying order of nature must, in virtue of some occult necessity, be always invariable. These reasons for depreciating miracle belong to the history of modern thought; and to import them into the interpretation of Scripture is to make an historical as well as another and graver mistake. But at the same time, nothing is more clearly stated in Scripture than that the effect of miracle in producing belief is not of a mechanical and resistless character. Miracle is God speaking emphatically from behind the veil of nature to a particular state of mind or conscience; and if the requisite state of mind or conscience does not exist, the miracle is fruitless; in order to succeed it requires a certain inward susceptibility on the part of the eye-witness, such as faithfulness to natural light would supply. No mere external force or fact can subdue the human will; if the will is determined against any spiritual impression, no material fact, however extraordinary,

[1] Heb. ii. 4.

Faith without Miracles. 255

wrought before the eye of sense, can compel internal sympathy and assent. If Moses and the Prophets do not persuade to repentance, men will not be persuaded though one rose from the dead.[1] Men will acknowledge the outward fact; but they will seek to diminish its importance, or they will refer it to some evil agency, to Beelzebub, in order to escape an unwelcome admission. Therefore our Lord distinguishes between merely eating of the loaves, and recognising the inner meaning of the miracle; and although He insists that to have seen and rejected His miracles entails "sin" upon the Jewish people, He speaks in the highest terms of the faith of the Pagan centurion, which did not wait for miracles to call it forth. And here indeed we may reverently trace one of the main objects with which the last Gospel was written. When, at the end of the first century of the Christian era, the first three Gospels had been for some thirty years in circulation, the question would naturally have occurred to their readers, Why it was that the people who had seen so many miracles of our Lord could have rejected Him? The fourth Gospel recognises the fact, and accounts for it. "Though Jesus had done so many miracles among them," says St. John, "yet they believed not on Him: that the saying of Esaias might be fulfilled, which he spake: Lord, who hath believed our report? and to whom hath the arm of the Lord been revealed? Therefore they could not believe, because that Esaias said again, He hath blinded their eyes, and hardened their heart; that they should not see with their eyes, nor understand with their heart, and be converted, and I should heal them. These things said Esaias, when he saw His glory, and spake of Him."[2] Prophecy pointed not merely to the glory and force of the miracle-working Christ, but to the state of mind of the generation which would reject Him; and St. John,

[1] St. Luke xvi. 31.   [2] St. John xii. 37-41.

by selecting certain representative miracles and attendant discourses of our Lord, and manifesting thus how close was the connexion between His teaching and His miracles, shows how the Jews, instead of believing His teaching on account of His miracles, rejected His miracles because they shrank from His teaching. We cannot be surprised then that the fourth Evangelist carefully recorded the triumphs of a ministry like that of the Baptist, which had been unattended by miracle, while yet it had achieved so much for faith. The case of the Baptist showed that, if miracles could not compel faith, faith might exist apart from miracles; and in this way it has also a permanent interest for the Christian ages, and for ourselves, the present or expectant members of the Christian ministry.

My brethren, I am far from saying that no miracles have occurred in the Christian Church since the Apostles' days, or that they may not occur in our own. Looking to the unaltered relations between God and His works, we must feel that what has been, may be. Looking to the unlimited character of the Gospel promises, we cannot wisely say that their complete fulfilment was meant to be confined to the age of the Apostles, or to the first three centuries, or to any one period of the history of the Church. But the possibility, or even the probability, of miracle is one thing; the proof that a reputed miracle has occurred is another. There are miracles in the Primitive Church so much in keeping with Apostolic precedent, and so well attested, that it is difficult to see how they can be set aside except by denying the possibility of their occurrence. On the other hand, a miracle like that of La Salette, and many of which it is a sample, is discredited by its typical character, and still more by the insufficiency of the producible proof that it ever occurred. Miracles at any rate have been dispensed with, as a rule, in the

Church of Christ, for reasons which we may reverently conjecture; the great miracles remain to us in the Gospel and the Apostolic records : and if it should be said, with or without truth, of the modern Church, " She does no miracles," there is no reason whatever why it should not be added by believing hearts, " All things that she has said of her Lord and King may be shown to be experimentally true."

II.

These considerations suggest encouragement and instruction for all of us, but especially for those who are about to be ordained to-day.

1. And first, encouragement. What a good man needs chiefly, when he is first setting his hands to the work of Jesus Christ in His Church, is encouragement. There may be, here and there, a self-confidence, a shallowness, a levity of temper which treats Ordination as it might treat a call to the bar,—as a piece of inevitable ceremonial in a professional career. To most men who have any seriousness of purpose or any approach to a real perception of what is at stake, the case must be far otherwise. A man who is on the eve of his ordination, if he is worth anything, feels, as he never felt before, the awfulness, the greatness, the holiness, the love, of the Being Whom he is freely undertaking to represent. He feels as it was impossible to feel it in the more ordinary levels of life, the intricacy, the mystery, the manysidedness of human nature—that human nature to which, for his whole life, he is going to address himself in his Master's Name. Above all, he feels, as never before, his own personal weakness—his insufficiency for these things, as well as the many sins and shortcomings of his past life : like the prophet, he feels himself a child;[1] or as a man of unclean

[1] Jer. i. 6.

lips, whose eyes have seen the King, the Lord of hosts;[1] or like the simple and sincere Christians of antiquity, when they were called to high office in the Church, he would fain hide himself rather than undertake "*onus reformidandum angelis*"—a burden from which the angels might wisely hold back.

"Ah!" many a man has said to himself in these solemn hours, "the case would be different if we were really on a par with those Apostles in whose steps we tread. We might do Apostolic work if we could really wield Apostolic weapons. But we are face to face with a world which looks with cynical calm, or with declared hostility, upon our work and message; and yet we do not, upon occasion, heal the cripple, or smite the sorcerer with blindness, or shake off the deadly serpent into the fire, or pass through prison bars under the guidance of angels, or expel the spirit of evil, or raise the dead. These things may happen; but, as far as experience goes, they do not happen; and we find ourselves, like the Apostles, in charge of a supernatural Creed, but without the supernatural aids which they could command."

Many a man has said this to himself, but surely he might find comfort in the Baptist. The Baptist was not a minister of the kingdom of heaven as we: he only announced it. He had no such chartered means of communion with the inmost Heart and Life of God such as we Christians enjoy through the mediation of the Only Begotten Son. He was more than a prophet! true, and yet the least in the kingdom of heaven was to be greater than he. Our Ordination at this hour confers a gift which in its fulness was certainly denied to him. Yet though the herald of an unrealised future, intrusted with no miraculous certificates of his mission, he made an impression upon the souls of men that was profound, ineffaceable.

[1] Isa. vi. 5.

Why should not we? He did not despair because at his word the desert did not again witness the miracles of the age of Moses or Elijah: why should we?

But many a man at his Ordination would state his grounds of discouragement in other words. " There are, if we may adapt the word, miracles within the sphere of nature and order; miracles of spiritual insight, miracles of persuasive eloquence, miracles of practical pastoral ability, miracles of biblical or theological acquirements. These, at any rate, are given in different measures to some in all ages of the Church; and yet we may feel that, for lack of aptitude or of opportunity, they each and all are denied to us. There might be some hope, if one such power were conspicuously ours; as it is, must we not feel that there is little or nothing that we can hope to achieve in the great kingdom of souls?"

No, my brethren, it is not so. These gifts of God, whether in nature or in grace, have their value; and we are all indebted to Him when here or there He bestows them on any one of His servants. We all of us, for instance, have gained by such gifts as those of the late Bishop Wilberforce; yet it would be an irreligious as well as a foolish idealism which should practically say, " I cannot hope to do any good, because I am conscious of not possessing this or that accomplishment which was so conspicuous in that remarkable man." Depend upon it, brethren, the real work that is done in the Church of God does not in the main depend upon splendid gifts of this kind, any more than it depends upon the power to work literal miracles. As a rule it is the outcome of certain spiritual forces and moral laws which may be appealed to by every one of us; the real Worker is the same, through the weakest and lowliest, as well as through the strongest and greatest, of His servants: and while it is well to " covet earnestly the best gifts," there is no reason for losing heart if we are denied them. We may work no miracles that will take the imagination of the world by storm, yet we may succeed in doing that which is of more importance, bringing men to see that the Church's teaching about Christ is true.

2. And this brings me to the instruction which is suggested by the language of these Peræan converts. What was it in the Baptist's case which secured the highest spiritual success, in the absence of what was supposed to be the ordinary instrumentality for commanding it?

There was, of course, first of all, the native power of truth, which cannot be wholly ignored,—which is honoured indeed by the ferocity and outcry of prejudice and passion; which may be resisted successfully by an evil will, but which always secures a certain measure of success. There was, secondly, the voice of an inward Teacher, not yet baptizing His people with Pentecostal Fire, but, as in all ages, sanctioning the ministry of His representatives and organs by seconding in the secret chambers of the soul their appeal from without. And we can fall back on this assistance with peculiar confidence, since it is the Christian Church to which this great gift is specially promised. "I will put My laws into their minds, and write them upon their hearts":[1] the Holy Ghost teaches, not in words of human wisdom, but by an inward persuasion, in demonstration of the Spirit and of power.

But the secret of the Baptist's ministerial power was still more peculiar to himself. Thousands of Christians have administered a larger and therefore more powerful truth, under the chartered promise of a richer measure of the Holy Spirit, but with far inferior results.

a. That which distinguishes St. John is, first, his clear, well-defined conception of the message he has to give. Repentance first, then the coming kingdom of the heavens,

[1] Heb. viii. 10.

then, and above all, the Person and Work of the coming King. Whether he is addressing scribes or peasants his message is the same. He is cross-questioned by a delegacy which is sent by the Sanhedrim at Jerusalem, and which would have placed a teacher who did not know what he meant in a serious difficulty. He was consulted by publicans, by soldiers, by people generally; his answers were clear and consistent with his whole representation of life and duty. It was consideration for his followers, not vacillation of his own, which dictated the message which he sent from his prison at Machærus, " Art Thou He that should come?" As reported in the fourth Gospel, he says more about the great Object of his teaching than in the first three; but there is no contradiction—only progress; the Divine Object before his mind is one and the same.

There have been ages when it would have been unnecessary to insist on the value of a clear mental conception of what we have to teach. But in our days the distractions of controversy and the sceptical feeling of the time combine to ascribe a certain merit to an indefiniteness which, if it could be justified on intellectual grounds, which I do not care here to discuss, would be, in any case, fatal to spiritual work in the souls of men. The human soul needs, above everything, a clear representation of truth and duty. Indefiniteness paralyses moral force: a cloud is not a thing to rest upon in the hour of temptation, or in the hour of bodily or mental agony. If we ourselves know little or nothing clearly about the unseen world, we had better, far better, hold our tongues; if we do know anything, we cannot be too explicit in stating what we know. Above all things, like St. John, we of the Church of Christ cannot point too clearly, too frequently, too earnestly, to the Lamb of God. For us He is not the beautiful theme of an old-world literature; He is a living Being, Who exerts upon the world and upon the soul at this hour a blessed and awful influence; Who is, or should be, more to us than any other is or can be. No sermon should be unconsecrated by a clear reference to His Person and His Work; no enterprise should be undertaken, save with an eye to His glory; no form of ministerial or personal effort should be entertained as practicable apart from Him to Whom—as the Lamb that was slain—the perfect homage of the intellect and the heart of His servants is pre-eminently due in earth as in heaven. His adorable Person, His unspeakable condescension, His bitter and world-redeeming sufferings, His resurrection glory, His endless intercession in heaven, His spiritual and sacramental gifts chartered to His Church until the end of time—let these truths have possession of our hearts and intellects, and we shall not need the power of working physical miracles.

β. St. John's strength lay, secondly, in his singleness of purpose. His mental energies, his moral aims, were not dissipated. That he might the better concentrate his powers upon the single object of preparing the way of the Lord, he lived apart from men, dwelling in solitude on the meaning and exigencies of his awful message, even when he was not announcing it. He would have been a weaker man had he lent himself to any one of the political or scholastic opinions which distracted Jerusalem: men soon lose sight of a supreme object of interest amid the claims of the social and intellectual world. "A double-minded man"—a man with two souls—says St. James, "is unstable in all his ways":[1] and instability, of course, means weakness. St. John was a man of one soul, a man who could take the Psalmist's words as his own: "With my whole heart have I sought Thee."[2]

This absolute simplicity of purpose, brethren, is a form of moral power which can dispense with miracle. It is

[1] St. James i. 8.   [2] Ps. cxix. 10.

unlike anything which the mass of men can recognise in their own lives, and it impresses them accordingly. A soul simply bent upon carrying out the Will of God, so far as it is known, is like a man pushing his way towards a definite object through a crowd of people who are huddling together in aimless confusion or pointless gossip. Depend upon it, St. John Baptist was a power—for this if for no other reason: he had only one practical object before him from first to last.

γ. And thus, lastly, St. John's strength lay in his consistency. He was a preacher of Repentance—of high and awful views of God's justice, and of His impending providences. He lived accordingly. As he was not a reed shaken with the wind, so also he was not a man clothed in soft raiment. And this had its effect in an age when the Idumæan Herod was doing what he could to introduce a Pagan standard of luxury into Jerusalem. The life of the Baptist reflected visibly the reality and power of another world; the bleak desert, the locusts and wild honey, the raiment of camel's hair and leathern girdle about the loins, were in keeping with the claims of the man who would dare, when true charity demanded it, to speak the language of the sternest reproof and address the most influential classes of his day as a "generation of vipers."

My brethren, in all probability, we of the Christian Church sometimes lose more than we think by an opposite course. Society has its claims, no doubt; but men look in the lives of all preachers of the Crucified for something that shall stand for the mark of the Nails. And if there be nothing, if all be easy, pleasing, smooth, then men say to themselves there is no real correspondence between our lives and our message. We may get through our days without trouble, but we shall not bring souls to faith in Jesus Christ. If we could make up our minds, in whatever degree, to do what we dislike, to undergo what we dislike, to "endure hardness," in that exact degree shall we secure moral power such as can sway the souls of men —moral power which is worse than worthless, if we do not use it to lead our brethren to the Feet of their and our Redeemer, but which, where it exists, can dispense with miracle.

On his Ordination day a man stands as it were upon an eminence from which he looks back over the path which he has hitherto trodden, and forward over the plains, which may or may not be long and weary, to that point on the horizon which all must reach at last. On an Ordination day a man does well to ask himself, What shall I desire to have been, to have done, when I come to die? All the intervening circumstances of clerical life, between Ordination and death, are really insignificant; marriage, promotion, change of work and scene, loss or acquirement of friends, the great joys, the great sorrows—they are everything at the time, but, in the long-run, they cannot be measured with that solemn incident which closes all. And if a man who has served our Lord simply in the Priesthood could choose an epitaph, not to be sculptured by human art upon his gravestone, but to be traced by God's finger on the hearts of his flock, what would he desire but that which was uttered by the Jordan converts over their martyred master: "John did no miracle: but all things that John spake of this Man were true"? What will it profit in those awful, searching moments, when we are passing into the presence of the Judge, that we have been literary or eloquent, or men of mark, or even men of great spiritual sympathy and penetration—if all this has not resulted in bringing our fellows to the foot of the Cross, if it has done nothing for the glory and the empire of our Lord and Saviour? What will the absence of these things matter, the absence of all gifts that impress the imagination, and win honour in the judgment of men, if quietly, perseveringly, unflinchingly, we have kept our eye on Him,—spoken, worked, suffered if need be, for Him—so that when we are gone, His Love and Presence are lodged for time and eternity in many a soul, and men arise to say of us, "He was a commonplace person; he did no miracle; but we shall bless him in the hour of death and in the day of judgment, and in the everlasting world, for we have found already, by a blessed experience, that all things which he spake, by his words and by his life, of the Redeemer of our souls, are certainly true"?

SERMON X.

APOSTOLIC LABOURS AN EVIDENCE OF CHRISTIAN TRUTH.[1]

ROMANS x. 18.

But I say, Have they not heard? Yes verily, their sound went into all the earth, and their words unto the ends of the world.

ON the Feast of the Apostle who was first converted to Christ, and who opens the list of festivals in the Christian Year, it is obvious to attempt a consideration of the work of the Apostolate under that aspect which is suggested by St. Paul in the passage chosen from to-day's Epistle. The whole context is in its style one of the most obscure portions of the Epistle to the Romans. The structure and connection are continually disjointed or broken by the introduction of quotations from the Old Testament: and in reading these quotations we are often supposed to be in possession of secondary or even of mystical senses, as well as of other underlying trains of thought which connect them. These, when detected and exhibited, enable us to trace the sequence of the argument, and to explain in detail the sense of a passage, which a too eager literalism might find hopelessly unintelligible. For the general scope of the Apostle is sufficiently plain. The Jew is taught his responsibilities in presence of the advancing Gospel from the pages of his Hebrew Bible. He learns to contrast the religion of the Synagogue with that of the Church, when viewed in its spirit, method, and end. And this, not from the lips of

---

[1] Preached in the Chapel of Lambeth Palace at the Consecration of the Bishop of Nassau, on the Feast of St. Andrew, November 30, 1863.

Evangelists, but from the books of Leviticus and Deuteronomy.[1] Prophets like Isaiah and Joel successively announce to him the reward of faith in Christ, and the intimate and beneficent nearness of the Lord of all to all His true worshippers,[2] and by consequence the abolition of the Judaic nationalism, and the Catholicity of the religion which was succeeding it.[3] And when the question is asked how there can be such true worship without faith in its Object, or faith without a religious education, or this again without a message from heaven, and an authoritative commission to proclaim it,[4] the reply is given in the words of the Evangelical prophet,[5] for whose entranced soul the intervening centuries have neither force nor meaning, and the distant and contingent future is a realised and present fact. Along with the messengers who announce to captive Israel the speedy return of peace and freedom, there mingle, in the prophet's vision, other forms of Apostolic mien and greatness, and their footsteps fall on all the mountains of the world, as they carry forward the message which emancipates mankind, and which proclaims an alliance between Earth and Heaven. Yet more, this greatest of the prophets foresees the partial acceptance of the Gospel as accurately as he foretells its universal promulgation:[6] and prophecy closes around the Jew, who refuses belief to the report of the Apostles, by describing not merely the Truth which confronts him, but his own attitude towards it. That there may be no mistake as to the weight and pressure of the Jew's responsibility, the Apostle asks in the text somewhat abruptly, whether the men of Israel[7] have not heard the Gospel-

[1] Ver. 5, Lev. xviii. 5; ver. 6, Deut. xxx. 12-14.
[2] Ver. 11, Isa. xxviii. 16; ver. 13, Joel ii. 32.
[3] Ver. 12.   [4] Ver. 14, 15.
[5] Isa. lii. 7.   [6] Ver. 16, Isa. liii. 1.
[7] So Meyer *in loc.* against Origen, Calvin, Fritzsche, etc., who refer the question to the Heathen, in spite of the obvious connexion.

message. And he answers not by pointing to the literal fact, that already the messengers of Christ had penetrated far and wide into either of the great branches of the Dispersion, while Jerusalem itself was the home and focus of Christian Doctrine: he quotes a psalmist who is singing of the heavenly bodies, and who tells how they speak for the glorious Creator in terms which all can understand, while from day to day and age to age, they hand on their mighty tradition of the Truth, which all the languages of man confess, and all the climes and regions of the earth have heard.

> "The heavens declare the glory of God,
> And the firmament sheweth his handiwork.
> Day unto day uttereth speech,
> And night unto night sheweth knowledge.
> There is no speech nor language
> Where their voice is not heard:
> Their line is gone out through all the earth,
> And their words to the end of the world." [1]

In the translation "their line" the Authorised Version keeps close to the etymology of the original Hebrew: but unprejudiced scholars (at least on such a point we may trust Ewald and Gesenius) will tell us, that the line was probably the chord of a musical instrument; [2] and that, by a common form of speech, the chord might stand for the sound which it produced. The sense of the LXX., which St. Paul quotes, is supported by the version of Symmachus, and by the Syriac translation: [3] and this rendering of the passage is further illustrated by the well-known representation of the morning-stars singing

---

[1] Ps. xix. 1-4.
[2] Gesen. Lex. *s.v.* קו. Compare too *Thesaurus*, p. 1201, where, however, Professor Roediger seems inclined to adopt Olshausen's "conjecture" of קלם for קום, in which he had been anticipated by Bellarmine (*de Verbo Dei*, lib. ii. c. 2), Ewald, *Dichter A. B.* ii. 28.

[3] LXX. ὁ φθόγγος. Symm. ὁ ἦχος. Syr. Pesch. ܐܢܘܢܩܝܐ "annunciatio eorum." Vulg. and St. Jer. *sonus eorum.*

Evidence of Christian Truth. 269

together, in the book of Job.[1] We might be tempted to think of a literal music of the spheres,—a conception familiar to the ancient world, and not unknown among Christian writers:[2] but the general features, and particularly the gravity of inspired Scripture, would lead us (with St. Augustine[3]) to recognise a satisfactory account of the metaphor in the order and harmony and proportion which rule the movements of the heavenly bodies, and from which the truths of his Creator's Being, as they flash upon the outward eye, pierce the inner ear of the soul of man. The Apostle in this very Epistle has shown how the Revelation of God in nature is only lost to man through his moral corruption.[4] And the Psalm throughout supposes a correspondence between God's original unveiling of Himself in Creation, and His second revelation of Himself in the Mosaic Law.[5] Let this, the internal thought of the Psalm, have been grasped, and it will be admitted that St. Paul cannot be accused of an arbitrary accommodation of language when he extends an analogy, recognised by the Psalm itself, as existing between the lessons of God's work in nature and the teaching of His Voice to Moses, to the wider comparison of the teaching of the heavens that shine on all climes and races of men, with the world-wide mission of the Church. He is indeed speaking of nothing less than the whole world,[6] yet there

[1] Job xxxviii. 7, where, however, the parallelism בְּנֵי־אֱלֹהִים shows that the Holy Angels are intended, although described under a metaphor which illustrates the text.
[2] See the authorities in Lorinus in *Psalm.* vol. i. p. 322.
[3] Quoted by Lorinus *ub. supra.* Compare too *de Civ. Dei,* xi. 18, where he expands the idea of Ecclus. xxiii. 15 in this sense.
[4] Rom. i. 20-23.
[5] Comp. Kuhn, *Dogmatik Einl.* vol. i. p. 6, for a clear statement of the sense in which the natural world is a Revelation.
[6] It would be absurd to pretend that in adopting the LXX. transl. τὰ πέρατα τῆς οἰκουμένης, St. Paul was thinking of the Roman Empire. The words εἰς πᾶσαν τὴν γῆν would correct this. St. Ambrose christianises the idea of the word οἰκουμένη (in Ps. xlviii. ver. 3, ii. 946).

is no real ground for maintaining that he is speaking hyperbolically; as though he were flourishing a quotation without having ascertained its range of meaning—in other words, without a due sense of the solemn responsibilities of language. We must at least endeavour to place ourselves in the position of the speaker, before we decide upon the force which must be attributed to words of doubtful import. Thus when Obadiah speaks of all the nations and kingdoms of the earth into which Ahab had sent to seek Elijah, he uses the language of an uneducated Oriental, with the narrowest political horizon.[1] But when our Divine Lord bids His Apostles go teach all nations, He speaks as One Who from all eternity had shared the Intellectual no less than the other Glories of the Everlasting Father.[2] So when St. Paul tells the Romans[3] that their faith was spoken of throughout the whole world, he means throughout the world of Apostolic Christendom: when, later, he assures the Colossians that the Gospel which had come to them "is in all the world,"[4] his intrepid faith already sees the end in its beginning, and like the prophets of the older Covenant he describes a future which had yet to unfold itself, as if it were an accomplished fact. So here, the true sense of the text must be looked for in the parallel which it assumes between the world-embracing light, which streams as a speechless utterance of self-evident Truth from the orbs of Heaven, and the Illumination of the Faith, radiating from the Person of Jesus, and diffused by His Apostles and their representatives through the centuries and countries of the world. It is obvious that St. Paul's quotation is more than sufficient for his immediate purpose. He might have told us much that we yearn to know, about

---

[1] 1 Kings xviii. 10.
[2] St. John xvii. 5; x. 30; xiv. 9. Compare Col. ii. 3 and Eph. i. 8, 9.
[3] Rom. i. 8.   [4] κόσμῳ, not οἰκουμένῃ, Col. i. 6.

the labours of his brother Apostles : he might have
pointed to his own constant presence in the synagogues of
the Hellenic Dispersion. But while his question touches
merely the labours of the first age of Christendom and
the needs and opportunities of a single race, the answer [1]
carries us up to an ideal or rather a prophetic vision—the
Jew and his responsibilities fade away into the background of thought—and before us there opens a panorama,
comprehending the whole Missionary action of the Church
from the labours of the first Apostle on the Day of Pentecost down to the last efforts of those servants whom our
Lord will find working and watching when He comes to
Judgment.. The Apostle reads the history of the Church
in the light of his Master's words: "Go teach all
nations." [2] The intervening centuries count for nothing;
just as when we gaze at the fixed star, we do not
ordinarily reflect upon that scintillation of the rays of
its light through almost measureless space which Science
yet reveals to us in all its wonder with minute precision.[3]
And the Apostle sees all at a single glance: he ignores
the alternation of ebb and flow—the constant play of light
and shade—which meet us in the actual history of the
Church; we forget, as we read his words, that struggle for
life, maintained for centuries,—maintained against overwhelming forces,—maintained amid tears and agony and
blood; we seem to be watching a process which has all
the beauty and ease of a natural movement; we have
before us what is less the history of an accomplished and
hard-won triumph than it is the spectacle of a beneficent
provision or law of the universe, in which there is no

---

[1] Some expositors seem to have inferred from the passage, that when St. Paul wrote it, the Gospel was actually being preached in China and America; cf. Meyer *in loc.*

[2] St. Matt. xxviii. 19; cf. Ps. lxxii. 11, Hag. ii. 7, St. Matt. xxiv. 14, xxv. 32, Acts xvii. 26, Rom. i. 5, xvi. 26, Gal. iii. 8, Rev. vii. 9.

[3] Humboldt, *Cosmos*, iii. p. 259 *sqq.* ; cf. pp. 110, 111.

struggle, no effort, no jar, no resistance, and in which the Heavenly Wisdom already reaches from one end to another mightily, and smoothly and sweetly ordereth all things.[1] "Their sound is gone into all lands, and their words unto the ends of the world."

The continuous missionary and self-expanding action of the Church is a truth which we generally fall back upon or enforce for the practical purpose of supporting Missions. But it has a distinct speculative value; it is in itself an evidence of the divinity of Christianity; its history, often intermittent and disappointing, is yet (taken as a whole) a living and perpetual testimony to the presence in Jesus of a something which was higher than the highest human foresight or human genius; it is a feature of Christianity which, if Christianity were not divine, would be nothing less than inexplicable;—it flows from Words of Christ, which if Christ had been merely human, would have been words of startling audacity or of unprecedented folly.

And here are two points that demand our consideration.

I.

For our Lord's command and the prophecy of His Apostle imply first of all that the Gospel would stand *the test of time*. Of all forms of power, as of all forms of thought that are merely human, time is the great enemy. No sooner has a doctrine or a system taken its place in the arena of human thought, than, like the ocean which imperceptibly fritters away the base of a mountain cliff, time forthwith begins its relentless work of progressive demolition. Take the case of any human doctrine which has gained the ear of classes or of races of men, and which accordingly has been formulated by genius and proclaimed

[1] Wisd. viii. 1.

with enthusiasm. A doctrine, let us suppose, which not merely does not rest upon revelation, but which is not exclusively based upon those axioms of mathematics or morals which themselves express truths of the Being and Mind of God. And I say, that such a human speculation will pursue a development of which the stages can be traced with certainty: it will pass from the energy of its youth to the self-reliant vigour and system of its manhood, and to the decrepitude and death which are beyond. For as time passes, men slowly learn the lessons of experience and reflection; and the titles by which a doctrine can establish permanent empire are very different from those which originally recommend it. It must not merely have created admiration at the first, it must bear the friction of a continuous scrutiny; it must be able to afford not merely the charm of an hour's entertainment, but the duties of a life-long friendship. Again, time brings with it what we term in our ignorance, chance; it brings combinations of circumstances, and of agencies to bear, upon which no genius can calculate, and against which no prudence can take its measures. Human annals are rife with the history of dynasties and empires which have survived the resistance of natural and mighty foes, and have succumbed to indirect and accidental dangers; and herein the thought of man resembles the organisation of his social life, and philosophies like empires have found their doom in influences upon which their framers never lavished so much as a suspicion. Once more, the lapse of time involves the liability to internal decay: those who have reached power, betake themselves to its enjoyment; those who believe that they are securely masters of the world of thought are not alive to the decomposition which awaits or preys upon their stagnant system. At one end of a dynasty you admire the hero who founds it by his toils and his sufferings, at the other you turn away in disgust from the effeminacies and luxuries and weaknesses which drain its strength and its life. On the birthday of a philosophy a presiding intellect is moulding thought into new forms, and imparting to it a new impetus; in its decline, his feeble representatives are defending positions which an intellectual enemy has already turned, or are obstinately clinging to phrases which have ceased to represent anything save the dogged determination of their maintainers. For, lastly, as the years pass over a doctrine or a system, they inevitably subject it to the decisive test of opposition. And this not necessarily because it has faults and failings, but because it exists, and by its existence invites hostile criticism, since it drains away something, however little, of the attention, and labour, and substance, which would but for the fact of its existence be bestowed elsewhere. Well has it been said, that, when there is a competition for the means of life, you need only live to provoke hostility: and where a doctrinal system lives in earnest, and demands sacrifice and submission elsewhere, it is certain to be breasted by an opposition as fierce as that which is provoked against political powers who threaten the independence of even the most misgoverned among nations, or the lives of the most guilty of men. To attempt conquest in the intellectual or moral world, cannot but expose the system which does so to a shock of opposition, which, combining with such tendencies to dissolution from within as are incident to all that is strictly human, must make its final overthrow a matter of time, and even a matter of approximate calculation.

Need I say it, brethren, that He Who came from heaven to redeem and save us knew what was before Him? He foresaw the coolness which would succeed to a first fervour of welcome to His Truth; He allowed for the unfavourable conjunctions of circumstance, and for the intimidation and the errors of those who might represent Him, and for the opposition which a Gospel, such as His (making, as it did, no terms with any human feeling or conviction that was inconsistent with the Rights of God), could not but encounter in the passions of man. He predicted a time when the love of many would wax cold, when His disciples would be brought before kings and rulers for His Name's sake, when false Christs and false prophets would arise, deceiving, if possible, the very elect.[1] He accepted, He embraced, He set forth the idea of the intense and fervid hatred which His Gospel must perforce encounter in the world, so energetically, that He, the Prince of Peace, described Himself as sending not peace but a sword.[2] Yet foreseeing these elements of destruction gathering around Him, He is calmly certain of the perpetuity of His Doctrine. Heaven and earth, He says, shall pass away, but My Words shall not pass away.[3] Surely the event has not falsified the prediction. Since the Incarnation, all else has changed; new races, new moulds of thought, new languages, new institutions, political and social, supplant others which once seemed destined to exist for ever, and which have passed away. But, reigning amid the ruins of the past, reigning amid the progress of the present towards the future, Jesus Christ is here; He reigns in the heart and intellect of modern Europe; He reigns here and there, if you will, amid the suspicion, and the feebleness of His worshippers, amid the upgrowth of forces which continually threaten His supremacy, and in spite of the efforts of men who succeed after eighteen centuries to the inheritance of Pilate and to the task of Judas. And yet, "Thy Throne, O God, is for ever and ever; the Sceptre of Thy Kingdom is a right sceptre. Thine arrows are very sharp, and the

[1] St. Matt. xxiv. 9, 11, 12, 24. [2] Ibid. x. 34.
[3] St. Mark xiii. 31.

people shall be subdued unto Thee, even in the midst among the King's enemies."[1]

You may contend that here and there His work is marred or broken; you may insist on the desolating spread of the great heresies of the first ages, or on the loss of the Churches of the East and of the Church of Cyprian and of Augustine—trampled as these are beneath the feet of the infidel. You may show from history that the great Roman Communion, the largest fraction of existing Christendom, has subjected its polity to an unprimitive jurisdiction, and has surrounded its creed with an incrustation of elements which were at least foreign to the belief of the Early Church. You may follow the track of the Reformation, and mark how all the Churches which took part in that movement, save only the Church of England and a possible fraction of Scandinavian Christendom, forfeited with the Episcopate the organic conditions of true Sacramental life. And then you may turn to our own England, and note our spiritual deadness during the last century, or the heathenism of our great cities, or the ravages of a feeble rationalism among a portion of our educated classes, or the attitude of those more imposing, logical, and fatal forms of destructive thought which rule in some of the Schools of Germany, and which threaten us with invasion, or the divisions, and heartburnings, and scandals which paralyse what else were at this hour our mighty strength, as a Church, for God. You may urge all this and more; and then ask if it be indeed true that our ascended Saviour has redeemed His promise. Certainly, I reply, He has redeemed it, and with a surplusage of honour; He has indeed rejoiced as a giant to run His course; He has trifled with foes and with dangers which a cautious timidity, could such an attribute have reigned in heaven, might have crushed or have avoided; His

[1] Ps. xlv. 6, 7.

Church, like His Body Crucified, is known by the Five Wounds and the opened Side, and her scars, like His, have been imprinted in the house of friends.[1] But now, as of old, He is crucified in weakness, while He reigns in power:[2] He is, by the very pressure and fierceness of His foes, uniting friends who have long been sundered: His vast Providences enlist the services even of men who know but fragments of His Truth: He has more loyal hearts who trust and worship Him than in any previous age: He has more tokens of present strength and of future victory than in the days when the kings of Europe were more ostentatiously the nursing-fathers of His Church, and its peoples more ready to own themselves her children.

For observe, that He does not merely hold His ground: He is extending His empire. He has already with but scanty exceptions and by various agencies made the New World his own: He is pushing His advances along the steppes of Northern Tartary and through the deserts of Central Africa. He is again laying siege to those citadels of superstitious yet of philosophical idolatry—the Oriental religions—which have so long resisted Him: He is, as we are this day reminded, bidding the islands of the sea wait on His advancing Footsteps. This would be indeed passing strange, if it could be supposed that His Gospel was really threatened with dissolution, whenever some fitful gust of negative criticism troubles the upper atmosphere of contemporary thought. They say that the legions of the falling Empire had no heart to face the barbarians on the frontier, while a principle of national and political ruin was throned and crowned at Rome. And the feet of the Church's missionaries might well falter, and their words would surely die away on their stammering lips, if they should admit the suspicion that

[1] Zech. xiii. 6.   [2] 2 Cor. xiii. 4.

the Faith they were bearing to the heathen could be proved to be less than absolutely certain in itself, or other than an imperious necessity for man. Only they who believe can speak prevailingly for God: Only He Who was, and Who knew Himself to be, the absolute and the highest Truth, could by proclaiming it assure Himself of the possession of an unfailing agency, streaming through the ages and the countries of the world, with the life-giving and penetrating ubiquity of the rays which speak of God as they fall on us men by day and by night from the orbs of heaven.

II.

And thus we are led to observe a second feature of the predicted missionary energy of the Church, which, no less than that already mentioned, would seem to possess an evidential value.

For our Lord did not merely ensure His Religion against the triumph of those causes which, in the case of human institutions or opinions, must ultimately produce decay and dissolution. The stone which you throw loses force and swiftness as it obeys the impulse you gave to it: it buries itself, we will suppose, beneath the waters of a still lake, and again the ripple which radiates from the point of disturbance becomes, moment by moment, less clear to the eye, as on this side and on that its widening circles approach the shore. So it is with human religions; they spend themselves while they gain the prestige of antiquity: and our Lord, as we have seen, reversed this law of exhaustion in the case of His Gospel. But He did more: He presumed upon, He appealed to, because He knew Himself able to create and to command, an ever-youthful and active enthusiasm, which in the last ages of the Faith, no less than in the first, would carry forward His doctrine into

Evidence of Christian Truth. 279

all the regions of the earth, and, at whatever risk, would press it closely in its perfectness and its power on the consciences of men. Look at the other great religions which have ruled, or which still rule, the thought or the heart of the human race. Some of them are of ancient growth; they are the religions of highly-gifted races: they are dominant throughout some of the fairest regions of the globe: nay more, in some cases they cumber lands which were once beautiful with the Faith and Worship of the Redeemer. We Christians indeed study their sacred books, their traditional polities, and their unlovely rites—as for other and graver reasons, so because in these we find interesting records of the early mind and fortunes of great divisions of the human family. But we send to these heathen our own Bible and our Missions, not by way of promoting literary or social intercourse, but as sending to them the message and the gift of Heaven. In wellnigh all the great cities of the East are to be found the representatives of Christ: in many of them the missionaries of our own branch of the Christian Church. But who ever heard of a Buddhist Mission in London or in Paris? Where are there societies for translating the Vedas, or the Zendavesta, or the Koran, into all the languages of the world? What effort that is felt beyond the natural limits of race, or the forced limits of empire, have the millions of India or of China made to propagate the thoughtful or the foolish superstitions which they hold for Truth? Where have ancient priesthoods, like the Egyptian, been missionary agencies? Where have philosophical speculations, like those of the Schools of Greece, been more than the luxury and the pride of the selfish few,—where and when have they shown any capacity of becoming the inheritance of the heart and thought of the struggling many? Certainly Mohammedanism has attempted, and at this moment it attempts a world-wide proselytism: but Mohammed had studied the first six centuries of the Kingdom of the Incarnation: and his great genius is more manifest in nothing than in the fact, that while he borrowed from the Gospel the idea of a mission to mankind without distinction of race or language, he differed from it in intrusting the propagation of his eclectic imposture, not to the native power of his boasted truth, but to the sharp edge of his scimitar, and to the courage of that warrior race from which he sprung. The first apostles of Islam were beyond doubt great military commanders: its earliest mission was one of the most ruthless wars which have desolated the East. And if to-day this creed may seem to address itself to thought and conscience, in regions where no other form of movement is possible, it is more true to its traditional methods of action when it organises a mutiny against Christian rulers in India, or when in the Syrian villages and the streets of Damascus it bathes its sword in Christian blood. It would not be difficult to show by an exhaustive induction, that the idea of a Truth—so beautiful in its evident symmetry as to compel the absolute homage of the intellect and of the heart—so strong in this compulsion, that alone and unarmed it can dare to pass forth on the lips of an unlettered Apostolate, to demand submission from the passions and the prejudices of man,—is strictly proper to our Redeemer's Gospel, and undiscoverable elsewhere.

Surely, brethren, it were not unreasonable to surmise, that if the Infinite and Eternal God has spoken in very deed to us His creatures, He can only so have spoken, as at the first He can only have given us being, out of the free and pure love which He bare towards us. And thus along with the gift of truth would come the accompanying gift of love; and we should anticipate, what is in fact the case, that He, our Incarnate Lord, Whom we worship as the highest and absolute Truth, is also the most tender and indeed boundless Charity. It is by combining in Himself Truth and Love so perfectly, that Jesus, from age to age, commands the most intelligent and the most heroic devotion of which man has ever been capable. For when by Faith and Love, and Sacramental Union, a man has not merely stood face to face with Jesus, but has drawn the strength of thought and desire and action from His Invigorating Life, he intuitively perceives that there is nothing beyond for which the heart or the understanding need further yearn, since in Jesus the understanding and the heart are satisfied. In such a man we may note this striking and characteristic symptom,— that the passion for novelty, so dominant elsewhere in human life, has ceased, at least to be a ruling power. Where Truth and the King of Truth are as yet unknown, the love of novelty is not merely pardonable, it is a virtue. It is a virtue, because it expresses the fact —that man's real end is an Infinite Being, as his true home is Eternity, and that he cannot so forget his original destiny as to find permanent satisfaction in anything that is finite and that belongs to time. But those to whom our Living Lord is more than a phantom or a phrase, can echo His Apostle's question from century to century, "Lord, to whom shall we go? Thou hast the words of Eternal Life."[1] Think not that true devotion to Christ our Lord is a luxury of the Primitive Church which can find no lasting home in the midst of our modern civilisation. It may be true that mutilated creeds cannot provoke, and that coward hearts cannot understand, such devotion. But wherever the truth is taught in its integrity to hearts that are "honest and good," the same phenomena of absolute self-devotion will be found to repeat themselves which illustrated so gloriously the first ages and children of the Faith. For Jesus Christ our

[1] St. John vi. 68.

Lord, in bidding His servants make disciples of all the nations, knew that He had endued human nature with new powers of thought and of action; He knew that He had raised the beggar from the dust to take a place among the princes of the moral world, and that His command, so impossible to unregenerate man, would be obeyed within the Church. He has, indeed, made men love Himself: He has made Himself the Object of an intense, tender, passionate devotion to millions who have never seen Him with the eye of flesh: and beneath His Throne, Christians have for eighteen centuries been crying with His Apostle, "Who shall separate us from the love of Christ?"[1] For around Him and His work there mantles such a robe of unfailing and ever-youthful beauty, that in His Divine Person, His Human Form, His Words, His World-redeeming Sacrifice, His ceaseless Intercession, His Gift of the Blessed Spirit, His oneness with His people through the Sacraments of His Church, the soul finds that which answers to its highest imaginings no less than to its deepest needs. It finds in Him, as in none else, its rest. And this absolute repose of the soul in the highest Object of truth and of love, does not (as Rationalism would pretend) destroy its intellectual or moral activity; it only changes their direction. The forces which were but now employed in the search for Truth are, when Truth is found, enlisted in its service and devoted to illustrate and explain and propagate it. Here is the raw material out of which our Lord fashions and carves by His Providences the missionaries and the martyrs of His Church. And the strong desire to proclaim Him which is inseparable from a true knowledge and love of Jesus, gains a new strength and motive in a contemplation of the nature and destiny of the soul of man. One single soul, one centre of strictly immaterial life, one abyss of being, which once existing

[1] Rom. viii. 35.

never can die, one tenant (it may be) of the most decrepit and unlovely form among the sons of men, yet in itself a capacity for boundless joy or boundless agony, nay more, a being freely moving towards, while absolutely destined to, an eternity of such agony or such joy,—who can contemplate this living fact, which each of us carries about within him, which to each is his inmost self, and which each may measure, in wellnigh its whole significance, by close and honest self-analysis,—who, I say, can contemplate it, and not gain a new power of living and of working for that Most Merciful Lord Who has made the contemplation something else than what but for Him it had been—a fearful, a mysterious agony? For He Who said, "What shall it profit a man, if he shall gain the whole world and lose his own soul?" said also (blessed be His Name!), "In Me ye shall have peace."[1]

Now the history of the Church is so interesting beyond any annals which merely touch the material, or social, or political life of man, because it is an unfolding of the forces thus placed at His own disposal by our Divine Redeemer in their conflict with the errors and selfishness of the race which He came to save. It is a long response to that command which He first, He last, He alone has dared to give,—to give without giving arms, and letters, and the ordinary weapons of social or political sway—to give with an accent of certainty that He was giving the motto of human history, and that He would be obeyed—"Go teach all nations." Certain of His Doctrine, and certain of His Empire over hearts; certain of the love, the courage, the patience, the heroism, which would from age to age draw strength from His Passion, and push its self-sacrificing devotion, if need be, even to martyrdom—He bade His disciples "Go teach all nations." Foreseeing that mankind, like a sick but wayward child, would

[1] St. Matt. xvi. 26; St. John xvi. 33.

refuse the draught of Truth, and would resent its being proffered; foreseeing that the intelligence and resolution of the race would be arrayed against Him; knowing well that the statesmen would resent a doctrine which respected Cæsar but which Cæsar had not authorised, and that the men of genius would be indignant at a Flash of Thought which owed nothing to their penetration and which condemned it as a blindness, and that the people would not brook a command to break with their time-honoured superstitions, and with their consecrated sensualities; foreseeing accurately and in all its bearings each step of that long and agonising struggle which began when Stephen knelt to die beneath the walls of the Holy City, and which, although it ceased for a while and in a sense with the world-famed Edict of Milan, yet under new conditions lasts and shall last to the end of time, whenever there is sin and error on the one side, and love and truth on the other—He bade His followers "Go teach all nations." And if ever Christians have forgotten the spirit of their Master's Word and the power of His Doctrine, and have invoked the proselytism of the sceptre or the worse proselytism of the sword, this has been mainly in dark times, or in diseased and enfeebled Churches. As a rule, in the primitive, in the mediæval, in the modern period, the Church has trusted herself to the Words of Christ, and has really triumphed just so far as she has done so. Among the many blessings of our modern civilisation, and the indirect advantages which God's goodness wins for us even from the hostile activity of the intellectual and political influences at work around us, we may reckon this;—that they force us Christians of the Church to look the terms of our Great Charter more fully in the face, and to intrust the interests which we prize most dearly more and more to those moral and spiritual forces, by which throughout the ages of Christendom the sound of Christian doctrine goes forth into all lands most persuasively, and its words unto the ends of the world.

Some thoughts such as these will have occurred to us, who are privileged to be witnesses of this solemn scene to-day. There are men who see in a Bishop's Consecration one of those graceful but meaningless proprieties, whereby high office in the Church as in the State is supposed to be recommended to the imagination and respect of the multitude. There are others who indeed see in it a religious act, but only an act of that character which is inseparable from the self-dedication of any human soul to the highest service of the Truth. Yet surely there is more here than a proffer of service, more even than a solemn acceptance and sanction of one who passes to a place of government among Christian people. For us, loyal children of the Church of England, such an event, if the most solemn of its uttered words and transacted forms are to be other than an unreality which yet challenges the Eye and the approval of the Most Holy; for us a Bishop's Consecration is the active assertion of an essential principle of organic Life in the Church of Jesus; it is an act, which at a period when the Canon of the New Testament was yet unformed, and for fifteen centuries continuously, was believed by Christendom to be absolutely indispensable to the transmission of Grace and Truth in their entirety, from the Redeemer's Person to the souls of men. And therefore to-day does not merely call up historical associations that tell of God's past mercies towards His Church;—such as are provoked, my Lord Archbishop, almost inevitably in this place, and by your Grace's presence, since they cluster in a profusion, unrivalled elsewhere in England, around your Throne of Canterbury. Nor may we pause too curiously to speculate upon the providential destinies of a See, whose occupant on the one hand might seem to have peculiar opportunities for carrying the Knowledge and the Love of Jesus among the fleets and seamen whether of the Tyre or of the Tarshish of the modern world; and who on the other may, from his geographical position, be enabled as none else to bind closer the bonds of belief and affection which already unite the English Church to the Church of the nascent Confederacy. Blessed privilege! thus even remotely by encouragement and counsel to aid in the overflow of that miserable legacy bequeathed by English rule to England's ancient colonies, and to free the African race from a bondage, which beneath the very shadow of Christ's Emancipating Cross, outrages the rights of our common manhood. But it were presumptuous to dwell on these high yet precarious anticipations; and duties of another order claim our earnest attention during the solemn moments which will presently follow. If our hearts swell with thankfulness to our Adorable Lord, for this fresh illustration of the living mission of His Church, certain of her doctrine and certain of her power to carry it forward; if with St. Paul, the present scene seems almost to fade from before us, as we lose it in the contemplation of that glorious whole of which it is a real albeit a fractional part—the perpetual Missionary Agency of the Church, radiating like the light of heaven through the countries and the centuries of the world;—let us at least not forget what is due to him, to whom beyond all others this day all true and Christian hearts will now turn with the homage of a sincere and respectful sympathy. He needs, he asks our most earnest prayers, that that elevation of his to the Chief Pastorate of a Flock of Christ, in which we gratefully own our share in the Church's joy and gain, may not turn to his own or to his Master's loss; and that he may carry forward Christ's true work, by attaining in himself more and more that which is indeed the spirit of predestined Apostles, and the earnest of their victories,— the spirit of freedom—of freedom from all fears save the fear of God, and of freedom from all ambitions save the one legitimate, masterful, life-absorbing desire to be Christ's alone,—His perfectly,—His for ever.

SERMON XI.

A FATHER IN CHRIST.[1]

1 Cor. iv. 15.

For though ye have ten thousand instructers in Christ, yet have ye not many fathers: for in Christ Jesus I have begotten you through the Gospel.

HERE is a contrast which never disappears altogether from Christendom, but which has not often been more vivid than it was at Corinth in the age of the Apostle. On the one side is a body of active-minded teachers, who within the Christian society are widely listened to and influential; and some of whom, without realising what Christianity really is and means, evidently aspire on its behalf to meet the cultivated Paganism around them on terms of something like intellectual equality. The faith of Christ had not been long enough in Corinth to have entirely forfeited its character of novelty, and they look upon it, possibly from other points of view, but mainly as a valuable stock-in-trade for lectures and dissertations. They are less concerned with its abstract truth than with their own skill in manipulating it. The divisions among the Corinthian Christians are interesting to them, as adding to the general mental fermentation, and as affording numberless opportunities for critical discussion, analysis, perhaps amusement. They are more concerned for their personal reputations

[1] Preached in St. Paul's at the Consecration of the Bishop of Lincoln and the Bishop of Exeter on the Feast of St. Mark, April 25, 1885.

than for the moral and spiritual effect upon their hearers of anything that they may say; and their reputations, no doubt, in that small Christian society of Corinth, are, in a sense, brilliant.

On the other side is the Apostle, not less alive to the intellectual aspects of Christianity than are his enterprising opponents, but with a totally different and far loftier conception of its awful meaning. To him it is valuable, not as a stepping-stone to personal importance, but as a message from God to man; as a body of truth compared with which the highest philosophy of this world is foolishness. To his own interests and fame he is sufficiently indifferent; but he is passionately concerned for the well-being of those poor souls at Corinth, and for their practical loyalty to the crucified Redeemer, Who had been the one subject of his preaching among them. He is bowed down with grief and shame at the report of their divisions, which might seem to surrounding heathendom to imply a divided Christ; he thinks cheaply enough of any intellectual activity which was morally so costly. But, if the premisses of his opponents were to be granted, no doubt they had the best of it :—" Now ye are full; now ye are rich; ye have reigned as kings without us. . . . We are fools for Christ's sake, but ye are wise in Christ; we are weak, but ye are strong; ye are honourable, but we are despised."[1] It is the contrast between the merely academical and the pastoral, between a business and a vocation, between the professor and the Apostle, between a religion in theory and a religion of practice, between the intellectual world in its solitary barrenness and the intellectual world illuminated and fertilised by the moral, between that which only interests and occupies the mind and that which rouses and quickens the conscience, and invigorates the will, and changes and purifies the life.

[1] 1 Cor. iv. 8-10.

But there is another point in the comparison which has yet to be mentioned. The Corinthians might have—he did not know how many—lecturers in Christianity at work among them, sufficiently versatile, clever, witty, even entertaining. Nevertheless only one person could claim to stand towards them in the sacred and tender relation of a spiritual father. For to his toil and prayers alone, under God, did they owe their conversion; and his authority had a claim on them such as that of no other could possibly rival. "Though ye have ten thousand instructers in Christ, yet have ye not many fathers: for in Christ Jesus I have begotten you through the Gospel."

I.

It would seem that when the Apostle looked around him for a metaphor which should describe his relations towards his flock, he could find nothing in life or nature which so nearly satisfied him as that of a father. It is not the only metaphor he uses to illustrate his Apostolic office. When propagating the Gospel he is a husbandman who plants while another waters;[1] when struggling with sin or error he is a soldier in the uniform of Jesus Christ;[2] when entreating men to accept God's promises of mercy in Christ, he is an ambassador furnished with Divine credentials;[3] when building up the fabric of the Church, or the Divine Life in souls, he is an architect, greatly concerned that the foundation of the edifice shall be solid.[4] But the figure on which his profoundly sympathetic nature loves to dwell as best expressing his permanent relation to those whom he has won to the faith of Christ is that which we are considering.

There is nothing in nature which so resembles God as a human father: for the strength, the majesty, the tender-

[1] 1 Cor. iii. 6.
[2] 2 Tim. iv. 7; cf. 2 Tim. ii. 3.
[3] 2 Cor. v. 20.
[4] 1 Cor. iii. 10, 11.

ness, above all, the authority of the universal Father, rests, in a measure, on each of His earthly representatives. This was instinctively felt by heathens who, when anxious to salute a civil ruler by a title that should invest him with associations such as might take captive the hearts of his subjects, have called him *pater patriæ*, the father of his country. This is the secret of an indefinable dignity that mantles over the great patriarch whose position is so unique in the history of the East and in the history of Revelation; as the father of many nations and the father of the faithful. The greater clearness and prominence which the Gospel had given to the fatherly attributes of God had enriched the word and the idea with a wealth of authority and affection that men had not before associated with it. Accordingly, when recommending Timothy to the respectful sympathy of the Philippians, St. Paul says that "as a son with the father he hath served with me in the Gospel."[1] When reminding the Thessalonians of those evangelising labours of his which had resulted in their conversion, "Ye know," he says, "how we exhorted and comforted and charged every one of you, as a father doth his children, that ye would walk worthy of God, Who hath called you unto His kingdom and glory."[2] Once, indeed, he recognises in a presbyter this character of spiritual fatherhood.[3] But, as a rule, he reserves this figure to describe his own office. "Though ye have ten thousand instructers in Christ, yet have ye not many fathers: for in Christ Jesus I have begotten you through the Gospel."

II.

When we say that Bishops are successors of the Apostles we are not formulating a theory, but stating a

[1] Phil. ii. 22.   [2] 1 Thess. ii. 11, 12.   [3] 1 Tim. v. 1.

fact of history. In one sense, indeed, every presbyter succeeds the Apostles; like them, he ministers the Word and Sacraments of Christ. In another the Apostles have no successors; they alone were privileged to found the Church of Christ, and while founding it to wield a world-wide jurisdiction. But substantially, and in a sense all its own, Bishops do, in the phrase of St. Cyprian, *Apostolis vicariâ ordinatione succedunt*.[1] If they do not singly share in the world-wide jurisdiction which belonged to the Apostles, and which could only now be wielded by the universal Episcopate acting together, they do in other respects reproduce from age to age among men the fulness of the Apostolic authority.[2]

There are in the last analysis two, and only two, coherent theories of the origin and character of the Christian ministry. Of these one makes the minister the elected delegate of the congregation; in teaching and ministering he exerts an authority which he derives from his flock.[3] The other traces ministerial authority to the Person of our Lord Jesus Christ, Who deposited it in its fulness in the College of the Apostles. "All power is

[1] S. Cypr. *Ep*. 66, ad Florentium, § 4 (ed. Hartel.).
[2] Bramhall, *Vindication of the Church of England*, Disc. iii. "Episcopacy was comprehended in the Apostolic office, *tanquam trigonus in tetragono*, and the distinction was made by the Apostles, with the approbation of Christ."— *Works*, vol. ii. p. 69 (Oxf. 1842).
[3] This would not be admitted by the deeper minds even among the Congregationalists. "The Church," says Dr. Dale, "determined what men should fill the office, but the office was instituted by Christ." . . . "It would be treason to Christ to obey the rulers of the Church at all, unless their authority were derived from Him." But then he adds, "In *electing* its officers, the Church acts not for itself but for Christ; it appoints the men whom He has chosen."—*Manual of Congregational Principles*, by R. W. Dale, LL.D., London, 1884, pp. 98-100. This might seem to confuse election to a Church office with a commission to discharge it. They differ alike in their origin and in their nature. Election is an act of the Christian people: ordination or consecration is a gift of Jesus Christ bestowed through the Bishops who represent Him. With us, it must be owned, the election of a bishop is now but a shadow. But the validity of an Episcopal Consecration is independent of the machinery which decides who is to be the subject of it.

given unto Me in heaven and in earth; go ye therefore
and make disciples of all nations."[1] "As My Father hath
sent Me, even so send I you."[2] The Apostles, thus
invested with the plenitude of ministerial power, detached
from themselves in the form of distinct grades or orders
of ministry, so much as was needed, at successive epochs,
for building up and supporting the Church. First, they
created an order which was charged with the care of
the poor and with the administration of Church funds,
although also specially empowered to preach, and to administer the sacrament of baptism.[3] Next they bestowed
on the Church a larger separate instalment of ministerial
power—that of the presbyters or bishops—as in those first
days the second order was called indifferently.[4] To this
order full ministerial capacity was committed, excepting
the faculty of transmitting the ministry. Lastly, St. Clement
of Rome tells us,[5] that desiring to avoid controversy which
they foresaw, the Apostles ordained certain men to the
end that when they should have fallen asleep in death
others of approved character might succeed to their special
office. Such were Timothy and Titus; not yet exclusively
called Bishops, but certainly Bishops in the sense of the
sub-Apostolic and of our own age; men who in addition
to the fulness of ministerial capacity had also the power

[1] St. Matt. xxviii. 18, 19.   [2] St. John xx. 21.
[3] Acts vi. 6, vii. 2, viii. 38; 1 Tim. iii. 8-13.
[4] Acts xx. 17, 28; Tit. i. 5, 7; cf. S. Clem. I. ad Cor. 42.
[5] S. Clem. I. ad Cor. 44: καὶ οἱ ἀπόστολοι ἡμῶν ἔγνωσαν διὰ τοῦ Κυρίου
ἡμῶν ὅτι ἔρις ἔσται ἐπὶ τοῦ ὀνόματος τῆς ἐπισκοπῆς. Διὰ ταύτην οὖν τὴν αἰτίαν
πρόγνωσιν εἰληφότες τελείαν κατέστησαν τοὺς προειρημένους, καὶ μεταξὺ
ἐπινομὴν δεδώκασιν, ὅπως, ἐάν κοιμηθῶσιν, διαδέξωνται ἕτεροι δεδοκιμασμένοι
ἄνδρες τὴν λειτουργίαν αὐτῶν. Compare the remarkable statement, quoted by
Eusebius (*H. E.* v. 6) from St. Irenæus, iii. 3. 3: θεμελιώσαντες οὖν καὶ
οἰκοδομήσαντες οἱ μακάριοι ἀπόστολοι τὴν ἐκκλησίαν Λίνῳ τὴν τῆς ἐπισκοπῆς
λειτουργίαν ἐνεχείρισαν. Eusebius says (*H.- E.* iii. 2) that Linus became
Bishop of Rome after the martyrdom of SS. Peter and Paul. But the language
of St. Irenæus, taken alone, might imply that the Apostles made him Bishop
of Rome during their lifetime. So Döllinger.

of transmitting it. In Crete, Titus receives explicit authority from St. Paul to ordain presbyters; at Ephesus, Timothy has particular directions from St. Paul respecting the way in which charges against presbyters are to be received.[1] Thus we see in Timothy and Titus the exercise of what is distinctive both in Episcopal orders and Episcopal jurisdiction; and unless the Pastoral Epistles are not of Apostolic origin, the three orders existed in their completeness under the eyes of St. Paul. Within the compass of the New Testament there are two other facts which point to the establishment of the Episcopate in Apostolic times. One is the position of St. James the Less at Jerusalem; he seems to have been an Apostle who already occupied the more localised and restricted position of a Bishop. This appears in the place assigned to him at the Council of Jerusalem,[2] and in the formal visit which St. Paul paid him at a later period,[3] but especially in the unanimous testimony of the second century, which spoke of him as Bishop of Jerusalem.[4] The other fact is the representation in the Apocalypse of the "angels" of the Seven Churches. What were these angels? Guardian spirits of the Churches they cannot have been, since some of them were guilty of grave faults. Nor can they have been the Churches themselves, since St. John distinguishes the angels and the Churches as having the distinct symbols of stars and candlesticks.[5] Each angel represents a Church, for the faith and practice of which he is responsible; and it would be difficult to express more exactly the position of a primitive Bishop.[6]

[1] Tit. i. 5; 1 Tim. i. 19, 20.   [2] Acts xv. 13.   [3] *Ibid.* xxi. 13-18.
[4] See reff. in Bp. Lightfoot, *Philippians*, p. 206, note 1.
[5] Rev. i. 20.
[6] Cf. St. Aug. *Ep.* 43, § 22; Abp. Trench, *Epistles to the Seven Churches*, pp. 52-57.

III.

The origin and claims of the Episcopate is a district of theology which English divines have made peculiarly their own.[1] The anti-Episcopal Puritanism of Elizabeth's reign, represented by Cartwright, provoked Bishop Bilson's great work on the "Perpetual Government of Christ's Church"[2] and the seventh book of Hooker's *Ecclesiastical Polity*. The more trenchant Puritanism of the next age necessitated those deeper studies to which we owe Pearson's *Vindiciæ*,[3] and Beveridge's annotations on the Apostolical Canons[4]—not to mention the often admirable, but less accurate, *Antiquities* of Bingham.

But some English divines may also have felt, that when insisting upon the Episcopate as organically necessary to the structure of the visible Body of Christ, —as necessary not merely to its *bene esse*, but to its *esse*, —they were indirectly strengthening a barrier against

---

[1] Perhaps the well-weighed words of Sanderson, as one of the most illustrious Bishops of Lincoln since the Reformation, may here be quoted: "My opinion is that Episcopal Government is not to be derived merely from Apostolical practice or institution, but that it is originally founded in the Person and Office of the Messiah, our blessed Lord Jesus Christ, Who, being sent by His Heavenly Father to be the great Apostle (Heb. iii. 1), Shepherd, and Bishop (1 Pet. ii. 25) of His Church, and anointed to that Office immediately after His baptism by John, with Power and the Holy Ghost (Acts x. 37, 38) descending then upon Him in a bodily shape (St. Luke iii. 22), did afterwards, before His Ascension into heaven, send and empower His holy Apostles, giving them the Holy Ghost likewise, as His Father had given Him, in like manner as His Father had before sent Him (St. John xx. 21) to execute the same Apostolical, Episcopal, and Pastoral Office, for the ordering and governing of His Church, until His coming again; and so the same office to continue in them and their Successors unto the end of the world (St. Matt. xxviii. 18-20)."—*Works*, vol. v. p. 191, ed. Jacobson. On the general subject, cf. Bp. Pearson, *De Successu Prim. Rom. Episc.* Diss. i. c. 9; Bp. Beveridge, *Theol. Works*, vol. i. Serm. i. ii. (Oxf. 1844); Rev. H. J. Rose, *On the Commission and Duties of the Clergy*, Serm. ii.

[2] Ed. Eden, Oxf. 1842, pref. vii.   [3] Ed. Churton, Oxf. 1852.

[4] *Works*, vol. xi. xii. ed. Oxf. 1848.

Ultramontanism.[1] Nothing is more remarkable in this connection than certain debates,[2] both in the second and third meetings of the Council of Trent. The Papal representatives, especially when discussing the question whether a Bishop's residence in his diocese was of divine obligation, or could be dispensed with by the Pope, minimised the authority and rights of the Episcopate down to the very verge of Presbyterianism. Indeed, it may be doubted whether any Presbyterian divine would easily rival the skill of the Jesuit Lainez, when, in a sermon historically famous, he essayed to reduce Episcopal jurisdiction to a shadowy impotence, that would make the way clear for exaggerated assertions of Papal supremacy.[3]

In our own days the question of Episcopacy is increasingly seen to be bound up with that of the Apostolic origin and authority of the Pastoral Epistles. The critics, who, from Schleiermacher down to Baur and Pfleiderer and others, have partly or wholly denied the Apostolic authorship of these Epistles, have insisted with much force and justice upon their so-called hierarchical characteristics;[4] and then they have proceeded to beg a very large question by arguing that these characteristics prove the Epistles to be of post-Apostolic origin. It is also observable that the ablest and the most destructive of recent English speculations on the early organisation of the Christian Church omit all reference to these

---

[1] Compare, *e.g.*, Skelton, *Works*, iv. 513, 514, ed. Dubl. 1770.
[2] For the *decision*, see Conc. Trid. sess. xxiii. cap. 4, can. 7.
[3] Phillipson, *Contre-révolution religieuse au xvie Siècle*, pp. 403, 513, 514. So Morinus, *De Sac. Eccl. Ord.* pars iii. ex. 4, c. 3, 4, gives a list of schoolmen and others who taught "simplicem presbyterum, delegatione Pontificis, posse diaconos et presbyteros ordinare." Even Vasquez, in iii. part. S. Thomæ, diss. 243, art. 3, 4, thinks the opinion probable. Cf. Palmer, *On the Church*, ii. 410.

[4] See Baur, *Die sogenannten Pastoralbriefe*, pp. 75-89; *Vorlesungen über Neutest. Theologie*, p. 344; Pfleiderer, *Paulinismus*, kap. xi; Holtzmann, *Pastoralbriefe*, p. 190 *sqq*.

particular books of the New Testament, which, surely, whatever their worth and character, most directly bear on it.

It is, indeed, a solemn question whether we hold the Episcopate to be enjoined by the Revealed Will of God, or, like archdeacons and capitular bodies, to be a feature of our Church arrangements, which, however admirable, may conceivably be dispensed with, without sacrificing anything organic in the conditions of communion with Christ. If, by suppressing Deans and Chapters, we could reconcile all the separated Protestant bodies to the unity and doctrine of the Church, who of us would not gladly make the sacrifice? And if Bishops are not of Divine obligation, is it right to maintain a cause and symbol of division with which essential Christianity could dispense? The Protestant historian Ranke[1] has drawn attention to the barrier which is raised by the Episcopate between the English Church and the Lutheran and Reformed communities on the Continent. The maintenance of such a barrier is more than intelligible if we believe that upon a true Episcopal succession depends the validity of the Eucharist—our chief means of communion with our Lord. But when we consider the present pressure of infidelity upon all reformed Christendom, is such an obstacle to unity even defensible, if in our hearts we deem the Episcopate to be only an archæological treasure,

[1] Ranke, *Hist. Engl.* iv. 375 (Oxf. transl.) remarks, that at the Restoration "no one was to obtain an ecclesiastical benefice or be intrusted with a cure of souls who had not been ordained by a bishop." He then indorses the observation that English Churchmen "thus renounced all connection with the Protestant Churches of the Continent." *Ibid.* iii. 495 : "Although the Anglican Church rose again, this was balanced by the fact that she had preserved and now restored to its full authority, one of the most important forms of the ancient Church, its Episcopal Constitution." Professor Ranke understands the importance of 1662, as putting an end to any apparent inconsistencies, in respect of the principle of ordination, which may be discoverable in the practice of some members of the Church of England during the preceding century.

or only, as the phrase goes, a very interesting form of Church government?[1]

IV.

It is time that we should return to the lessons which the Apostle would teach us by his expression "a father in Christ."

The first and great characteristic of the earthly father is that, under God, he transmits the gift of physical life. This is his prerogative distinction; it most nearly likens him to the Father of heaven; it raises his relationship to his children above any other between human beings.

The Bishop, too, is a father in this sense; that he alone can transmit ministerial power to others. "Whereas," says Hooker, "presbyters by such power as they have received for administration of the sacraments are able only to beget children unto God; Bishops, having power to ordain, do by virtue thereof create fathers to the people of God."[2] "The Apostles, being Bishops at large, ordained everywhere presbyters."[3] "Titus and Timothy having received Episcopal power, as Apostolic ambassadors or legates, the one in Greece, the other in Ephesus, they both did by virtue thereof likewise ordain, throughout all churches, deacons and presbyters, within the circuits allotted unto them."[4]

---

[1] By the existing law of the Church of England any Roman Catholic or Oriental priest may be admitted to a cure of souls, on producing his Letters of Orders, and subscribing the English formularies, while the most gifted and experienced of Presbyterian or Congregationalist pastors would have to be ordained deacon and priest. This indeed is inevitable if we hold the Episcopate to be indispensable to the conveyance of a true ministerial commission. But if episcopal ordination be only a matter of ecclesiastical taste, or usage, or propriety, have not our separated brethren among the Protestant dissenters some right to complain of the slight which is thus put upon their ministry? And if Presbyterian or Congregationalist ministers have been really ordained, is there no risk of sacrilege in repeating an ordination? But cf. Law's Second Letter to Hoadley, p. 31.

[2] E. P. vii. 6. 2.   [3] Ibid.   [4] Ibid.

But was this prerogative shared by presbyters? The admission of presbyters to lay their hands on the ordained conjointly with the ordaining Bishop, as implied in the Pastoral Epistles,[1] and explicitly recognised by the Fourth Council of Carthage,[2] and in our own Ordinal, does not prove it, any more than the promise to the Apostles that they should judge the twelve tribes of Israel confers on them the office of the one universal Judge.[3] The presbyters who assist in laying on hands give token of moral approbation and sympathy with the act of the chief pastor; but their presence adds nothing to, as their absence would subtract nothing from, the validity of the rite.

Not that the power of ordination exhausts the creative functions, so to call them, of a Bishop. He is not only a ruler but a parent, not merely a *caput* but a *radix ecclesiæ*; the author or nourisher of all activities for good among those whom he rules. He perpetuates, from age to age, the work of the missionary Bishop in whose chair he sits; and from him every useful effort within the scope of his jurisdiction should receive, if not its original impulse, at least its ready encouragement and consecration. He is by the terms of his office the originating, and creating, and impelling, as well as or rather than the controlling force in his diocese;—it was, perhaps, his keen realisation of this aspect of his ministry which made the episcopate of Bishop Wilberforce so fruitful in its results both to his own flock and to the Church at large.

Out of the father's relation to his children, as the

---

[1] 1 Tim. iv. 14: μετὰ ἐπιθέσεως τῶν χειρῶν τοῦ πρεσβυτερίου. Cf. 2 Tim. i. 6: τὸ χάρισμα τοῦ Θεοῦ ὅ ἐστιν ἐν σοὶ διὰ τῆς ἐπιθέσεως τῶν χειρῶν μου.

[2] Con. Carth. iv. 3: "Presbyter cum ordinatur, episcopo eum benedicente, et manum super caput ejus tenente, etiam omnes presbyteri qui præsentes sunt, manus suas juxta manum episcopi, super caput illius teneant."

Hooker, *ubi sup.*

earthly author of their life, arises a natural authority which has three distinct departments for its exercise.

The father is the natural teacher of his children. Their intelligence opens under the rays of his instruction. His is the highest wisdom of which they have any experience, and he brings truth home to them by the voice of love. If he cannot himself teach his children, he not only has the right but is under an obligation to choose a substitute —a master who shall stand in his place, and administer that which it is beyond his power to supply.

The Bishop, too, as the father of his diocese, is the one teacher within its limits. In the eye of the Church all the clergy are his substitutes; he can, by the law of the Church, whenever he wills, take their place. This is his *jus magisterii*. Holding as he should in his mind and conscience the deposit of the true faith, his first duty is to see that it is taught to his flock, that it is taught in its integrity, that it is defended when assailed, that it is reasserted in its purity when corrupted or disfigured. For he is not the versatile exponent of a human theory, but the keeper and teacher of a Revelation from God.[1] He can

---

[1] 1 Tim. i. 3, iii. 2, iv. 13, 16. This passage has been understood to mean that every Bishop is infallible; that no circumstances can warrant the dissent of his clergy or flock from their Bishop's judgment; and that Church history, ancient and modern, amply illustrates the inconsistency of those who make thus much of a Bishop's authority, yet pay scant respect to its actual exercise.

General principles must sometimes be stated, especially in sermons, without discussing exceptional cases to which they do not apply; and especially is this inevitable at times when such principles are in danger of being lost sight of. But the analogy of a father's relations to his children, appealed to in this sermon, might have prevented the misunderstanding in question. The duty enjoined by the Fifth Commandment is not less generally a duty because some parents teach their children to lie and steal. And yet it is undoubtedly a child's duty to disobey the father who should thus employ his authority to discredit that moral law which is its real sanction.

Certainly bishops have been heretics, like Nestorius; and bishops have been infidels, like Talleyrand. A bishop can only hope to be obeyed, while he himself holds the faith, and believes in the Divine Commission, which alone render his office something distinct from an imposture. And if earnest believers in the necessity of Episcopacy have sometimes used stern language

neither reject an old doctrine nor welcome a new one; he can only decide whether a given doctrine which falls in his way is conformable or contrary to the truth which he holds and teaches, and which his spiritual children may expect at his hands. His intellectual outlook will indeed be wide: he will keep his eye, as far as may be, on all the surging currents of thought, along which souls are carried hither and thither in our distracted modern world; and as he will welcome from any quarter any ray of truth, so he will pay no feeble compliments to any shade of error. Before all things he will be jealous for the honour of our Lord—His eternal Godhead, His Incarnation in time, His infallibility as a Teacher, the Atoning power of His Death, the literal truth of His Resurrection and Ascension and perpetual Intercession, the converting and sanctifying influence of His Spirit, the life-giving and life-sustaining power which He exerts through His Sacraments, the endlessness, for weal and woe, of the life to which He points, beyond the grave. But an Apostle must trace a Bishop's duties in this department. "Take heed unto thyself and unto the doctrine." "Hold fast the form of sound words which thou hast heard of me, in faith and love which is in Christ Jesus." "That good thing which was committed unto thee, keep by the Holy Ghost Which dwelleth in us." "The things which thou hast heard of me among many witnesses, the same commit thou to faithful men, who shall be able to teach others also."[1]

about the conduct of individual Bishops, this language has not been necessarily inconsistent with their belief. *Corruptio optimi pessima.* To understand the unique malignity of Judas, a man must believe in the greatness of the Apostolic office. The immortal letters which describe Hoadley's unfaithfulness to the English Church were not due to the acuteness of a worldly cynicism, but to the deeply-wounded faith and piety of William Law. Nevertheless the rule is that the Bishop is the teacher and guardian of the faith of his flock, and that it is at once their happiness and their duty to obey him. And there are sufficient reasons for insisting on this in our own day.

[1] 1 Tim. iv. 16; 2 Tim. i. 13, 14, ii. 2.

Not only does a father teach; he governs. Like every society, a family must have a government; and the modern theory of a government of all by all is not well calculated, at least in a family, to ensure the general wellbeing. And since children lack the requisite experience, and a mother the necessary vigour, the natural and undisputed ruler is the father.

As the father of his diocese, the Bishop is its ruler. His right to rule is derived, not from a body of electors who have made him, for their common good, a chief magistrate, but from the character which he inherits from the Apostles of Christ. Timothy and Titus are addressed as rulers of Churches; they are to examine the conduct and bearing of their clergy; and in particulars which are specified in detail.[1] They are to see that presbyters who labour in the word and doctrine are counted worthy of double honour.[2] But their rule extends to all descriptions of persons within the Churches over which they have jurisdiction. Timothy is to superintend, according to rules delivered by the Apostle, the ecclesiastical order of widows;[3] Timothy and Titus are to have especial regard to the condition of the numerous Christian slaves;[4] Titus is to look after whole classes of Cretans separately, the young and the old of both sexes.[5]

The Bishop rules, not only the outward circumstances and departments, but also the inner life of his flock; he has, within limits, the *jus liturgicum*; the right and duty of providing that prayers, supplications, intercessions, and eucharists should be made for all men, and especially for all in authority.[6] Everything liturgical, according to primitive Church law, save the matter and form of the Sacraments and the language of the Catholic Creeds, is subject to his discretion. In later ages, as we know, this

---

[1] 1 Tim. iii. 2-13; Tit. i. 5-9. [2] 1 Tim. v. 17. [3] *Ibid.* v. 3-16.
[4] 1 Tim. vi. 1-5; Tit. ii. 9, 10. [5] Tit. ii. 2-6. [6] 1 Tim. ii. 1, 2.

discretion has been limited, almost to the point of annihilation, by Congregations of Rites, and by Acts of Uniformity; yet it may be well, on an occasion like the present, to recall the sense of early Christendom.

But government is impossible in any society without the sanction of punishment. If rules are to be made their violations must be punished; if command is to be a reality, there must be a means of enforcing obedience. The best father who governs but cannot punish would soon discover that the sceptre of his authority was already falling from his feeble hands.

Nor is the Episcopate able to discharge its true duties unless the Bishop can enforce obedience to the faith and discipline of the Church; unless he have some kind of coercive jurisdiction. Already in St. Paul's First Epistle to Timothy, Timothy is addressed as if he were the *judex ordinarius* of a later age. "Against a presbyter receive not an accusation, but before two or three witnesses. Them that sin rebuke before all, that others also may fear. I charge thee before God, and the Lord Jesus Christ, and the elect angels, that thou observe these things, without preferring one before another, doing nothing by partiality."[1] In the same sense Hymenæus and Alexander are pointed out to Timothy as having "made shipwreck concerning the faith," and as having been "delivered unto Satan."[2] And to Titus the order runs: "A man that is an heretic, after the first and second admonition, reject."[3]

V.

The fatherly character of the Bishop is sometimes traversed by the accidents of age or attainments. He may find among his clergy men who are older, or more generally accomplished, or better divines, or of higher spiritual

[1] 1 Tim. v. 19-21.   [2] *Ibid.* i. 20.   [3] Tit. iii. 10.

experience than himself. Of these the best will always echo St. Jerome's exclamation to St. Augustine—"Amice carissime, ætate fili, dignitate parens."[1] They will remember that a Bishop's fatherly character is independent of his personal characteristics; that it belongs to an office which comes from Christ.

A like result may follow on the relations of the Church to the civil law. We may well, indeed, be grateful to the law for the position which it secures to the clergy by making every benefice a freehold; yet a freehold may be converted into a fortified castle, from within whose walls a rebellious son sets at nought the counsels of a spiritual father. But that which of late years has most frequently veiled from the eyes of the clergy the kindly face and hand of a father in Christ, is the unhappy fact that under the form of interpreting documents which have a legal aspect, the most sacred questions of doctrine and morals are not decided in the last resort by the commissioned guardians of the faith, but by accomplished lawyers, who may or may not be Christians. This fatal weakness in our Church polity was aggravated by the provisions of the Public Worship Regulation Act. We can indeed defend existing arrangements if we can suppose that St. Paul would have allowed the questions pending between himself and the Galatian Judaisers, or the Corinthian deniers of the Resurrection, to be settled by the nearest proconsul. Only those who wish ill to the English Church can desire to perpetuate a state of things which is not necessary to the union of Church and State, or to the maintenance of the Queen's Supremacy, and which, among the many mischiefs which it entails, does more than anything else to impair, in the eyes of faithful clergy, the fatherly character of the Episcopate.

But a father does not, unless in the last extremity,

[1] *Opp.* iv. pars ii. p. 613, *Ep.* 71, ad Aug. ed. Martianay.

A Father in Christ.

insist upon his rights; he takes them for granted; he recommends them to his children by the love which makes authority more than welcome. When the machinery of Church government, especially in its penal aspects, is rudely exposed to view, it is plain that there has been somewhere a serious failure in duty.

So delicate a relationship as that of a father in God does not depend for its working efficacy on the amount of authority which can be arrogated for one side, or on the submission which can be extorted from the other. It depends on moral influences; on the respect which is inspired by high and disinterested character; on the attraction which is exerted by a true love of God and man. Like the most beautiful things in the moral world, this authority is of tender growth, and it is easily impaired or forfeited. A scornful or impatient word, scarcely intended by the irritated and, perhaps, overworked speaker, will rankle for years in the mind of a young curate, and colour his whole conception of the relation in which he stands to the fathers of the Church.

It is difficult to say how much is lost to the moral force of the Church and to the character of her ministers when a Bishop is thought and spoken of as a good man of business, or a man who might have been a judge, or a very accurate scholar, or even a well-read divine, if besides and beyond all these he is not recognised as a father of his flock, both lay and clerical; the one man to whom men instinctively turn for advice and counsel in moments of moral or mental perplexity; the man on whose wide knowledge and kindly temper and simple disinterestedness of purpose they know that they can depend for trustworthy guidance; and of whom they think habitually as of one whose blessing would be dearly prized as a message of encouragement from another world in the dark hours when its shadows are already falling thick across the path of life.

VI.

Of public institutions in modern Europe the Episcopate is in years the most venerable. It is older than any secular throne; it is by some centuries older than the Papacy, which was an outgrowth from circumstances unknown to the first Bishops of Rome.[1] The Episcopate had reached its prime while the Empire was still standing. It could shed its blood with Cyprian; it could illuminate the world by the consecrated genius of an Irenæus, of an Augustine, of Chrysostom and Basil and the Gregories. It seemed to undergo a weird transformation at the hands of feudalism. We think of the Bishops clad in mail armour who fought at Senlac or in the wars of Stephen, or of later prelates whose brasses in our older cathedrals represent them as blessing us in cope and mitre out of their battlemented castles. Of the sixteen sculptured compartments which record the events of the episcopate of Guido Torlati at Arezzo, only the first, in which he takes possession of his See, and the last, where he lies upon his deathbed, exhibit him in any pastoral character or have any relation to his work as a father in Christ. After the soldier Bishops come the great statesmen; it requires an effort to recollect the true character of Wolsey and Richelieu, or of certain of those prince-electors who so largely swayed the fortunes of Germany. Then appeared the literary Bishops; men

---

[1] Professor Hussey observes that the first step towards the establishment of the supremacy of the See of Rome was taken "in the fourth century," when an appellate jurisdiction was given to its Bishop by the Council of Sardica, A.D. 347. "Then for the first time the precedence among equals, willingly conceded to Rome in early ages, was turned into a claim of authority."—*Rise of the Papal Power*, by Robert Hussey, B.D., late Reg. Prof. of Eccl. Hist. Oxford, Clarendon Press, 1863, 2nd Edition, Lect. i. p. 1, note 3, and specially Pref. p. xxxii.

often greater in profane than in sacred letters. And now, as in many other ways so in this, we are apparently re-entering upon the earliest conditions of the Church's life. But the intervening periods were not, as we may too hastily think, periods during which the real objects of the Episcopate were utterly lost sight of. The soldiers, the diplomatists, the men of general literature, were always a small minority of their order, which, as a whole, quietly and unostentatiously pursued its course of ruling churches and guiding souls. Let us remind ourselves of such language as that of the Sixth Council of Arles,[1] held at a time when the Bishops of France were largely great feudatories under Charlemagne. "Let the Bishops bear in mind," says the 17th Canon, "that they are intrusted with the care of the people and of the poor, as their guardians and protectors. If, then, they see the unfortunate oppressed by the powerful and the highly placed, let them charitably remonstrate; and, if their advice is disregarded, let them carry their complaints to the Sovereign, that he may correct by his supreme authority those who would pay no regard to the advice of their pastor." And as for Wolsey, let us not recall the years when—the most powerful statesman in Europe—he was wont to appear in this cathedral as Legate *a latere*, and indeed proudly held the balance between France and the Empire; let us think of the discredited and broken man who had retired from the Court of the sensual Tudor to his northern diocese, there to win almost at once the hearts of the clergy and the poor by his pastoral care and tenderness.[2] The Episcopate, as it traverses the centuries, is like a weather-beaten barque on whose hull clusters many a shell and weed that tells of the seas of feudal or political life behind it; but as these

[1] Conc. Arelat. vi. (a. 813) can. 17. Hefele, *Conciliengeschichte*, iii. p. 757.
[2] Cavendish, *Life of Wolsey*, p. 202 (ed. Morley).

incrustations fall away we discover that the essential features of a spiritual fatherhood, which were always there, remain intact. The title, father in God, has never disappeared, whether from the language of the Church, or of the law, or of general literature; and the reality, even in the worst times, has never been without a witness. The century which beheld Hoadley on the English bench was also the century in which men knelt down in the streets of London to ask for the blessing of Bishop Wilson.

VII.

Certainly we meet to-day on an occasion when we may insist on this characteristic of the highest order in the sacred ministry with more than usual hope and confidence. The eminent scholar and poet, not less saintly in his life than remarkable for his acquirements, who has lately left us,[1] is to be succeeded in the See of St. Hugh by one whose nomination has thrilled the hearts of his brother Churchmen with the deepest thankfulness and joy. Never, probably, in our time has the great grace of sympathy, controlled and directed by a clear sense of the nature and sacredness of revealed truth, achieved so much among so many young men as has been achieved, first at the Theological College of Cuddesdon, and then from the Pastoral Chair at Oxford, in the case of my dear and honoured friend. He is surrounded at this solemn moment by hundreds who know and feel that to his care and patience, to his skill and courage, to his faith and spiritual insight, they owe all that is most precious in life, and most certain to uphold them in the hour of death; and their sympathies and prayers are shared by many others who are absent from us in body, but present with us in spirit. Certainly, if past experience is

[1] Dr. Christopher Wordsworth, Bishop of Lincoln.

any guarantee of what is to come, if there be such a thing as continuity of spiritual character and purpose, then we may hope to witness an episcopate which, κατὰ τὰς προαγούσας προφητείας[1]—if current anticipations are not wholly at fault—will rank hereafter with those which in point of moral beauty stand highest on the roll of the later English Church—with Andrewes, with Ken, with Wilson, with Hamilton.

And, if I may not presume to speak from such personal knowledge of the successor of our own Bishop[2] in the great See of the West, it is at least allowable to dwell on the hopes which gather round an honoured name, and on the wide reputation for devotion and spiritual experience which has been gained by a long and fruitful ministry in this metropolis. He, too, will carry with him into his new field of labour the prayers and sympathies of grateful friends, known and unknown, who earnestly desire that he may long rule and feed his flock in the fulness of the blessing of the Gospel of Christ.

Men say that hard times are coming upon the English Church; and, outside her walls, voices, like those of the children of Edom in the day of Jerusalem, may even now be heard to cry, "Down with her; down with her; even to the ground!" And, in truth, she has already lost much which was of no mean value for our Master's service. The Education Act of 1870 has largely withdrawn the people from her schools, and recent legislation has swept away all but a rapidly diminishing fragment of her old position at the Universities. With largely secularised populations, with our higher class increasingly trained by infidel teachers, and with our vastly extended franchise, it is not unnatural to anticipate for the Church in the coming years sterner experiences than have befallen her

---

[1] 1 Tim. i. 18.
[2] Dr. Temple, Bishop of Exeter, had been translated to the See of London.

since the middle of the seventeenth century. But the prospect is by no means an entirely dark one; and among its brighter features is the wealth of generous devotion which young men and women in increasing numbers, and of various conditions in society, are freely offering, almost day by day, to the sacred cause of our Lord and Saviour. It is as though the anxieties of a loved and aged parent could open and melt hearts which were closed against her in days of more assured prosperity: and surely no token of God's present favour could inspire more courage for dealing with the problems that may be in store for her sons. To all who are thus, in their opening life, giving their best to God, the event of this day will be full of encouragement and of hope. For it is the consecration to the highest duties in the Church of sympathies which, next to His own supernatural grace, have drawn them, most persuasively, to the feet of the Redeemer; it is an assurance that they will find on Apostolic thrones that union of tenderness and wisdom which recalls while it transcends all that is most revered and loved in an earthly home.

SERMON XII.

BISHOP SAMUEL WILBERFORCE.[1]

1 COR. ix. 22.

I am made all things to all men, that I might by all means save some.

NO one, perhaps, of St. Paul's sayings describes the general effect of his life and character with such terseness, or so vividly, as this. Not that the Apostle can be thought of as deliberately framing an epigram which might afterwards do duty in a biography. He is, as you know, on his defence, as against the charge, widely circulated by his Corinthian opponents, that he was really a selfish person, who was making a good thing out of the Gospel; he is showing that, if he chose to stand upon the letter of his rights, he might have claimed more, and done less, than he did. Had silence been possible, we may be sure that he would gladly have said nothing about himself; but since there is this hostile criticism in the way of his usefulness, and he is forced to speak, he boldly asserts the rights which he had waived, and the loftiness of the motives which governed him. It is with this last part of his apology that we have to do; for in making it he incidentally draws a picture of himself which is especially entitled to claim our attention. In so varied and complex a life as his, there was of course much which

[1] Preached at the Parish Church of Graffham, Sussex, November 2, 1875.

could not be compressed into any single saying; but nowhere else does he so nearly bring himself before us as a whole, or trace with so delicate yet powerful a hand the leading feature of his great career, as in the words, " I am made all things to all men, that I might by all means save some."

I.

The great gift which St. Paul had received of God—next in order of importance after that of God's grace and truth—was the power of making himself at home with all classes, races, and degrees of men. A practical capacity like this cannot be learnt up like an art or trick; it must be rooted in and spring from those affections and sympathies which are at the base of human character. Nor, although this gift was undoubtedly developed and shaped by grace, can we suppose it to have had no place in the character of St. Paul until he became a servant of Christ. Nature would have contributed to it at least somewhat of the raw material. As a Jew, we may be sure, Saul of Tarsus—apart from the limits which Rabbinical narrowness would have assigned to his sympathies — could already have said, with the heathen poet, that, being a man, he deemed nothing human strange. His broad and genial humanity would have belonged to the original outfit of his nature: for in him, the sympathies of our race seemed to live with extraordinary freshness and power. The fact that he was a member of the great human family would always have had a great place in his consciousness; he was indeed, if any man ever was, enthusiastically human. For such as he, to see another man is forthwith to be drawn to him; it is to take for granted, although in spite of appearances, that there is in him something—nay, much—to love, if you could only get at it: it is to sink the sense of all that repels in the individual in a stronger sense of all that combines all members of the race; it is to meet each one as far as possible; to become "all things" to him,—as the Apostle puts it; to yield to the full force of that true human impulse towards sympathy and service which knows no frontier save that of the human family itself.

This, I say, is a rich natural endowment of which we are speaking; and, as such, it is to be found beyond the frontiers of the Church of Christ. But, apart from Christianity, it commonly fares like a fastidious plant in an uncongenial climate; it is only exposed to become deformed or to die. Too often it sickens into a vague, dreamy sentimentalism; or it loses itself fairly, as unsanctified sympathies will, in the mire of animal passion; or it provokes against itself, as if it were a hollow unreality, some fierce reaction within the character, which seeks to crush out the original impulse in tears and blood. What St. Paul's fervid nature would have become, had he been left to himself, it is useless to inquire; we only know that by the grace of God he was what he was, as we know him in his Epistles. The wonder-working grace of our Lord Jesus Christ did not expel from or suppress in this man those impulses of a wide and genial humanity: rather was it the effect of that grace to refine, to spiritualise, to transfigure, without weakening or maiming, what nature had given. For, in truth, One had appeared among men Who alone and adequately represented them; in Whom our race found at once its centre-point and its ideal; in communion with Whom all the finer common sympathies of men are strengthened and refined; and in bringing men to Whom the virtue of true humanity finds its best and highest exercise. When, then, Paul became a servant of Christ, the natural gift was taken, as it were, under a higher protection; it was illuminated by the rays of a loftier motive than nature could supply: "I am become," he said, " all things to all men, that I might by all means save some."

The Apostle himself has traced this versatile sympathy in three of its fields of operation. " To the Jews I became as a Jew, that I might gain the Jews; to them that are under the law, as under the law, that I might gain them that are under the law. To them that are without law, as without law (here he explains and guards the expression), that I might gain them that are without law. To the weak became I as weak, that I might gain the weak: I am become all things to all men, that I might by all means save some."

"All things to all men." In his own words, the Jews had both killed the Lord Jesus and their own prophets; and, he proceeds, " have persecuted us; and they please not God, and are contrary to all men."[1] In their eyes Paul was the apostate who had endeavoured to revive the memory of the false and dishonoured Prophet of Nazareth. In his eyes they were the race which had come nearest to God, and had most decisively rejected Him. And yet how tender and affectionate is he in his dealings with his poor countrymen, or with Christians who shared, less excusably, their hereditary prejudices! It might almost seem at times as if he had turned his back upon the Cross;—so careful is he not to wound the sensitiveness of the adherents of the old religion. He, the Apostle of the grace of the Crucified, must take and circumcise Timothy at Lystra, " because of the Jews that were in those parts, for they knew all that his father was a Greek."[2] He must shave his head in Cenchrea, " for he had a vow."[3] He must, at the instance of the Apostle James, " purify himself," along with four Jewish devotees, and " enter into the Temple, to signify the accomplishment of the days of purification, until that an offering should be offered for

[1] 1 Thess. ii. 15.   [2] Acts xvi. 3.   [3] Ibid. xviii. 18.

every one of them!"[1] And even when he is compelled, by virtue of his Apostolic commission, and by the imperious Truth which fills and rules him, to utter the stern and awful sentence, that by their infatuated rejection of the True Messias, Who was the Crown and Promise of their history, they had rejected their God—how does he soften his message by all the resources of sympathy and affection! At the thought of their fall, he protests that he has "great heaviness and continual sorrow in his heart."[2] He cannot forget that to them pertains "the adoption, and the glory, and the covenants, and the giving of the law, and the solemn service of God, and the promises"; that theirs are the fathers; that of them—the last distinction and the greatest—"as concerning the flesh, Christ came, Who is over all, God blessed for ever."[3] He remembers that he too is an Israelite, of the seed of Abraham, of the tribe of Benjamin.[4] He even "could wish that himself were accursed from Christ for his brethren, his kinsmen according to the flesh."[5] He will not believe that they are finally rejected: he must soften down his own description of their ruin: "Blindness," he says, "in part is happened to Israel, until the fulness of the Gentiles be come in, and so all Israel shall be saved."[6]

"All things to all men!" He, the Apostle of Revealed Truth, the preacher of that One God Who is only known to and approached by man through our Lord Jesus Christ, how does he make himself at home with the men and thoughts of the heathen world! Read his Epistles, and see how he can sympathise with the happy conqueror in the Greek games "who receiveth the prize";[7] or with the old Latin idea of the city or state, imagined as a

---

[1] Acts xxi. 26.   [2] Rom. ix. 2.   [3] *Ibid.* ix. 4, 5.
[4] Rom. xi. 1.   [5] *Ibid.* ix. 3. [6] *Ibid.* xi. 25, 26.
[7] 1 Cor. ix. 24.

political transcript of the human body.¹ How does he study each detail of the dress and accoutrements of the soldier who watches him as he writes to the Ephesians![2] How interested he is in the details of the administration of the empire when addressing the Romans![3] How tenderly does he survey the heathen world at Athens, as "feeling after God" as though on its way to "find Him!"[4] Nay, the writers of Pagan Greece,—and, as has been more than once observed, not always those whom, we may think, a Christian would have chosen,—are constantly on his lips, or in his thoughts; he refers to them when he is preaching at Athens, or writing to Corinth, or even privately exhorting a trusted disciple.[5] In St. Paul's eyes heathenism was not all bad; there was in it much to love and to sympathise with; it was being prepared for Truth, without having yet reached it; in it, as in the irrational creation at the fall, higher aspirations had been for a while made subject to vanity, not willingly, but in hope; and before it was extended, not indistinctly, the prospect of a deliverance from this service of corruption into the glorious liberty of the children of God.[6]

"All things to all men!" There were "weak" Christians, as the Apostle gently calls them, who clung to observances, or who entertained scruples which were at variance with the import, freedom, generosity of the Gospel. And of that Gospel, in its unstinted liberty and grace, St. Paul was the jealous and passionate champion. He, if any man, might have been expected to pour contempt upon a worthless scruple—to brand, with the sternest note of disapprobation, the forms, whether of life or of thought, which, however

---

[1] 1 Cor. xii. 12-27. Compare Livy, ii. 32; Seneca *De Irâ*, ii. 31. This image furnishes the Apostle with his opportunity for unfolding the nature of the Church as the σῶμα τοῦ Χριστοῦ.

[2] Eph. vi. 14-17.   [3] Rom. xiii. 1, 4, 6, 7.   [4] Acts xvii. 27.
[5] Acts xvii. 28; 1 Cor. xv. 33; Titus i. 12.   [6] Rom. viii. 20, 21.

unintentionally, did dishonour to the work of the Redeemer. We know how he could express himself upon occasions when great principles were at stake, as when he told the Galatians sharply that if they were circumcised Christ would profit them nothing.[1] But, as a rule, how tender he is, how full of consideration and charity, how tolerant, how hopeful! The prejudice against the meat exposed for sale in the Corinthian market was a weakly superstition; but for himself he would rather eat no flesh whatever while the world lasted, than offend the conscience of a weak brother.[2] The private observance of days, Jewish or other, at Rome, was no part of the Church's rule, and might easily engender Jewish errors; but the Apostle insists that those who kept these days did so to the Lord, and should be respected in the observance.[3] The strong, he says, with a touch of quiet irony, ought to bear the infirmities of the weak, and not to please themselves.[4] And—to the scandal of some, no doubt, at the time, but for the instruction of the Church of all ages—what he preached he practised.

We cannot too often remind ourselves that all this was not mere natural sympathy run wild; it was throughout prompted and controlled by a powerful motive. That motive was not, "That I may be agreeable to all the world," but that "I may by all means save some"—save them from the sin which besets and from the eternal death which awaits them; save them by bringing them into living communion with the Almighty and Crucified Saviour. Not "all"—that were too much to hope—but "some." God knows who they will be, but the duty of His servant is plain. Thus, while Paul's heart is on fire his reason is cool; after all this expenditure of feeling and effort he looks for very partial results. But

[1] Gal. v. 2.   [2] 1 Cor. viii. 13.
[3] Rom. xiv. 5, 6.   [4] Rom. xv. 1.

whether in the Jewish synagogue or on Mars' hill in Athens; whether among scholars or the unlettered; whether amidst friends or foes; whether he stands face to face with multitudes or is pleading with a single soul; —he keeps one purpose steadily before him; he is what he is—he does what he does—that some at least may know the power of that faithful saying which is ever worthy of all acceptation, that "Christ Jesus came into the world to save sinners."[1]

Mere human sympathy, however strong, wears itself out; it is at least half physical in its nature, and its energy shares the vicissitudes and decay of our bodily frame. One motive only—the love of God—really lasts; and of the love of God, the love of man, whom God has loved so well as to create and to redeem him, is in reality the consequence and the attestation.

II.

The motto of the Apostle might well serve for that of the Church of Christ. Just as the Divine Redeemer, although born of Jewish parentage, and nurtured in a Syrian village, belonged already, by the representative character of His perfect Humanity, to all the world, so that in Him was found exactly and exclusively neither Greek nor Jew, nor barbarian nor Scythian, nor bond nor free; so was it to be—so in fact it was—with the society which He established upon the earth, in order to represent Him in history. Hardly had the Apostles passed away when the Church was, in a large measure, at home among races and in civilisations the most various and distant. Her missionaries were upon the Euphrates or beyond it; she was penetrating the southern desert: scarce any city in the Lesser Asia had not become familiar with her

[1] 1 Tim. i. 15.

presence; she was planted in strength upon the Tiber; she had already her eye, if nothing more, on Gaul and Spain and Britain. Everywhere she learnt the speech, the habits, the social and national temper of her children; she identified herself, so far as the law of Christ allowed, with the life of the races to which she came. One treasure, indeed, to be guarded at all costs, she brought them; it had come from heaven. But in all else she was a willing learner—I might say, a faithful domestic. So it was at the first, when the idea of an ecclesiastical absolutism—which, after confiscating the ancient liberties of the Christian Churches, should control the action of kings and governments—had not yet dawned upon the world; when as yet too it was not supposed that a true Christian must perforce dress, talk, and read after the fashion of a particular civilisation, or must uphold a particular political polity, or must be strictly independent of it. To men of many climes and races the Church of Christ appeared in those bright and early days as a perfectly disinterested friend and adviser: she made herself "all things to all"; not that she might win place, or wealth, or power—though these things came to her in time, and inevitably, from the hands and hearts of her grateful children—but that out of the vast mass of human beings to which she addressed herself she might by all means "save some."

III.

My brethren—if we could forget the Apostle's words—there is, here and to-day, one subject, one character, one name, which, next to that of our Lord and Master, has a first place in every heart. This Church, which, although not under his pastoral jurisdiction, was peculiarly controlled by him, and at his disposal; this Church, which, in its older guise, was for so many years and so repeatedly the scene of his ministrations; this Church, which is so near to his honoured grave, and which, in this its reconstruction, is associated with his dear memory, we hope, for ever, obliges us, if nothing else, to think of him. And surely our thoughts will have been already turned towards him by our contemplation of the great Apostle, of whose character, in one significant respect, he was, as it appears to me, so remarkable a reproduction. There were indeed, in St. Paul—not merely as an Apostle, but as a man—many elements which do not suggest themselves to-day. In particular St. Paul was, by business, not merely a pastor and missionary, but a formal theologian. First of all, he had clearly before his mind the idea of a body of certain truth which had come to him from above, and which was in his keeping for others; and then he set himself to unfold, to recommend, to fortify, to define, to ascertain precisely what was meant and what was not meant,—to guard on every side against assaults and misconceptions, to illustrate out of the resources which were supernaturally given him,— this priceless treasure. In this, as it would seem, St. Paul has had, amongst ourselves, others, who, at however vast a distance, have more nearly imitated him. One such, perhaps, beyond any, will be in our minds just now, as he has lately been lost to the Church of Scotland; for he, like the Apostle, moved with severe accuracy, yet with reverent passion, amid the things of God, and he heightened the natural skill of an accomplished thinker and dialectician by the fervour and intensity of a devoted heart.[1] But he to whom our thoughts turn to-day, although indeed he found time to read, and to learn more than do the majority of students by profession, yet was wont to say of himself that he had to deal not with books,

---

[1] Alexander Penrose Forbes, Bishop of Brechin. He died on Friday, October 8, 1875.

but with men. Bishop Wilberforce's mind was practical rather than speculative; he was better able to make the most of concrete and historical fact than to feel his way, with patient and measured hesitation, among the bewildering heights and passes of abstract truth. And therefore he is nearer the Apostle, not when the latter, as if looking upward, scans the sublime mysteries of Revelation, but when, looking downwards in the fulness of his compassionate sympathy, he addresses himself as one of themselves to the race of beings whose ignorance and wants the message he bore was destined to relieve. He was peculiarly like St. Paul in the strength, in the tenderness, in the versatility of his humanity—in his power of becoming all things to all men, that he might by all means save some.

This was, I say, among his many great gifts, the prerogative endowment of this most remarkable man—that he could, without effort, and with the readiness and grace of a perfectly natural instinct, identify himself with human beings who agreed in almost nothing except the being human. He was ever ready for intimacy with people of all stations and temperaments : he was courtier and peasant by turns; the friend of kings and ministers, and the familiar and accustomed inmate of the penitentiary or the workhouse. He could approach, with the same resistless persuasiveness, the most cultivated and the roughest of mankind ; and, up to the last year of his life, he could exchange the gravest business of his high office at a moment's notice for a children's game, into which he entered with the natural and unconstrained enjoyment of a child. He was at home with the most religious, and, in a sense, with the least religious of men; ever aiding and elevating the one, and doing what he could—in fact, doing much—for the other. He was the friend, the trusted, sympathising, intelligent friend, of the

studious and the practical, of the enthusiastic and the
cautious, of the prosaic and the imaginative, of the light-
hearted and the sorrowful; of the young man, whose
robust health and untamed spirits vented themselves in
boisterous and joyous speech, and of the sick or the dying,
treading fearfully amid the shadows which fall along the
frontiers of the eternal world. With perfect ease he
could pass from scene to scene, from man to man, the
most dissimilar, as though, so far from experiencing any
strain upon his sympathies, he found positive relief in
the sharpest ethical contrasts; and he made each one
feel that his sympathy was perfect, so perfect as to seem
for the time to preclude the possibility of sympathy in
any opposite direction. What he was to those nearest
and dearest to him,—how unwearied in his interest, how
passionate yet tender in his affections—I must not
attempt to say in this presence. But you, my brethren,
who have lived in this parish, will remember what he
has been in past years among you; how he came to you
as your own pastor; how, without condescension on his
part or effort on yours, you felt at once at home with
him; how he entered with a true human interest into
your cares, your occupations, your efforts, your failures;
how from this pulpit he set before you, in all its simple
tenderness, the grace and Gospel of our Divine Saviour,
and as you listened and looked at him, you knew that in
him you had a friend whom you could trust so to guide
you through things temporal that you should finally lose
not the things eternal. And when he left you, it was
probably to appear before his own University, where the
ripe learning and the choicest youth of England hung
upon his lips; where, if he could not command universal
assent—that, in a very chaos of disintegrated convictions,
was, alas! impossible—yet his eloquent and intrepid
voice could never be heard, even by the least friendly

hearers, without imposing or rather exacting attention and respect, when indeed it did not, as it often did, achieve so much beyond. And then, perhaps, within twenty-four hours, he would be found in the national Senate, swaying by his speech that most unsympathetic and frigid of audiences, and holding his own amid veteran politicians, as if he had been a statesman all his life; or at some social gathering, where his brilliant powers of conversation, and the incomparable grace which he could throw into all the minutest details of intercourse, made men think for a moment that he only lived for the entertainment of good society. And then, as if to show what all along had been his governing motive, he would suddenly pass to some home of strict Christian devotion, tenanted by those who knew nothing of the outer world, and who, as having given up all for God, spent their whole time in works of mercy and of prayer; and here,—in this rare spiritual atmosphere,—nothing was strange to him, and he could breathe it and express it so joyously and perfectly that, as a Sister of Mercy once exclaimed, after hearing him preach on the joys, and risks, and enthusiasms, and depressions of a consecrated life—"You would think that he had been himself a Sister for at least thirty years."

This astonishing social and mental versatility, this combined flexibility of heart and head, so entirely beyond the reach and even the comprehension of ordinary men, could not but expose him to misconstruction. Too often in matters of character men judge hardly what they cannot understand from a personal experience. And so it came to pass that the question was seriously raised whether this great servant of Christ was not, after all, merely a worldling, who used Church language, Church occasions, even Church ordinances, as instruments to promote and subserve a selfish, social triumph. It is hard, but it is necessary to mention, that we may brand, as it deserves, the foolish and odious charge not seldom made against him, as indeed against St. Paul—the charge of insincerity. How could he really mean this universal sympathy, men have asked, with persons, and classes, and characters so dissimilar? How could he rightly be thus the country pastor, the academical preacher, the far-sighted statesman, the favourite of all that is brilliant and fastidious in society, the wise spiritual guide of devoted souls, the ruler of the Church, and the sympathising friend of every class of Churchmen, so perfectly and all at once? How could he truly love truth himself, whilst he lavished such care on those who doubted or rejected it? how could he thus, without wrongdoing, essay to combine the incompatible? to ignore thus audaciously the moral and intellectual chasms which part men asunder in this modern world? Was he not, though he sat in the chair of the Apostles, only after all a consummate actor, who could, in matters of practice, assume any character at will, and who, in matters of speculation, while professing loyalty to absolute truth, really strengthened the impression, that the most cultivated and subtle minds of our day know that nothing beyond the field of sensible experience is ascertainably true, and make the best of the whirl of contradictory opinions which surrounds them, by being intellectually civil to everybody?

It may be said that this estimate of him, however unwarranted by facts, was, in intention, honest. Honest it may have been, as the hard judgments of contracted sympathies, and dull and sluggish feelings, and a very narrow field of thought and observation, are wont to be honest. Men who themselves love only with a very tepid affection, when they love at all, and who can only concentrate affection on a single object at the price of denying it to others, or of viewing others with active dislike; men who cannot understand that it is possible to be sincerely loyal to truth, and yet generous in the estimate and treatment of its opponents;—these had before them, in the language and action of Bishop Wilberforce, an inexplicable problem. In their eyes he was a standing paradox. And as they were unwilling to think that he was wholly beyond the scope of their moral comprehension, they explained him, as narrow natures will, by asking instinctively what, in his circumstances, would too probably have been true about themselves.

Thus, indeed, it had fared eighteen centuries before with St. Paul. The gossips of Corinth or of Ancyra had anticipated the ill-nature of some among ourselves in this nineteenth century. St. Paul, also, it seems, had too large a heart to be always understood; and so it was suggested that his work was tainted throughout by a selfish aim; that he sought not men, but what he could get from them; that, "being crafty, he caught them with guile."[1] It is the penalty, or rather it is the distinction, of moral genius to be thus misunderstood; thus to be credited with that which it abhors; thus to be painted, though on the very steps of the throne of Christ, in the likeness of the enemy.

Did not He Himself, our adorable Master, forewarn us that it would be so; and was this warning meant to hold good only of the first age of His Church, as though after that human nature would all of a sudden change fundamentally, and unwelcome truth would always command the welcome of generous or ungenerous hearts?

For what is it that at once provokes these criticisms, while it is at the same time the warrant of their injustice? What is it but the strong, simple motive which in such a man underlies the varieties of the outward life; what but

[1] 2 Cor. xii. 16.

the stern determination by all means to save some, to bring, at whatever cost, some souls for pardon and peace to the feet of the Crucified? Criticism of this kind does not waste itself upon the inert respectability which dreams of nothing less than a serious effort for God and for righteousness; and, if Bishop Wilberforce had been less like the Apostle in his unresting work for souls, he would have escaped, we may be sure, the calumnies which he has shared with Christ's earlier and greater servant. The stupidity—to use no harsher term—of these criticisms was in reality most apparent to those who knew him best. Certainly he did not always say or leave unsaid that which some of us, looking at portions of truth from a somewhat different standpoint, could more than once have desired. But he was often credited with opinions which he did not really hold; he was charged with disloyalty to beliefs which those who knew him knew he did not share. Certainly, he may at times have felt the moral pressure of a personal sympathy more strongly than the intellectual pressure of an abstract principle; he may, on some occasion, have faltered in the actual maintenance of truth; at least, he would not now wish me to say that this was impossible. But that he ever consciously betrayed it, who that knew him can imagine? He need not have shrunk, I firmly believe, from the Apostle's words: "Our rejoicing is this, the testimony of our own conscience, that in simplicity and godly sincerity, not with fleshly wisdom, but by the grace of God, we have had our conversation in the world."[1] Take his life and work as a whole, and let me dare to say, in virtue of the long friendship with which he honoured me, that it was penetrated throughout by sincerity of purpose. Yes; if any man, he was sincere: sincere in his assertions; sincere in his hesitations; sincere in his negations; sincere in his

---

[1] 2 Cor. i. 12.

belief that much which seemed to be contradictory might ultimately be reconciled, and that men were often on two sides of a hedge, while they thought themselves on different continents; sincere when he seemed to be inconsistent or exaggerated; sincere too in the trivialities of intercourse as in the great resolves and concerns of life. Like the Apostle, he was "a deceiver, and yet true."[1] An insincere man would have been less careless of appearances, less ready to expose himself again and again to hostile criticism for the sake of doing a kindness; but he,—as strong men will,—knew that he could dare to be misunderstood, since God and time would correct the misunderstanding.

One consideration indeed there is which of itself should enable all thinking and fair-minded persons to do justice to the disinterestedness of his character. High as was the position which he held at the time of his death, it was not that which the earlier opinion of his countrymen, or his vast practical abilities, or the unexampled scale and character of his public services, had long marked out for him. By common acknowledgment the natural chief of the English clergy, a man who maintained his ascendency among his fellows with that careless ease which forbids the thought of rivalry, he must have known, nay, he knew, that he would have been carried by the popular voice to one of the two historic seats of honour and authority in the English Church, if he would only have consented to make popular prejudice the measure of his utterances. If he could have brought himself—they were nearly his own words—to ignore the spiritual character of the English Church; to treat her practically as a State department; to appeal to Acts of Parliament for her highest claims upon the conscience of the English people; if he could have sincerely echoed those popular deprecia-

[1] 2 Cor. vi. 8.

tions of the Christian Sacraments, which make them the barren and graceless symbols of an absent and shadowy Christ;—the higher ecclesiastical honours could not, in the nature of things, have been withheld. Not that I would be understood for a moment to imply that others have consented to that which he refused. But, in his case, popular errors would have exacted pledges and conditions which others may have been spared, and which he could not have given without moral loss. And full well he knew that these matters are ordered by the Church's invisible Head; that His decisions must be really best; that such earthly rewards, if they are rewards, are not what a Christian should desire.[1] Assuredly happy is he now in that world where all is true, that he put from him the temptation to which many a man, conscious of his vast abilities, might so easily have yielded; put it from him so decidedly, that only when life's evening was closing in upon him, and his strength was failing, and the end was near—how near we little thought—was there any, and that but a slight, as it was an unsought, recognition of his altogether unrivalled services as a Bishop, to the Church of Christ in England.

Yes! Two years and a quarter have passed since his removal from among us—since that tragic moment on a summer afternoon, when, without warning, he passed from the very dust and turmoil of busy human life into the silence of eternity. Two years and a quarter; and even yet it seems but yesterday. The flowers have long since grown on his grave; but his place in memory—the vast blank which he has left in the heart and thought of the Church—is still what it was on the morrow of his death. Nay rather, as we do justice to the real height of a lofty mountain when we are no longer in contact with it at its base, but have left it in the distance, and survey it across

[1] St. Matt. vi. 2, 5.

a larger and larger foreground of vales and hills, so is it with a really great character. We see our late Bishop more nearly in his true proportions, as we gradually leave him in the distance of history; we have slowly learnt to do him justice, when we find that even now his real place in the Church of England is still unfilled. It is not that the Holy and Eternal Spirit, Who made this great and gifted man what he was to all of us, cannot raise up and fashion new instruments for that Divine work, which belongs to no one generation, or set of circumstances, or type of character. But it would seem as if, all through Church history, God was purposely sparing of these more magnificent creations. A really great prelate—it was the remark of a German historian—is of rare occurrence in the history of the Church of Christ. So high is the true ideal of that august office, so exacting are its requirements, so much does it demand of the loftiest qualities which are supplied from earth and of the choicest graces which are sent down from heaven, that even in earlier and better times than these a great bishop was accounted a signal token of God's favour. And, like other blessings, so this is barely recognised at the time; it is taken as a matter of course, or it is depreciated: we only do it justice when it is withdrawn. Certainly we have learnt, in his absence, whom and what we have lost. How many a mourner, how many a doubter, how many a struggling, perplexed, bewildered man, has sadly felt, that the one friend who could and would have brought sympathy and relief is no longer in sight! And amid the public events which have passed since his death, and which are as yet scarcely history, how have thousands of hearts turned back in memory to one who would have done so much; who would have prevented so much; who would have understood and explained motives, and repressed extravagances, and soothed irritations; who would surely, amid the wild tumult of an irrational panic, have raised his voice on behalf of charity and justice; who would have bridged over chasms and healed wounds which even yet bode no good for the peace and wellbeing of the Church of England; who in his own person, and by the magic power of that grace and charity and humanity which God had given him, would have done much to turn the hearts of the children to the fathers, and of the fathers to the children, wherever they have been or are unhappily estranged!

But it is neither wise in itself, nor loyal to his great memory, to dream away what remains of life in longings for the impossible. Rather let us endeavour to-day to make our own—not indeed all that he has to teach us— that were far from practicable—but the single and most important lesson which the text suggests. To become, as nearly as may be, all things to all men from a purely unselfish motive is to make a great step in Christian practice. Honesty of purpose is not necessarily unsympathetic and repellent; nor has lack of sympathy, felt and owned, any special title to the praise of Christ. Never, perhaps, was the grace so conspicuously illustrated, first by the Apostle and then by our late revered Father in God, more urgently needed in members and ministers of the English Church than now;—when she has so much reason both for fear and for hope; when she is pressed so sorely by Ultramontane propagandism on that side, and by dark negations of all fundamental truth, theistic not less than Christian, on this; when within her there are so many and such various elements of interest and anxiety, which it is so easy to alienate irrevocably, so all-important to conciliate and combine, if it may be, into a new and vigorous unity. And be we what or where we may, grace and courtesy of speech and manner, tenderness and consideration for others, the becoming all things to them—even to their prejudices and weaknesses —short of sin, is a debt which we owe to our fellow-creatures; and it should be paid, not out of a stock of blind though kindly impulse, or at the chance suggestions of an easy temper, but with a view, if possible, to do them in time the highest of all possible services. For such a habit is the salt of human society; it is the enrichment and bloom of the individual Christian life; nay, it is the fruit of intimate personal knowledge of and contact with that Living Saviour, Who opens His arms and His heart to the whole human family, and Whose love reflects itself in the lives and conduct and speech of those who live with Him and for Him. God grant that this occasion may be fruitful in something better and more enduring than the deep and strong feelings which are inevitably called forth by it; that it may leave an impress of unselfish and active charity upon our lives, and may be looked back to with thankfulness by each one of us from his place in the eternal world!

SERMON XIII.

JOHN KEBLE.[1]

COL. iii. 10

The new man, which is renewed unto knowledge, after the image of Him That created him.

THE day which is now drawing to its close, and the incidents of which will not be soon forgotten by those who have taken part in them, has had a double significance. It is almost the second birthday of an institution which must interest all who care for education, as being an experiment at once bold and successful. Founded at a critical moment in the history of the University, and, as was felt at the time, on the eve of changes of momentous importance, this College has, by God's kindly providence, rapidly attained a position of usefulness which exceeds the most sanguine hopes that prompted its foundation. The devoted industry, the foresight, the high administrative genius which have been placed at its service, are, within these walls, matters rather for thankful remembrance than for eulogy; but to such qualities as these it is immediately due that less than ten short years have sufficed to convert a timid suggestion upon note-paper into one of the largest and most vigorous of the colleges of Oxford. And when we look around us at this chapel—the crown and flower of the surrounding buildings—we may also thank God for not having denied

[1] Preached at Keble College, Oxford, on occasion of the opening of the Chapel and laying the foundation-stone of the Hall and Library on the Feast of St. Mark, April 25, 1876.

to our generation either the impulse to a splendid munificence, or the reverential instincts of sacred art, when endeavouring to set forth, however faintly through material things, the supersensuous realities, or the desire to make whatever He has given—whether it be wealth or genius—promote His glory. "Blessed are they which love thee, O Jerusalem, for they shall rejoice in thy peace; blessed are they which have been sorrowful for all thy scourges, for they shall rejoice for thee when they have seen all thy glory, and shall be glad for ever. . . . For Jerusalem shall be built up with sapphires and emeralds and precious stones; thy walls and towers and battlements with pure gold; and the streets of Jerusalem shall be paved with beryl, and carbuncle, and stones of Ophir; and all her streets shall say Alleluia, and they shall praise Him, saying, Blessed be God, Which hath extolled it for ever."[1]

But to this aspect of the occasion justice has already been done; while in the years to come it will naturally command an increasing share of interest. And, as has been already intimated, the day has another meaning—a meaning which will be hereafter insisted on at a comparative disadvantage. The time cannot be very far distant when all those who have known the gifted and saintly man whose name has conferred such lustre and sanction upon this college will have gone to their account. And criticism of the dead past, however acute it be, and however furnished with the necessary material, yields a poor substitute for that incommunicable freshness of impression which actual contact with a living man alone can give. Let us, then, endeavour once more to-day to place ourselves in the company of the dear and honoured servant of Christ, whose life and work has inspired the idea and urged forward the completion of this foundation, as an acknowledgment of the gratitude which is due to

[1] Tobit xiii. 14, 16-18.

Almighty God for all that is best and most invigorating in a noble model of the Christian life.

And here, lest we should lose our way in so wide a subject, the Apostle comes to our assistance in the text with a particular suggestion. He is speaking of the New or Ideal Man—realised perfectly in our Lord Jesus Christ, and imperfectly, although, so far as it goes, truly, by each of His servants. This new humanity comprises every department of human nature; for its Divine Author makes all things new. A new heart, a will free because regenerate, an illuminated and sensitive conscience, the passions controlled by will, and the will controlled by conscience, and conscience enlightened by the Holy Spirit;—this is its meaning. Of this complete renewal the germinal force is given in baptism, whether baptismal grace be developed in accordance with God's Will, or checked and lost by unfaithfulness or sin. And of this New Man, "created in righteousness and true holiness," a renovated intellect is not the least important feature. Although the moral side of human nature, the passions, the heart, the will, gain most conspicuously through the re-creative power of the grace of Christ, because they exhibit the ravages of sin most glaringly; yet the intellect is too closely associated with moral character not to be largely affected by it for good and evil. Doubtless, there have been bad men of the highest ability, and saintly men of no ability at all; but at least in dealing with one, and that the highest, class of subjects, this absolute dualism of the two departments of the soul is impossible. In this sphere of attainments, general intellectual dulness is no bar to quick spiritual penetration; and the acutest of intellects may be fatally blinded by a bad or perverse heart.

"Renewed unto knowledge," says the Apostle—ἀνακαινούμενος εἰς ἐπίγνωσιν—in process of being so renewed as to enter upon a higher knowledge than that to which unregenerate nature could attain. "Renewed," he says elsewhere, "in the spirit of your minds";[1] and once again, "Be ye transformed by the renewal of your minds."[2] Whether it be the intuitive faculty, or the practical intelligence, or intermediate powers and functions of mind, it is mental renovation on a large scale that St. Paul is contemplating. Such renovation is an integral portion of the renewal of human nature through union with the New Manhood of the Divine Redeemer; and a striking illustration of its reality and of its far-reachingness is afforded by him who is the subject of our thoughts to-day.

For there are three characters under which the remarkable man whose name is identified with this College may be considered. He was a poet; he was a man of eminent goodness; and he was a great Christian thinker and theologian. Of these characters the first has mainly riveted the attention of the world. The name of the author of *The Christian Year* is known to thousands who know nothing, whatever they may infer, about his life and character. And a scarcely smaller number who are aware that he was a man of singular purity and simplicity of life have no idea that his intellect was one of unusual strength and beauty, and that he wielded decisive influence at a crisis pregnant with consequences to the religious future of his country. "The poet Keble!" The phrase is used, often indeed as a title of honour, but sometimes also to imply that he was only a maker of religious verses, and not properly a leader or guide of men. It is meant to suggest that, while the fitful and turbid stream of passion and thought which we term modern life was rolling impetuously onwards, he sat pensive but helpless on the brink of the torrent, and warbled soft strains of mournful half-intelligible song which could not even catch the ear of those who were battling with the angry waters. It is

[1] Eph. iv. 23.   [2] Rom. xii. 2.

with a view to correcting this impression that I shall say what little I have to say this evening. His poetry already belongs to the literature of the country; and it has been criticised, and will be criticised yet, by those who may rightly venture upon the task. Of his daily life the governing feature which illuminated all else, and in which all else found its centre and its harmony, has been unveiled to you this morning by one who speaks on such a subject with a higher authority than any other living man. It will not be wrong, in a place of mental as well as moral training which bears his name, to direct attention to the characteristics of his mind, especially as his mind flashes through his poetry, and is shaped by and inseparable from the elevation of his moral nature.

And here let it be said once for all that in such a matter as character, whether mental or moral, the eye of an observer will embrace only a part of the whole, probably a very small part; and that he reports what he sees, not as it is in itself, but only as it appears to him. Yet, on the other hand, in the case of a beautiful and highly endowed soul, each one of us perhaps recognises something which others might miss; and each may therefore hope, in spite of inevitable one-sidedness and imperfection, to contribute towards a final estimate some feature or detail that may be worth remembering.

I.

Of Mr. Keble's mind, then, the inspiring, controlling, penetrating principle was a sense of truth—a sense so keen-sighted and imperious, yet withal so delicate and tender, as to form a specific variety of what may be thought a commonplace excellence in honest men. And such a sense of truth, as is plain from the context,[1] was the governing quality of that new intellectual man whom

Col. iii. 9.

St. Paul describes in the text. Certainly, the noble passion for truth, the passion which would woo and win her, though it were through toil and suffering, is not so exclusively a Christian excellence that it is undiscoverable elsewhere. Greeks could desire to perish in the light; and the records of Eastern mysticism, associated though they are with odious and grotesque idolatries, describe some of the noblest efforts and aspirations of the human soul. The love of truth is, indeed, part of the outfit of every noble nature: its inspiring and purifying force cannot but be recognised in some of our day, who, alas! sit loosely to the creed of the Church of Christ, or are bitterly hostile to it. Admitting, or rather premising this, let us, on the other hand, observe that, in its higher and more delicate forms, the love of truth is of Christian growth. It ranks with charity and purity among the fairest flowers which grow on the Tree of the Cross. By His revelation of Himself our Lord brought the human mind into direct contact with the highest and absolute truth; and this contact had the effect of awaking in it new faculties, almost a new sense of loyalty to truth, just as the sight of a great masterpiece endows the young artist with a new world of ideas as to the power and demands of art. With his sense and love of truth as such, the Christian received from Christ a capacity for working, daring, and enduring much on truth's behalf; a capacity which, in its intensity and range, was a new thing among men. Not merely old and thoughtful men, but weak women, slaves, and boys, caught the heavenly and ennobling flame, from the fire which Christ came to kindle; and by their lives, their works, and their deaths they illustrated the power of the Divine words, "To this end was I born, and for this cause came I into the world, that I should bear witness unto the truth."[1] If any man ever shared the spirit of

[1] St. John xviii. 37.

this noble company, it was the author of *The Christian Year*.

It is no objection to this feature of his character that he was a poet. Poets, it has been said, avail themselves of the services of a slave who is wont to get the better of them, and who is named Imagination; and there have been and are poets enough of whom this is true. But it is not necessary that poetry should be hostile to truth, or other than one of the most effective of its exponents; some of the truest poetry that ever was uttered was uttered at the bidding of a burning sense of truth, and owes its lasting power to the circumstances of its origin. Everything will of course depend upon the particular work and range of activity which is assigned to imagination; and in the case of a Christian this will be decided, not by the impetus of passion, or the supposed exigencies of art, but, like other matters, by conscience. Imagination may invent that which is known to have no basis in fact, or to be contrary to fact; but it may also place itself under the guidance of fact, and recover or fill up more or less successfully the minor features of an outline which already exists. The cultivation and employment of what is termed the "historical imagination" is held, when it is under sufficient safeguards, to be ancillary and not antagonistic to truth. Even physical science—I do not here say how prudently or otherwise—has claimed the services of imagination, to anticipate its triumphs, to fill up the gaps which yawn between its successive discoveries, or,—more doubtfully,—to elaborate the theories which it constructs from time to time about the origin and object of the universe. Religious poetry, then, if it is to be worthy of its name, must enlist imagination in the service of fact; poetry, like that of the *Paradise Lost*, has indeed other titles to admiration which are not here in question; but the invention of a new Satan and a new

Christ prevents a Christian from regarding it as religious poetry. In religious poetry, properly so called, imagination never lets go its hold upon the hand of truth.

With the author of *The Christian Year*, it may safely be affirmed, the creative instincts of the imagination were never consciously indulged at the expense of truth. To him revealed truth was too serious a reality to be obscured or contravened, on any occasion or for any purpose whatever. Certainly he allowed a chastened fancy to play around his creed; he brought, as few could bring, the whole play and activity of awe, wonder, eager desire, rapture, fear, into contact with the divine realities; he did not shrink from filling up the canvas—as in those exquisite lines on the compassion of the mother of our Lord for the mother of Judas in the *Lyra Innocentium* [1]—where Holy Scripture, however distantly, had pointed the way. But he never resembled the artist who sacrificed the brightness of his soul to the exigencies of his craft; he was not first a son of poetry and then of truth; he was first a son of truth, and then, or perhaps therefore, a son of poetry.

Still less is this governing feature of his mind inconsistent with the fact that he was a sincere believer in all the truths of the Christian Revelation, as understood by the ancient and undivided Church of Christ. It is sometimes hinted that a man with a large, fixed, and exacting creed cannot really love truth, subjective truth, as such; that being committed to one view of things, he is of necessity debarred from inquiries which a love of truth is always prosecuting in all directions. At least such a man, it is said, can never think his creed out; he can never examine his premises; he can never do more than arrange and rearrange details which flow from a source which he treats as beyond discussion. Any one who knew Mr. Keble at all intimately would know that this view of

[1] *Lyr. Inn.* ii. 13, "Judas' Infancy."

religious men was to him at least inapplicable. That he held his faith with sensitive and jealous tenacity it is unnecessary to say; he held it, not as his own opinion, but as God's truth. But although it was in the main hereditary, at least in respect of its principles and outline, he was always inquiring, learning, supplementing, correcting; he was continually tracing the first principles of his faith back to those facts of history or facts of moral consciousness to which they appeal; and he was constantly, to use his own expression, examining his major premises to see what they really did involve. Thus, without any change of principle, he wrote at one period of his life his poem on Gunpowder Treason, and, at a later, his treatise on Eucharistical Adoration. "I have learnt to see," he said, "what Scripture, explained by Christian antiquity, really meant." Certainly, he was as alive as the youngest of us can be to objections which might be urged against his faith; in former years he had breathed an atmosphere of discussion at Oriel, where nothing that passed was likely to have escaped him. Whatever sorrow he might feel on account of those who yielded to the pressure of modern negative systems, these systems, so far as I know, never seemed to take him by surprise, whether on the score of their audacity or their ingenuity. He had maturely traversed and explored the ground; he had surveyed his faith in detail, and had already made up his mind as to the force of theories that were urged against it. This side of his intellect came as a surprise upon a young man who only knew him as a poet or a devotional writer, and who, perhaps, thought that the current criticisms on the evidences or subject-matter of revealed religion or parts of it, in the Universities or elsewhere, belonged to a more modern world than his. Utterly as his moral nature shrank from conclusions which imperilled faith, he could measure the depths of the abyss as accurately and as coolly as most men; and could, to save a friend, venture as chivalrously near the brink. But, in this class of questions, the truthfulness of his mental character was especially observable. You felt it in his hesitations;—the product, as they were, of his far-sightedness, already anticipating and answering an objection to that which he was about to say, and weighing out to himself the exact value of the answer. You felt it in the concessions which he would make quite abruptly to the side against which he was arguing, with a full conviction of the damage he was doing to his own conclusion. His sudden reservations, dictated by a fear that he might have said more than his knowledge of a subject warranted, or that he might have said less than truth required; his tender but resistless expostulations with those who seemed to be playing with arguments instead of using them seriously; his frequent protestations of inability to grasp a given subject—as pathetically sincere as they were really unnecessary—all belonged to this great feature of his mental character. For the attainment or expression of truth, no amount of trouble seemed to him to be superfluous. Travellers in Palestine[1] have remarked the accuracy of the references to the flora and natural features of the country which are found in *The Christian Year*: the author had never been out of Europe in his life. And when he was an old man, and had nearly written his last book[2] —" I find," he said, "that I must write a great part over again, as it does not express exactly what I meant to say."

It was not an imaginative temper or warm friendships, but this same imperious sense of truth, that determined his relation to the great religious movement which dates from the year 1833, and from Oxford. That movement would never have been what it has been, and is, had it

[1] Stanley's *Sinai and Palestine*, p. 19, note.
[2] *Eucharistical Adoration*.

been only, or chiefly, an enthusiasm for art, or for antiquity, or for ceremonial. The real spirit of that movement was an appeal to reality; it was based on a sense of truth. The indifference and torpor of the eighteenth century had been in part, but only in part, counteracted by the one-sided religious revival which succeeded it; for this revival, while stimulating the consciousness of personal sin, and dwelling with praiseworthy earnestness on our Lord's Atonement and the work of the Holy Spirit in the Christian's heart, knew little of the real value of the Christian Sacraments, or of the divinely ordered structure of the Christian Church, or indeed of the social and objective, as distinct from the purely subjective and individual aspects of Christianity. Yet the hierarchical fabric of the Church of England, and the public language of its formularies, and the traditional appeal of its greatest divines to that Christian antiquity which alone could justify them in the block, still remained. The venerable words of the Ordinal and the Sacramental services remained, but on the lips of a generation which to a very serious extent, ignored or rejected their natural meaning. In 1833 the questions for sincere minds were such as these:—Ought such institutions as the Episcopate to be swept away in order to promote unity among Protestants, or for the sake of economy? Are the ordinances of the Church really necessary, or are they only matters of antiquarian interest? Should the doctrine and forms of our Sacraments be assimilated to those of the Protestant sects? Or can a satisfactory account be given of these things which would address itself to religious minds, as distinct from the minds of statesmen, anxious only to guard the rights of property and the historical institutions of the country? We know what answer was given to these questions by the Oxford Movement, which, in fact, as Mr. Keble thought, appealed to the only principles on which the Church of England, as now constituted, has any *religious* right to exist at all. If the leaders of the movement appealed to the authority of that Primitive Church, which had, as a matter of fact, decided no less serious a question than what was and what was not canonical Scripture; if they insisted upon the reality of sacramental grace, and upon the Divine authority of the Episcopate; it was, in the first instance, because they believed that an honest recognition of the real frontier and contents of the Christian Revelation, and of the conditions under which it had been given to the world, obliged them to do so. But secondly, and as it were incidentally, they felt that they were doing a good work for the Church of England. The days were passing, or had already gone, when sincere and religious minds could suppose that difficulties about the system or language of a Christian Church could be silenced at the mere instance of the State. If loyalty to Church institutions and ordinances was to continue, it must rest on some deeper ground than this; and when the Oxford leaders pointed to the Apostles and Fathers of undivided Christendom, they were kindling a new enthusiasm for the ecclesiastical structure and for the distinctive sacramental teaching of the Church of England.

Into this vivid appeal to the true area and character of the primitive Christian creed Mr. Keble threw himself heart and soul. The new warmth, the fervour, the unworldliness, the enterprise, the poetry of the Movement, its firm attitude towards history, its nascent relations to philosophy—these had their charm for him; and "especially," as he once said, "the power of feeling at home in the whole Bible, if a man would; instead of being afraid, in his heart, of what some parts of it *might* be found to sanction if interpreted fairly, and so keeping timidly to a narrow interpretation of portions of some two

or three of the Epistles, and practically ignoring the rest."
For Mr. Keble the Christian creed was a living whole;
it was not, he held, really possible for any thoughtful
man to deny as much as he liked and retain faith in the
rest at will. "I cannot understand," he once said, "how
good and thoughtful people can employ arguments
against sacramental grace which are serviceable, *mutatis
mutandis*, against truths which they hold as truly as we
do; the Atonement, for instance, or the Personality of the
Holy Ghost." The Oxford Movement was a protest
against this inconsistency; and in this way too it
recommended itself to Mr. Keble's sense of truth.

This Movement was in different degrees under the
influence of several gifted men, who enjoyed no chartered
immunity from error and exaggeration, and who would
have been the first to own that they too might make
mistakes. But its results might have been different had
it been welcomed intelligently and generously in quarters
where such welcome might have been anticipated. As it
was, when defections to Rome clouded the fair prospects
of its earlier years, Mr. Keble's sense of truth again
determined the direction of his life. Like others, indeed,
at that tragic "parting of friends," he strained his eyes,
filled as they were with tears, across the frontier which
others were passing; but he never thought of following.
Between him and Rome there was the old barrier of
Scripture as interpreted by antiquity—scanned now more
jealously, more closely than ever, by his governing sense
of truth,—by his clear, unwavering sense of the original
conditions under which the Christian revelation had been
given to mankind.

II.

With this love of truth we may connect some other
marked characteristics.

1. Of these, one was his estimate of the value of a moral argument. The perception of the value of arguments of this kind is in reality a refined form of the sense of truth. It contrasts with the coarser habits of mind which clamour, on all subjects alike, for sensible experience or mathematical demonstration,—rather because these kinds of proof, to borrow an Apostolic expression, "make a fair show in the flesh,"—because they admit of being stated effectively,—than for a higher reason. Accordingly Mr. Keble was in an eminent sense a disciple, I might almost say a continuator, of Bishop Butler. "When a man reads Butler seriously," he said on one occasion, "I always hope the best of him." In those days Butler still reigned in the schools and mind of Oxford. It had not yet been whispered by brilliant critics that as he did not demonstrate the Being of God—an end, by the by, which he never proposed to himself,—he was out of harmony with the spirit of the time, and ought to be put upon the shelf. But Mr. Keble did not simply read Butler as ninety-nine out of a hundred of us do, only in order to master Butler's own great argument against the Deists of the last century; he extended him, if I may so speak, into the mind and circumstances of his own day. First of all, he met the criticism which has been so often made on Butler's argument from probability, that its tendency is to destroy absolute certainty, and to resolve all truth into opinion which it is safe to obey or to profess, but not possible to embrace with unhesitating inward assent. How he did this has been stated, with his usual clearness, by Dr. Newman. "Mr. Keble," he says, "met the difficulty by ascribing the firmness of assent which we give to religious doctrine, not to the probabilities which introduced it, but to the living power of faith and love which accepted it. In matters of religion, he seemed to say, it is not merely probability which

makes us intellectually certain, but probability as it is put to account by faith and love. It is faith and love which give to probability a force which it has not in itself. Faith and love are directed towards an object; in the vision of that object they live; it is that object, received in faith and love, which renders it reasonable to take probability as sufficient for internal conviction."[1] Such an account of Butler was open, of course, to criticisms of which its author was well aware and not slow to meet in detail; but Butler did not merely furnish materials by which Mr. Keble threw up new works in not a few minds around belief in Revelation. The considerations which induced some of his own dearest friends to transfer their allegiance to the Church of Rome in the year 1845, and afterwards, led Mr. Keble to ask himself how far Butler's method afforded any guidance as to the question of duty in presence of the Roman claims. The answer to that question he gives in a paper which to me at least recalls the substance and the flavour of his thought in many a conversation, more than anything else that he has left. I refer to the Preface to a volume of "Sermons, Academical and Occasional." In that preface he traces the applicability of Butler's argument in favour of revelation to the claims of the English Church upon her children; and the arguments by which Roman Catholic critics disputed this application at the time suggest other arguments with which we have subsequently become familiar, and which are urged by writers of a very different character, against Butler's method as a whole.

It was this same delicacy of mental texture which led Mr. Keble to pause reverently before Patristic reasonings or principles of interpretation in which many modern critics have only discovered materials for ridicule. He

[1] *Apologia*, p. 79.

used to dispute the assumptions of that phantom authority, common sense, on questions in which, if anything was to be decided at all seriously, it could only be by methods and after a patient investigation beyond the reach of the majority of men. He once brought a fluent critic of St. Ambrose as an interpreter of Scripture to a standstill, by asking him what he should propose to say to an unbeliever who ridiculed the principle of St. Paul's allegorical argument about the two covenants in the Epistle to the Galatians. On another occasion he expressed himself as follows: "People talk as if the Fathers, instead of arguing, wrote mere rhetoric: we want a monograph (that, I believe, is the modern word) to show that they were like the rest of us in meaning what they said, and unlike the great majority of us in seeing a great deal further into divine things than we at all suspect."

2. A further quality of Mr. Keble's intellect was a certain severity. His mind, like his body, seemed to be schooled to endure hardness like a good soldier of Jesus Christ. He who ministered to others such soft, tender, consolatory thought, was eminently unsparing towards himself. He was, to begin with, a scholar of the old robust type, for whom nothing had as yet been made easy in the way of modern grammar and dictionary, and who preferred the old methods by which knowledge was acquired at the cost of much greater labour than now. He would read by preference the old Greek editions of the classics and the Fathers (I remember especially his copy of Savile's St. Chrysostom, now I suppose in the library of this College); he was almost impatient when the more effeminate scholarship of the next generation stumbled over the quaint conceits of those early printers. This side of his mind appears in his defence of the use of Latin as the language of his exquisite Prælections on the healing virtue of Poetry. The preference for the

vernacular, which has long since banished its rival from the field, was just then making itself felt in the University; but Mr. Keble was not disposed to entertain the idea of a concession. He admits, indeed, characteristically, that in using Latin his powers of expression as a lecturer are fettered; he owns that there are modern compositions to which Latin could scarcely, in whatever sense, do justice; he knows that to lecture in Latin is not the way to fill a lecture-room with young men of the present day; but he would retain the language, not only as the historical tongue of the University, and the medium of communication between the learned throughout Europe, but as befitting the lofty severity of true criticism, and as a corrective to the relaxed tone of the literature of the age. "Facile patiemur plura nobis deesse, maxime alioquin optata atque commoda, gratiam, favorem, plena subsellia; tum, quod longe est gravius, multis ac præclaris locis, et qui ad rem bene gerendam vel præcipue possent adjuvare, æquo satis animo carebimus; modo nihil putidum, nihil fœcatum, nihil non vetus atque simplex in sanctissimâ re proferatur."[1] This scruple was not merely or chiefly literary; it was moral and religious. It was nearly allied to the habitual bent of his thoughts on holier ground. He had no sympathy with the self-deceiving theories which make much of the Benevolence of God at the cost of His Justice, or which ignore the nature and consequences of sin in order to flatter the fond hopes of the sinner. He pressed this side of truth home to himself with inexorable determination. He dwelt on God's Justice, as "the Attribute which I have most reason to think about." He loved Lent as "the season which best suited a person who ought always to be repenting." His mind rested continuously on the graver statements of Holy Scripture; not from any merely mental enterprise

[1] *Prælectiones Academicæ*, tom. i. pp. 7, 8.

or speculative curiosity, but as "the best for me." After the decision of the Privy Council in the *Essay and Review* case, he composed a Litany from Holy Scripture to "remind himself and others of what God had really revealed about the state of the lost, however men might deceive themselves." His intrepid study of the sterner sides of divine Revelation was not the least characteristic part of his renewal in knowledge after the image of Him That created him.

3. A third characteristic was courage,—courage of that simple unconscious kind which undertakes invidious or perilous duty without effort and as a matter of course. With his gentleness of disposition, and utter dislike of prominence in any form, Mr. Keble was incapable of silence when conscience bade him speak, and of speaking when conscience enjoined silence. Those who know the history of Oxford from thirty-five to thirty years ago, or of the Church of Scotland after the Primary Charge of the late Bishop of Brechin, or of the Church of England during each of the graver controversies which convulsed her within the last twenty years of Mr. Keble's life, will feel the truth of this. No fear of unpopularity, no frowns or menaces of the highly placed or the influential could weigh for a moment with that clear and delicate conscience; again and again, with chivalrous devotion of time and learning, he threw himself into the unpopular side, and, as he said, "never lived to regret it." A visitor one day observed to him that toleration was the order of the day, and that certain proceedings to which reference had been made would soon become impossible. "For myself," he said, "I do not expect to be included in the amnesty." On another occasion, quite towards the close of his life, he was conversing with an influential friend, who thought that he might venture to make a distinction between the author of *The Christian Year* and another

great name, which in a much greater degree than his own, was at that time the object of vulgar prejudice and abuse. "My lord," said Mr. Keble sternly, and using the epithet which had been just employed, "your lordship must have made a mistake. We are all of that kind here; I, perhaps, more than any one else." On the other hand, he was an example of that higher courage which is ready, not merely to confront an opponent, but to disappoint a friend. In the excited years which followed upon the Gorham decision he was more than once pressed to say or do things which were beside or beyond his convictions as to truth and duty. Impetuous friends, carried forward on the high tide of panic or of enthusiasm, could not understand the reserve of a highly instructed and sensitive conscience; and they would often, if they could, have forced his hand. But his gentle, unyielding resistance to pressure of this kind was not less instructive or fertile in results than his generous self-sacrifice under other circumstances. It made every one—friend and foe alike—feel that when he did speak, he meant what he said. Much against his will, but for a great many persons of very various characters who but for him might have fallen under very different influences, he became a sort of religious "court of final appeal." When all else had been said and done, people would wait and see what came from Hursley before they made up their minds as to the path of duty.

In nothing was the simple truthfulness of Mr. Keble's mind more observable than in his freedom from the spirit of paradox; it was indeed in this respect that the really philosophical character of his thought made itself especially felt. Paradox is the *ignis fatuus* which beguiles many a noble nature from the pursuit of strict truth; and paradox is apt to be proselytising, partly from an uneasy suspicion on the part of those who accept it that all is not absolutely right, and partly from the impulse which may be due to a subtle sense of humour. Twenty-five or thirty years ago, paradox, at least in certain regions of thought and discussion, was a more powerful temptation than it is now. Since those days there have been catastrophes; the ground of religious controversy has been strewed with ruins; and everybody who can feel or think at all is more or less saddened and sobered. In those days, too, sheer unbelief was still a rare and distant enemy, and Christian controversialists did not shrink from an appeal to weapons which seemed to promise an effective surprise. The supposed dilemma between Rome and infidelity was brilliantly manipulated; and men played with a terrible alternative because they honestly believed it to be strictly impossible that their countrymen could accept an infidel conclusion. It was in reviewing these arguments, as they were put before him by the perplexed, the impetuous, and the young, that Mr. Keble's mild wisdom shaped convictions which are still energetic; in how many cases, and how decisively, will only be known hereafter. But who that has ever had the experience can forget how patiently he would consider propositions which less clear-sighted men would have at once scornfully set aside as ridiculous; how tenderly he would identify himself with the exact prejudice or point of view of his questioner; how he would apologise for saying anything at all upon a point which it was suggested to him was obvious; and then how he would gently lay his finger upon some intercepting or disturbing fact, which shivered the whole fabric of abstract logic, and lowered the discussion to the *terra firma* of sober reality? Those who know the *Life of Dr. Arnold* will remember at least one instance in which Mr. Keble sacrificed to what he believed to be the voice of duty a personal friendship of no common order. And in intercourse with

Mr. Keble, his younger friends felt the presence of an intrepid sincerity, which they knew would never scruple to tell them the truth, however tenderly, or at whatever cost. Indeed, if the illustration might be permitted, he sometimes in his conversation recalled his old rival, the venerable Provost of Oriel, by his gentle but severe insistence upon accurate thought and language on the part of younger men. Certainly, his most ordinary table-talk had about it a soothing charm, which defies description or analysis; and those who came to him, tired by work, or worried and depressed by controversy, will often have applied to it the lines which have been suggested as a motto for *The Christian Year*:

> " Tale tuum carmen nobis, divine poeta,
> Quale sopor fessis in gramine, quale per æstum
> Dulcis aquæ saliente sitim restinguere rivo."

His conversation would flow on, constantly suggesting the deepest thoughts, while expressed in the simplest language, and rising not seldom into ripples of quiet humour, or of moral enthusiasm, or into some brilliant sally that might seem an echo from the Oriel Common-room of another generation, until at last a remark was hazarded by his companion which was showy rather than true, or a word was employed, intended to produce effect, but the true meaning of which had not been considered by the speaker. Then, all at once, in the gentlest, but, on that very account, the most formidable way, Mr. Keble would wield—if I may so speak—the "Socratic Elenchus." What was exactly meant; what was the exact element of truth in what was meant; whether something was not to be said in favour of an opposite position or phrase; whether, in short, what had been advanced had not better have been avoided;—this was the series of topics, embodying his quiet but irresistible protest in favour of the sacredness of truth,—of the duty of doing it rightful homage in language,—of the duty of avoiding all that was merely showy or paradoxical.

There were other qualities of his mind which ought perhaps, if time sufficed, to be insisted on. Such was an intellectual rectitude which never seemed to miss the relative proportions of truths, and never to be disturbed by a passing enthusiasm or a temporary panic. Such again was a tenderness, all his own, in explaining or communicating truth; such, above all, was the profound, the awful reverence with which, without alluding to them, he bent low before those unseen realities which had ever a first place in his heart and thought. No man, perhaps, ever lifted others to heaven without mentioning it, more persuasively than he; his own eulogy on the poet Wordsworth had a wider application to himself which he little suspected: "Cui illud munus tribuit Deus Optimus Maximus, ut sive hominum affectus caneret, sive terrarum et cœli pulchritudinem, legentium animos semper ad sanctiora erigeret, . . . atque adeo, labente sæculo, existeret, non solum dulcissimæ poeseos, verum etiam, divinæ veritatis antistes."[1]

The days will come, I suppose,—if indeed they have not yet come,—when young men, looking at these buildings, will ask the question, "Who was Keble?" To have made it inevitable that that question should be asked by successive generations of Oxford students is to have added to the moral wealth of the world. For the answer to that question cannot but do good to the man who asks it. It is not high station, or commanding wealth, or great public exploits, or wide popularity of opinions, which will explain the foundation of this College;—raised as it is to the memory of a quiet country clergyman, with a very moderate income, who sedulously avoided public distinc-

[1] *Præl. Ac.* tom. i. dedication.

tions, and held tenaciously to an unpopular school all his life. Keble College is a witness to the homage which goodness carried into the world of thought, or, indeed, into any other sphere of activity, extorts from all of us, when we are fairly placed face to face with it; it is a proof that neither station, nor wealth, nor conspicuousness, nor popularity is the truest and ultimate test of greatness. True greatness is to be recognised in character; and in a place like this character is largely, if not chiefly, shaped by the degree in which moral qualities are brought to bear upon the activities of mind. The more men really know of him, who, being dead, has, in virtue of the rich gifts of grace with which God had endowed him, summoned this College into being, the less will they marvel at such a tribute to his profound and enduring influence. May this College, for long years to come, be a home of teachers and students, whose clear strong faith, and general intellectual and moral mould as servants of truth will not be altogether unworthy of the great name it bears!

SERMON XIV.

EDWARD BOUVERIE PUSEY.[1]

ST. MATT. v. 19.

Whosoever shall do and teach the same shall be called great in the kingdom of heaven.

OUR Lord here implies that the standard of greatness in His Church—the kingdom of heaven upon earth—would differ from that which commonly obtains in the world outside. A claim to greatness among mankind at large is made good by that quality or circumstance which, in whatever way, increases a man's present importance among his fellows. And thus by a great man is meant a man of great intellect, or of great wealth, or of great social position, or of great reputation for some form of capacity or distinction. Greatness, so understood, does not even involve personal obedience to the law of truth and duty, much less any anxious effort to promote the ascendency of truth and duty in the life of other men. If, indeed, loyalty to a conviction or moral height of character can be combined with the conditions which in the world's estimate are of the essence of greatness, so much the better ; only, of itself, this practical devotion to truth and duty has nothing to do with greatness, as conceived among ordinary men of the world. For it does not necessarily enhance the relative power of the individual man among his fellows; and many, if not most, of

[1] Preached in St. Margaret's Church, Prince's Road, Liverpool, on the Second Sunday after the Epiphany, January 20, 1884.

those to whom the world has accorded the title of "great" have been conspicuously without it.

In the Church of Jesus Christ it was to be otherwise. The claim to greatness was to be weighed in the scales, not of immediate social importance, but of correspondence with an absolute test of excellence. Nothing that is purely external to a man himself, such as income or rank, can in the strict sense of the term make him great; simply because it *is* thus outside him, and therefore it does not touch that which in himself he is. Even great powers, whether of body or mind, do not of themselves, in our Lord's judgment, make men great. The Pagan Greek might crown the victors in games whose memory will last as long as men care for the finest creations of human literature; but "the Lord hath no pleasure in the strength of an horse, neither delighteth He in any man's legs." And the highest created intellect may be utterly fallen and perverted; there is no reason to think that the greatest powers of a human mind, cultivated to the utmost in the first Universities of Europe, could for a moment compare with the intellectual splendour of the hateful and apostate spirit who reigns in hell. Greatness in man is that in man which corresponds with the eternal moral Nature of God; it is obedience to the law of truth and duty, first of all controlling a man's own life, and then radiating from him with the persuasive eloquence as well of example as of language upon the lives of those around him. "He that shall do and teach the same shall be called great in the kingdom of heaven."

I.

This evening I am allowed to lead you to think of one who was taken from us some sixteen months ago, and whose career recalls the solemn words of our Lord which are before us in the text. At first sight, indeed, it might almost seem as if Dr. Pusey's greatness were of another order than that of the Divine Kingdom; since it had something to do with more than one form of greatness that is recognised by human opinion in general. What sort of place he held in the minds of his countrymen and of the world became plain when, at last, in the fulness of his years, he passed away from us. The press of this country, and in particular that powerful journal which stands at its head, treated his death as a matter of at least national concern. His family circumstances, his literary and theological work, his relations with distinguished contemporaries, his influence upon the religious convictions of our day, were discussed at much length, and, generally speaking, with an obviously anxious effort to be just and accurate. And since then notices of him have appeared in organs of foreign opinion, which show that his disappearance from the world is regarded as an event of European importance in countries where the death of those who hold the highest places of dignity in the English Church would commonly pass unnoticed. This is the more remarkable, because Dr. Pusey did not occupy any official position in the Church of commanding eminence. He was merely Canon of a Cathedral; and in a body of six theological Professors he held a chair which is by no means the first, either in its rank or in its natural opportunities for influencing theological thought. A position of this kind does not of itself imply any very particular claim to world-wide notice. It had already been occupied by a long line of predecessors, whose names, with some three or four exceptions, had been unknown beyond the walls of their University. The least important circumstance in connection with Dr. Pusey's death was that it placed a piece of Cathedral and University patronage at the disposal of the Government.

II.

But when Dr. Pusey died those who knew or cared anything about scholarship knew that the world had lost one of its foremost scholars. With him scholarship—the scientific knowledge of language—was even less of an acquirement than of an instinct. He had that fine perception of the vital genius of human speech which often enabled him to dispense with the machinery of grammar and dictionary, because he could, in fact, anticipate their verdict. The author of *The Christian Year*, who was some ten years his senior, used to say that he never knew how Pindar might be translated until he heard Pusey translate him in the schools. To the ordinary classical languages, and—what fifty years ago was a rare accomplishment—a thorough familiarity with German, Dr. Pusey added, while still under thirty, an exact knowledge of Hebrew, and, as there is reason to think, a still more intimate knowledge of Arabic, with its rich vocabulary and literature. He spent from fourteen to sixteen hours a day for a great part of two years in acquiring it, partly under the guidance of Freytag, the first Arabic scholar in Europe; his main reason for this great expenditure of labour being the light which Arabic throws upon the cognate language of the Old Testament. The habit of constantly enlarging his intimacy with language never deserted him when he was an old man. When he was more than sixty years of age he made himself entirely master of Ethiopic. And his enthusiasm for language was intimately connected with his profoundly religious idea of what language really is. In our day many ingenious theories have been put forth as to the origin of language. But Dr. Pusey believed that the only one which does justice to what it is in itself and to its place in nature as a characteristic of man is the belief that it is an original gift of God; the counterpart of that other and greater gift of His, a self-questioning and immortal soul. Language is the life of the human soul, projected into the world of sound; it exhibits in all their strength and delicacy the processes by which the soul takes account of what passes without and within itself; in it may be studied the minute anatomy of the soul's life— that inner world in which thought takes shape and conscience speaks, and the eternal issues are raised and developed to their final form. Therefore Dr. Pusey looked upon language with the deepest interest and reverence; he handled it as a sacred thing which could not be examined or guarded or employed too carefully; he thought no trouble too great in order to ascertain and express its exact shades of meaning; and this anxiety, so religious in its origin, had a certain temporal reward in the character of the philological work by which he was known to the world, and which made him the scholar that he confessedly was. Those critics in Germany who have been least able to agree in his general conclusions as to the Hebrew Scriptures have not been slow to express their respect for the scholarly learning by which he supported them.

III.

With Dr. Pusey, however, language was a means to an end beyond itself; it was the means by which he examined God's unveiling of Himself to man in His written Word. There have been many scholars who have treated scholarship, even the scholarship of the Bible, as an end in itself; while they have sometimes seemed to regard the Christian Revelation as mainly interesting on account of the consideration which it secures for philological studies. To adapt a famous saying—they encourage the suspicion that God had become Incarnate in order to aid the sale of their grammars and dictionaries. This singular and weird inversion of the true relative proportions of things, it is needless to say, found no sympathy in Dr. Pusey. In him scholarship was entirely divorced from the pedantry and self-display which has at times disfigured the labours of scholars. With him scholarship was ever the handmaid of Divine Truth; never so happily employed as when guarding or exploring it; and, as he thought, little worthy to engage the attention of dying men, if divorced from this high association and treated as a subject with no higher end in prospect beyond.

Accordingly, if Dr. Pusey was well known as a scholar, he was still better known as a divine. For him nothing was comparable in interest or importance to the Revelation which the Infinite and Eternal God has deigned to make of Himself to man; and to study and explore this Revelation, its governing and constitutive truths and principles, and its various and minutest details, was to the last moment of his earthly life his greatest joy. Long before he took Holy Orders, his interest was thoroughly engaged in questions of religious truth; and throughout his life whatever else might occupy him for the moment, the study of studies, to which all else was relative and subservient, was theology. He had in great perfection two natural qualities which go far to make an accomplished theologian. He combined with an intellectual sensitiveness, which rendered him alive to the claims of separate truths, and to distinctions between truths apparently similar, a remarkable sense of balance and proportion, which never allowed one truth to obscure in his mind the claims of another, and thus saved him from passing the line which separates the clear expression of very strong conviction from this or that kind of perilous exaggeration. This might, as I think, be shown by an examination of his most remarkable efforts in theology; or even of such sermons as those on the Holy Eucharist, on Absolution, on the Rule of Faith, on Darwinism—sermons which are of such a character as to form epochs, it is not too much to say, in our recent religious history.

Of this knowledge Holy Scripture was the great source. To him the Bible was in fact, what to all of us it is in name, but to some of us only in name—the first of books. Intimately as he was acquainted with the great writers of Christian antiquity (to use his own words, he "lived for some years in St. Augustine") he never lost sight of the vast interval which parts the sacred canon of Scripture from all other writings in the world. If you would know how he thought and felt in presence of the Sacred Text, read his Commentary on the Minor Prophets. If you would understand his jealous care for the claims of Scripture when assailed by modern unbelief, read his book on Daniel. He saw clearly that if Daniel was really written in the days of Antiochus Epiphanes, if its author was really describing the past when he professed to be foretelling the future, the book was not merely an uninspired book, but a dishonest one. And therefore he put forth his whole strength to meet the infidel criticism on its own grounds; and in none of his writings—to omit other characteristics of this effort of his pen—do we see his scholarship more entirely at the disposal of theology.

IV.

But theology, like scholarship, may be so handled as to lose altogether its grace and purpose. It may be resolved into the arid study of ancient texts, or into an almost mechanical play upon a set of propositions, while He, Whose living presence alone gives life and animation to all, is really lost sight of. Something of this kind seems to have been the case in Lutheran Germany during the years which preceded the rise of what is known as the Older Rationalism. The danger is a very real one, especially in days of controversy; and there is only one possible safeguard against it.

Dr. Pusey's accomplishments in scholarship and theology would have availed little to make him the really great man he was, unless they had been accompanied by that deep personal interest in Divine things—that sense of boundless indebtedness to the redeeming love of our Lord Jesus Christ—which he displayed even in early life, and which grew with his years up to the moment when he was taken from us. No one, most assuredly, could be long in Dr. Pusey's company without discovering that his thoughts, his feelings, his motives, his entire conception of the meaning and end of life, were practically different from and higher than those of the majority of men, even of men who are seriously interested in matters connected with religion. He did not merely now and then talk and think about God: in the language of the Bible, he "walked with God." No facts were so constantly present to his mind as God's encompassing closeness, His Mind, His Will, in their bearing on the thoughts and duties of our daily life. None of the human beings among whom he lived and worked visibly influenced him, as did this gracious and awful Friend, with Whom throughout the day he was constantly communicating in prayer. And thus to visit him was, as has often been said, to move out of the world into another atmosphere, where the language of the Bible was translated into reality; where St. Paul and St. John did not seem to be out of harmony with accepted principles of thought and action; where the unseen reckoned for more than the seen; and where all persons and events were looked at from a distant and higher point of view. Those words in to-day's Epistle

which seem to most of us to describe a purely ideal life—
"Fervent in spirit, serving the Lord, rejoicing in hope,
patient in tribulation, continuing instant in prayer,
distributing to the necessity of saints," [1]—were, all of them,
real in him. When he was most likely to be off his
guard, and engaged in intimate converse with those whom
he could perfectly trust, he was true to the most serious
language which he used in the pulpit. When other men
would say that a difficult question of conduct must be
decided by this or that consideration of immediate expediency, he would observe quietly, "Of course the first
thing for us to settle, so far as we may, is, what our Lord
is thinking about the matter." The only events which
really gave him pleasure were those which he believed to
promote the will or glory of our Lord. The only events
which long distressed him were those which appeared to
bode no good for the cause and kingdom of Jesus Christ.
He surveyed men, occurrences, politics, literature, education,
simply from this point of view; it shaped his judgments;
it at once controlled and animated his sympathies. He
was as far as possible from being morose or low-spirited:
no man was more equal in temperament, or more capable
of bright and hearty joyousness, or more free in his
expression of it than he. This is only a way of saying
that he was perfectly at peace with God, and happy in
the conviction, moment by moment, that he was living in
the grace of our Lord Jesus Christ. Indeed, our Lord
was literally to him, as St. Paul says, "wisdom, and
righteousness, and sanctification, and redemption";[2] and
the Infinite Love Who for us men and for our salvation
took human flesh and died upon the cross, and pleads
incessantly in heaven, and bestows on us His new Nature
through the sacraments of His Church was the constant
Object of His adoring praise.

[1] Rom. xii. 11-13.   [2] 1 Cor. i. 30.

V.

Early in Dr. Pusey's life he was brought privately into contact with a very pronounced form of infidelity, and this circumstance seems to have exerted a decisive influence on his later career. It certainly determined his studies during two years in Germany; and it had a great deal to do with his adhesion to the Church Movement of 1833. That remarkable Movement, which has had such various attractions for different minds, and which has done, and we may trust is still doing, so much for the spiritual wellbeing of the Church of England, was chiefly welcome to Dr. Pusey as a providential reinforcement of the cause of Christian faith. It owed its first impulse to the poet of *The Christian Year*, and its earliest phase of activity to that strong and beautiful mind who alone of its three great chiefs still lingers here below, though lost, alas! to the English Church. In its first days the Movement addressed itself largely to the task of supporting and defending threatened institutions: but it was soon perceived that institutions can only be defended successfully when the truths which they are intended to guard and set forth are sincerely believed. Thus, if the Episcopate was after all merely an ancient feature of Church government—a Bishop differing from a presbyter only as a Lord-Lieutenant might differ from a county magistrate —it was too cumbrous and costly a whim of ecclesiastical antiquarianism to be maintained in the long-run against the spirit of reform. But if the Christian Bishop, whether holding his stately receptions at Lambeth, or wandering about in search of souls among the solitudes of Central Africa, is an essential element of the organic structure of the Church of God, he will surely outlive any social or political vicissitudes that may await the modern world.

When men believe in the spiritual powers bestowed by Christ on His Church, the shell which enshrines them, or so much of it as is really necessary, will always be safe. But then every truth, however incidental, is to be prized for its own sake, and not only or chiefly for the sake of that which it supports. Thus the Movement found itself engaged in the work of proving and reasserting large elements of the Church's creed and system; and it was this which chiefly and early attached Dr. Pusey to its ranks. For he had come to see that the canon of the New Testament itself cannot be defended on purely internal evidence, and apart from the authority and witness of the Apostolic and primitive Church; and if Church authority is to be used in arriving at so momentous a conclusion as the true contents and frontier of Scripture and the nature of its claims on man, it is not possible in consistency to discard that authority when it also claims to interpret Scripture. And thus the Movement proceeded systematically to reassert the whole body of truth committed by Christ and His Apostles to the Ancient Church, and still substantially taught us in the Prayer-Book. There was, indeed, need of this. For not a few of the defenders of Christianity in previous years had thought to defend it best by the method of incessantly making concessions to its enemies; like those unarmed travellers who, when pursued by hungry wolves, threw first one and then another of their company to the savage brutes, in the hope that if not sated, they would be appeased, or at least occupied, by what had been so easily surrendered. Such theological methods are dangerous in practice as well as wrong in principle; and what is given up in one generation, as no part of the so-called "simple Gospel" of the Apostles, is discovered by the more penetrating criticism of the next to be so intimately linked with it, that the surrender becomes a good logical reason for demanding a concession of what is still unconceded. And thus men came to see that in abandoning faith in the grace and presence of Christ in His Sacraments, and in the necessity of an Apostolical ministry, they had really in ways little suspected at the time made the assaults of scepticism on such central truths as the Atonement and the Holy Trinity much more difficult to resist. For truths are related in numberless ways to each other; or rather, Revealed Truth is a great whole, no part of which can be withdrawn or denied without impairing what remains. A deep conviction of this was at the bottom of Dr. Pusey's theological activity during the most active years of his life; and it laid under contribution his acquirements as a scholar and theologian, while it brought great satisfaction to his piety as a devoted servant of our Lord.

VI.

It would be impossible for me to attempt within the limits at our disposal an account of Pusey's labours in the field of theology. Suffice it to say that for forty-eight years he was engaged in almost incessant production; while before that period began he had spent himself on two works which would suffice for the life of an ordinary man. Pamphlet after pamphlet, sermon after sermon,— each prepared with the care and thoroughness that befits a theological treatise,—book after book, attested the strength of his convictions, the depth and width of his learning, the indomitable tenacity of his purpose. His facile pen traversed in succession nearly the whole series of questions on which modern theories respecting the nature of the Church and the Sacraments are at issue with primitive Christianity. The grace of a new birth bestowed in Baptism; the truth of that Presence, inaccessible to sight and sense, whereby nevertheless in the Sacrament of His Death our ever-living Redeemer is wont to be among us that He may feed and bless His adoring family; the reality of the pardon which is uttered in His Name over all those who truly repent and unfeignedly believe His holy Gospel; the Catholic rule of faith as maintained in the Church of England; the authority and constitution of Church Councils; and then the various aspects of the personal and devotional life of the soul; the duty and privilege of self-denial in all its forms; the many and various activities of prayer; the complete case, in short, of the single soul, learning at the foot of the Redeemer's Cross to prepare for death and judgment—all in turn were passed in review. And in dark days, when hearts were failing, and friends were straying away from the fold of the English Church, and beckoning him to follow; whilst a vast mass of obloquy and misunderstanding, taking every shape that could wound a sensitive and affectionate nature, fiercely bade him begone, he had to defend himself more than once against the double assault; to show that in his loyalty to Christian Antiquity he had only taken the Church of England at her word; to show that she offered all the blessings, while she was free from great drawbacks that are to be found elsewhere; but also to show that in resolutely making the most of all the positive truth that she directly or implicitly sanctions, lies the best safeguard in the long-run against disloyalty to her claims. We must abandon the attempt to follow him through districts of thought so interesting and so vast;—his works are the property of the Christian world, and they will set me or any one else right, who has said or suggested too much, or too little, respecting them.

VII.

Dr. Pusey's life had two marks especially set in it by Divine Providence: it was a life of controversy and a life of suffering.

He often deplored the necessity which obliged him to spend so much of his time and thought in religious controversy. It was, he firmly believed, "the Lord's controversy" in which he was thus engaged; and he accepted a task from which much in his character would have held him back, as a duty laid on him by Providential Wisdom. Never did any man less forget that to treat the defence of truth as if it were the defence of a personal opinion, is to degrade it immeasurably; and the temper which he habitually cultivated, would have made those petty ferocities which so often disfigure controversy utterly impossible for him. Indeed, he carried into controversy great self-control. Of this those who have few or no convictions to animate them may well imitate the outer bearing; but it is difficult of attainment for men in whom devotion to known truth has assumed the proportions of a strong and ruling passion. Certainly he did all that could be done to sweeten controversy by the charities and courtesies that were natural to his chastened temper; but, after doing his best, he disliked heartily what he could not help. In the agony of one of the most trying episodes of his life, he made the words of Jeremiah his own, when addressing the venerable parent, Lady Lucy Pusey, who had so large a place in his filial heart: "Woe is me, my mother, that thou hast borne me a man of strife, and a man of contention to the whole earth."[1]

And his life was largely a life of suffering. Assuredly it did not lack the Print of the Nails. He had his full share of home sorrows, which the affectionateness of his

---

[1] Jer. xv. 10.

character sharpened to the utmost. His young brother, his father, his wife, his eldest daughter, his eldest brother, his mother, his only son, were successively taken; and what the loss meant for him in some of these cases it would be impossible to convey in a few words. Troubles there were of another order which wounded him even more deeply. The separation which for some years followed the secession of Dr. Newman, the desertion of friends who remained, and from whose sympathy he might well have hoped for much, the coldness or active hostility of persons in high authority, the failure of younger men to answer to his reasonable expectations or to be true to themselves, above all the lacerations of the Church, to whose wellbeing and growth he was devoted heart and soul—these things cut him to the quick. Some day expressions of sorrow which escaped him may see the light, and may illustrate what I am saying. Sorrow, we know, is a mark which God never fails to trace on the lives of the predestinate, and Dr. Pusey's life was no exception to the rule.

And this intimacy with suffering was probably one chief secret of his moral power, because it endowed him so richly, as it had endowed St. Paul, with the gift of sympathy. Within the last three days twenty-three poor young women, engaged in setting up types in London, have sent to me what they could save from their scanty earnings as a tribute to the memory of one whose helpful kindness in leading them to God they could never forget. And at the same time a student in the University of Giessen, who reads our language with difficulty, writes, evidently under the spell of that true sympathy with mental trials which breathes in Dr. Pusey's writings, that his great object in life will be to tread in Pusey's footsteps, and that his earnest wish is to visit the scenes of Pusey's life, and to join in the worship of the Church to which Pusey belonged.

VIII.

A great life, such as that before us, is a great gift of the Author of all Goodness to His Church, and especially to that part of it which is the immediate scene or recipient of the endowment. And let us not forget that all God's blessings are tests of the faithfulness of those who receive them. To treat the memory of Dr. Pusey as we might that of an ordinary man of good abilities, who, as men speak, had "succeeded" in his sacred profession, and had won the applause of the world, and had died full of honours, but without doing and teaching in the sense of the Sermon on the Mount, would argue serious moral dulness; an incapacity to see the difference between what passes for greatness in the world, and that which is called great in the kingdom of heaven. Not that Dr. Pusey's memory would die, if Churchmen could have resolved that nothing should be done to perpetuate it. His writings will command attention long after our generation has passed away; he lives and will live in his commentaries on Holy Scripture, in his doctrinal treatises, in his heart-searching sermons, in the abundant provision which God guided him to make for the spiritual life of men. Yes, he lives at this moment in the devotional life of thousands, in their prayers, in their repentance, in their efforts to love and serve God, and to correspond with His grace; he lives in them too constantly, too intimately, to be forgotten, if it were possible that others could conspire to forget him. But to forget him would be to injure not him, but ourselves. My friends, what is the best endowment, the true treasure, of a Christian Church? Not, surely, the material wealth which ancient piety has placed at his disposal, whether in land or tithe; not the noble piles, raised in some distant century, around which there cluster a thousand associations which take the heart and the imagination captive; not even the great minds which might have achieved any success in a worldly career, and which have enriched with new glories the vast literature of Christendom. No! Let us not underrate the value of these things; but they do not constitute the real capital or sinews of Christian Churches. That which invigorates a Church, rendering it independent of outward circumstance, and endowing it with a promise of perpetuity, is —next to His Presence, Who is the Source of all created good—the spiritual beauty of its members, and especially that union in them of knowledge and holiness which invites the sympathies, nay the entire confidence, of their fellow-men. Had Dr. Pusey been learned without being a devoted Christian ; had he been a true servant of Christ but ignorant of what is to be said for and against Christianity, for and against the position and claims of the Church of England, he would not have been what he was, or what he is to multitudes of souls. As it is, men look at his life and work, and they say, and they say well— "Where he could live and die, I may well be content to follow." And thus his life and death are a stay to many a soul, which but for him would be wandering far away, whether from the Church of England or from the Faith of Christ. To have been enriched with such a life, and to forget or disparage it, would be, on the part of a Church, an infatuation of which a country only could be guilty if it should take no account of the great statesmen or soldiers who have built up its fortunes, or should encourage reports likely to be fatal to its public credit. In honouring a man of this elevated stamp we recognise at one and the same time the claims of learning, the claims of piety, the claims, above all, of that portion of the Church of Christ in which Divine Providence has placed us.

IX.

An institution, as you know, is being founded in Oxford, which will bear Dr. Pusey's name, and of which his own library will be the nucleus. It will, at least, lead coming generations of Oxford students to ask the question, Who was Dr. Pusey? And the true answer to that question cannot but be very improving. But, as its promoters hope, this institute will do more. It will form, in the University of the future, a home of sacred learning, and a rallying-point for Christian faith; and thus it will strengthen all that is dearest to a sincere Christian at what, so far as we can judge, must always be one of the chief centres of the mental life of this country. For such an institution there would have been neither place nor need thirty years ago; but during the last thirty years very great changes, amounting to nothing less than a revolution, have passed over the University of Oxford. At the beginning of that period the University was still what, with a brief interruption in the seventeenth century, she had been for a thousand years—the handmaid of the Church of Christ in England. Clergymen and laymen, students and teachers, made public profession of allegiance to the Church; and the whole life of the place, literary and scientific, as well as theological, was moulded and inspired by her sons. Such was Oxford, as described in her own statutes; but I am not prepared to say, either that the Church made the best use of the splendid opportunities which were thus secured to her, or that it was possible in the present condition of the country to exclude much longer from a share in University education—I do not say teaching—those who might be neither Churchmen nor Christians. Yet, at the least, recent changes might have taken a religious direction as distinct from a direction which, while maintaining a semblance of deference for religion, is, upon the whole, hostile to it If only two or three colleges, out of her great inheritance—if only those founded since the Reformation —had been left to the Church of England, the remainder being frankly and at once secularised, her prospects would be better than they are ; when extracts from her Prayer-Book are made by bodies of Fellows of any or no creed, for use in chapels, which few care to attend; and when any tutor is at liberty to tell his pupils, of course in academical language, that the Body of our crucified Redeemer rotted in His grave, and that Almighty God does not really reign on earth or in heaven. Nor can the little that is left—the single clerical Fellow in certain colleges, and the Professorships of Divinity—be considered secure. Every argument that has been used in favour of secularising College Fellowships is waiting in readiness to be employed against these few remaining guarantees for Christian teaching, when the hour for further spoliation shall have struck. Meanwhile, young Englishmen continue, and will continue, as heretofore, to flock to what has been for so many centuries a home for learning; but when the recent changes have had time to take effect, and the representatives of the old order of things have quite died out, students will not find that the home of learning is also a home of religion. Indeed, already the extent and meaning of the change is often too apparent. A young man has been trained in a Christian family, and is looking forward to serving God in Holy Orders; but he comes to Oxford to unlearn one by one the convictions which his mother had taught him, and to make up his mind that he cannot become a clergyman, on the ground that he doubts whether he can still honestly profess himself a Christian. This is no imaginary picture; nor should it, in reason, occasion us any surprise. Young men are naturally influenced in religious matters by those whose information and powers of thought they have learnt to respect when studying other subjects; and if those who teach are, in whatever sense, unfriendly to the claims of Divine Revelation, it is not singular that their pupils should be so too. No doubt there are evidences of religious earnestness at Oxford as elsewhere; there is interest in missionary and philanthropic efforts; there are sincere attempts at self-improvement, and other encouraging symptoms. But these depend on individual influences, and the question is as to the general drift and system of the University. It was, until our day, in alliance with the Church of Christ; it is now at best neutral; it is not unlikely to be actively hostile.

The institute which is to shape itself around Dr. Pusey's Library will, as we hope, under God's blessing, do something to arrest the further decay of faith in Oxford. It will exhibit, as the old colleges of Oxford were meant by their Christian founders to exhibit, solid learning allied to Christian faith and piety. It will keep its eye not only on those great and majestic studies which attend on Christian theology; not only on the inheritance of thought and knowledge which comes down to us from the sacred past; but also on those speculations which, with the caprice of ever-changeful fashion, occupy in successive years the thoughts of young men, and particularly on the drift of the studies which may be from time to time prescribed by the University authorities as necessary to a degree. In this way the new institute will be, as we hope, useful to the old colleges, or to whatever may hereafter remain of them. It will foster studies for which they may naturally be expected to feel an increasing disinclination; and it will supply, in a humble measure, that which thirty years since was supplied to young men by college tutors of the best type, who lived unmarried among their pupils, and who thought of them not merely as paying attendants at their lectures, but as Christians committed to their pastoral charge. And thus, as we trust, it will form a centre of moral and intellectual and spiritual enthusiasm, in which all that is solid in inquiry and learning, and all that is lofty and aspiring in moral effort, shall find encouragement under the consecrating shadow of a great name.

X.

These are our hopes. And if we ask you, my brethren, to help us, when you have in this vast city so many claims, present and prospective, upon your care and charity, it is because our institute will, as we anticipate, powerfully, although indirectly, strengthen all that you have most at heart. No one need is likely to press more heavily upon the Church in the future which is before us than that of placing highly educated men in the great centres of our population; men who shall be abreast of the thought and research of the day, and well able to point out with the authority of knowledge, as well as with the authority of office, how modern learning is related to the faith which our Lord has brought from heaven. Your Bishop, I believe, has, at least on one occasion, expressed his sense of an increasing necessity for highly educated men among the clergy of the Church. Well, such a need will, no doubt, be partly supplied by the higher class of theological colleges, the importance of which is happily, year by year, more and more recognised: but we must still look to the Universities for the main supply. And depend upon it the question whether England is hereafter to remain Christian will be largely decided at the Universities, and not least at Oxford. This momentous question, I say, does not only concern those who live at Oxford; it interests all who think seriously about the future of the Church and the country; all to whom the temporal and eternal wellbeing of the great masses of our countrymen, and the honour and triumph of the faith of Christ, are in any sense dear. And therefore we ask you to help us while we endeavour to combine the duty of handing on with honour a great memory to those who will come after us, with the even higher duty of providing, so well as we may, at a time of grave changes in University education, for the already impaired, and still more seriously threatened, interests of the faith. If that great and humble servant of God, to whom I have referred at such length, could ever have thought with pleasure upon the prominence which we are asserting for his life and work, it would have been solely for the sake of those objects to which in life he habitually sacrificed his personal inclinations, namely, the glory of God and the good of souls. It may well be that he was taken from us at a time when his memory would best perpetuate the results which he was privileged to achieve in life; when a work, the foundations of which were laid amidst suffering and anxiety, amidst obloquy and misunderstanding, amidst toils and disappointments such as fall to the lot of few men in a century, would be completed amidst honours to which rich and poor, the simple and the learned, the aged and the young, rulers of the Church and the humblest of her children, have joyfully contributed.

And there is one consideration which will appeal to those who worship God in this church. You have an especial interest, my brethren, in him who is to undertake the great responsibility and labour of inaugurating this work.[1] You know something of his devotion to truth and duty, of his high and varied capacity, of the unstinted charity which has spent in the service of your souls, year

---

[1] The Rev. C. Gore, M.A., Fellow of Trinity College, Oxford, and first Librarian Residentiary of the Pusey Library, Oxford.

after year, the few weeks of leisure which could be spared from exacting labours. To others who have had opportunities of studying his mind and character he has seemed to combine, as few young men in our day combine, a lofty simplicity of purpose with that insight and knowledge in the things of faith, which makes him not unworthy to represent, even in Oxford, the great name of Dr. Pusey. It would be impossible, at least for me, to say more of him.

Again and again, during the last two months, have we looked upon the western sun, as, wellnigh shrouded by masses of lowering clouds, he hurries to hide himself, as if in shame, beneath the line of the horizon. But lo! no sooner has he disappeared from sight, than the heavens are suffused with tints and hues of unaccustomed beauty, and the very clouds which but just now seemed to gather that they might cover up his face while his time of departure had not yet come, are touched beyond others with the radiance which he flings in such profusion from his place in a sky which is beyond our sight. So it is with the servants of God; only with this difference—that while the splendours of the natural sunset die away before the advancing night, the path of the departed just, alike in the memory of the faithful here, and in the world of glorified spirits, is "as the shining light, which shineth more and more unto the perfect day." Surely we do well to bear our part, however humble, in proclaiming the moral beauty of one such life; since thus we may hope the better, through Christ's grace and guidance, to do and teach after our measure also, and to have our share in the promise of a name and place in that Kingdom which will last for ever beyond the grave.

www.ingramcontent.com/pod-product-compliance
Lightning Source LLC
Chambersburg PA
CBHW032031220426
43664CB00006B/431